GRAMMAR GAMES
FOR TEACHERS OF ADULT ESL

GISELE L. WHITE

To the city of Munich

Text, Illustrations & Cover Art
Copyright © 2013 Gisele L. White.
All Rights Reserved.

ISBN 978-0-578-08028-4

The Professor Melonhead logo is a registered trademark.

Table of Contents

5 Introduction

ACTIVITIES

SIMPLE PRESENT TENSE
- 7   Countries, Nationalities & Languages
- 17   Questions & Negative Statements
- 25   Word Scramble: Simple Present + Adjectives

PRESENT CONTINUOUS TENSE
- 37   Questions & Negative Statements
- 45   Present Continuous vs. Simple Present

SIMPLE PAST TENSE
- 53   Simple Past: Irregular Verbs
- 61   Simple Present to Simple Past: Irregular Verbs
- 69   Questions & Negative Statements

PRESENT PERFECT TENSE
- 77   Present Perfect: Irregular Verbs
- 85   Simple Past to Present Perfect: Irregular Verbs

PREPOSITIONS
- 95   Prepositions of Time
- 103 Prepositions of Place
- 111 Phrasal Verbs with Prepositions

COUNTABLE VS. UNCOUNTABLE
- 121 Countable vs. Uncountable Nouns
- 129 Noun Quantifiers

ADVERBS VS. ADJECTIVES
- 137 Adjectives: Vocabulary Building
- 147 Adverbs vs. Adjectives

Table of Contents

4

QUESTIONS
Question Words 157
Simple Present vs. Present Continuous 167
Word Scramble: Common Questions 177

VERBS
Definitions 189

IDIOMS
Idioms of Comparison 197
Business Idioms 205
Body Idioms 217

MISCELLANEOUS
Adjectives of Nationality 227
World Capitals 235
The U.S. & Capitals 243
Mystery Cards 251

BOARD GAMES

AROUND THE WORLD 261
FRUIT SMASH 267
SHOP OWNER 275
CONNECT FIVE 283
WHODUNIT? 291
PLAY BALL! 305
SOCCER TOURNAMENT 317

APPENDIX
U.S. Currency 326
Paper Die Pattern 327
Idioms Lists 328

Introduction

This book is designed to help students interact with and learn from each other through fun and engaging grammar activities and board games.

Each chapter consists of game cards that focus on a specific grammar point or which can be combined with different chapters to create customized activities.

Game cards can also be combined in a multitude of ways with the 7 board games in the back of the book.

All board games come complete with full-size gameboards, photocopiable game pieces, U.S. currency, and a paper die pattern.

The game cards from each chapter are uniquely designed, thus allowing them to be easily recognized at a glance should they need to be returned to their original groupings.

If you're using thin photocopy paper, Game Card Covers (274) are available to prevent the answers from being read through the paper.

Game Card Cover & Label

LARGE CLASSES:

Because the answers are included on every game card, your students will be able to play the grammar activities and board games with minimal supervision.

GRAMMAR ACTIVITIES:

Divide the class into groups. Photocopy a set of game cards for each group. If you are having pairs of teams play against each other, you'll want teams of 2-3 students; therefore groups of 4-6 students.

You can also divide the class into groups of 3 or 4 students and have each student play for themself.

BOARD GAMES:

Divide the class into groups as specified by each game. Photocopy enough materials for each group.

Introduction

PREP TIME:

Preparation for grammar activities takes about 15 minutes and primarily consists of photocopying and cutting out the game cards.

Upon completion of each grammar activity, the game cards can be collected in labeled envelopes to use again for future classes; thus greatly reducing prep time.

Prep time for board games depends on the complexity of the game and how many game components have already been cut out and collected in labeled envelopes.

DURATION:

Each grammar activity lasts approximately 20 minutes. The board games can last 30 minutes to over 2 hours, depending on the game and how many rounds are played.

Optional study sheets are included in the beginning of most chapters.

Additionally, there are game cards to add variety to the board games or as enjoyable activities on their own.

Idioms of Comparison	197
Business Idioms	205
Body Idioms	217
Adjectives of Nationality	227
World Capitals	235
The U.S. & Capitals	243
Mystery Cards	251

Finally, there are 7 BONUS sheets located throughout the book on:

Modal Verbs	36, 136
Yet, Still, Always	162, 172
A, An, Some	184, 210, 252

Enjoy and happy teaching!

Countries, Nationalities & Languages

LESSON PREPARATION:

Photocopy and cut out the GAME CARDS.

Divide the class into 2 teams or divide the class into groups of about 4 students and have each student play for themself.

A STUDY SHEET is provided (8).

If possible, it might be fun to have a globe or world map handy during this activity.

BEGIN:

Stack the GAME CARDS, face down, on the table.

Student A takes the top card and reads the country and the pronoun to Student B. Student B must correctly say the pronoun's nationality, country, and (official) language in complete sentences to earn the card and thus the point.

If Student B makes a mistake, the card is put off to the side and no point is earned.

Student B then chooses a new card and reads to Student C, and so on until there are no more GAME CARDS left.

The student or team that earns the most GAME CARDS at the end of the game wins.

BEGINNER

OBJECTIVE:

To learn the simple present tense using the verbs *be* & *speak*.

Upon completion of this lesson, students should know:

1. How to correctly use the simple present tense forms of the verb *be*.

2. When to add an *s* to the end of a present tense verb.

3. How to use adjectives of nationality.

OFFICIAL LANGUAGES:

Only one language needs to be given for countries that have two or more languages.

CIA.gov was used to compile the data for this chapter.

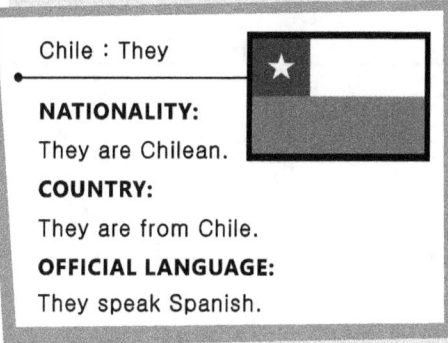

Chile : They

NATIONALITY:
They are Chilean.
COUNTRY:
They are from Chile.
OFFICIAL LANGUAGE:
They speak Spanish.

8 Countries, Nationalities & Languages STUDY SHEET

VERB: BE

I	**am**
he, she, it	**is**
we, they, you	**are**

VERB: SPEAK

he, she, it	**speaks**
we, they, you, I	**speak**

I *am* from France.　　**(Country)**
I *am* French.　　**(Nationality)**

I *speak* French.　　**(Language)**

He *is* from China.　　**(Country)**
She *is* Chinese.　　**(Nationality)**

He *speaks* Chinese.　　**(Language)**
She *speaks* Chinese.　　**(Language)**

We *are* from Mexico.　　**(Country)**
They *are* Mexican.　　**(Nationality)**

We *speak* Spanish.　　**(Language)**
They *speak* Spanish.　　**(Language)**

You *are* from Brazil.　　**(Country)**
You *are* Brazilian.　　**(Nationality)**

You *speak* Portuguese.　　**(Language)**

PRACTICE: Complete these sentences.

Canada : You

NATIONALITY:

You _____ _____ .

COUNTRY:

You _____ from _____ .

OFFICIAL LANGUAGE:

You _____ _____ .

Japan : I

NATIONALITY:

_____ .

COUNTRY:

_____ .

OFFICIAL LANGUAGE:

_____ .

GRAMMAR GAMES FOR TEACHERS OF ADULT ESL

Countries, Nationalities & Languages GAME CARDS #1

United States : I

NATIONALITY:
I am American.
COUNTRY:
I am from the United States.
OFFICIAL LANGUAGE:
I speak English.

Belgium : I

NATIONALITY:
I am Belgian.
COUNTRY:
I am from Belgium.
OFFICIAL LANGUAGE:
I speak French / Dutch / German.

Australia : We

NATIONALITY:
We are Australian.
COUNTRY:
We are from Australia.
OFFICIAL LANGUAGE:
We speak English.

Bolivia : We

NATIONALITY:
We are Bolivian.
COUNTRY:
We are from Bolivia.
OFFICIAL LANGUAGE:
We speak Spanish / Quechua.

Austria : They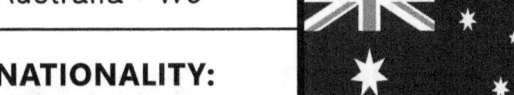

NATIONALITY:
They are Austrian.
COUNTRY:
They are from Austria.
OFFICIAL LANGUAGE:
They speak German.

Brazil : I

NATIONALITY:
I am Brazilian.
COUNTRY:
I am from Brazil.
OFFICIAL LANGUAGE:
I speak Portuguese.

Afghanistan : She

NATIONALITY:
She is Afghan.
COUNTRY:
She is from Afghanistan.
OFFICIAL LANGUAGE:
She speaks Persian / Dari / Pashto.

Cambodia : I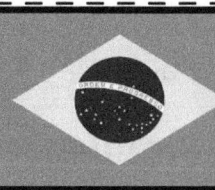

NATIONALITY:
I am Cambodian.
COUNTRY:
I am from Cambodia.
OFFICIAL LANGUAGE:
I speak Khmer (or Cambodian).

Countries, Nationalities & Languages **GAME CARDS #2**

Chile : They

NATIONALITY:
They are Chilean.
COUNTRY:
They are from Chile.
OFFICIAL LANGUAGE:
They speak Spanish.

Denmark : They

NATIONALITY:
They are Danish.
COUNTRY:
They are from Denmark.
OFFICIAL LANGUAGE:
They speak Danish.

China : We

NATIONALITY:
We are Chinese.
COUNTRY:
We are from China.
OFFICIAL LANGUAGE:
We speak Mandarin (Chinese).

Egypt : We

NATIONALITY:
We are Egyptian.
COUNTRY:
We are from Egypt.
OFFICIAL LANGUAGE:
We speak Arabic.

Colombia : I

NATIONALITY:
I am Colombian.
COUNTRY:
I am from Colombia.
OFFICIAL LANGUAGE:
I speak Spanish.

England : She

NATIONALITY:
She is English.
COUNTRY:
She is from England.
OFFICIAL LANGUAGE:
She speaks English.

Costa Rica : She

NATIONALITY:
She is Costa Rican.
COUNTRY:
She is from Costa Rica.
OFFICIAL LANGUAGE:
She speaks Spanish.

Estonia : She

NATIONALITY:
She is Estonian.
COUNTRY:
She is from Estonia.
OFFICIAL LANGUAGE:
She speaks Estonian.

Countries, Nationalities & Languages **GAME CARDS #3**   11

Finland : They

NATIONALITY:
They are Finnish.
COUNTRY:
They are from Finland.
OFFICIAL LANGUAGE:
They speak Finnish / Swedish.

Haiti : They

NATIONALITY:
They are Haitian.
COUNTRY:
They are from Haiti.
OFFICIAL LANGUAGE:
They speak French / Creole.

France : We

NATIONALITY:
We are French.
COUNTRY:
We are from France.
OFFICIAL LANGUAGE:
We speak French.

Honduras : We

NATIONALITY:
We are Honduran.
COUNTRY:
We are from Honduras.
OFFICIAL LANGUAGE:
We speak Spanish.

Germany : She

NATIONALITY:
She is German.
COUNTRY:
She is from Germany.
OFFICIAL LANGUAGE:
She speaks German.

Indonesia : I

NATIONALITY:
I am Indonesian.
COUNTRY:
I am from Indonesia.
OFFICIAL LANGUAGE:
I speak Indonesian.

Greece : She

NATIONALITY:
She is Greek.
COUNTRY:
She is from Greece.
OFFICIAL LANGUAGE:
She speaks Greek.

Ireland : They

NATIONALITY:
They are Irish.
COUNTRY:
They are from Ireland.
OFFICIAL LANGUAGE:
They speak English / (Irish) Gaelic.

Countries, Nationalities & Languages **GAME CARDS #4**

Japan : They

NATIONALITY:
They are Japanese.
COUNTRY:
They are from Japan.
OFFICIAL LANGUAGE:
They speak Japanese.

Lithuania : I

NATIONALITY:
I am Lithuanian.
COUNTRY:
I am from Lithuania.
OFFICIAL LANGUAGE:
I speak Lithuanian.

Jordan : We

NATIONALITY:
We are Jordanian.
COUNTRY:
We are from Jordan.
OFFICIAL LANGUAGE:
We speak Arabic.

Malaysia : We

NATIONALITY:
We are Malaysian.
COUNTRY:
We are from Malaysia.
OFFICIAL LANGUAGE:
We speak Malay (or Malaysian).

Italy : We

NATIONALITY:
We are Italian.
COUNTRY:
We are from Italy.
OFFICIAL LANGUAGE:
We speak Italian.

Mexico : We

NATIONALITY:
We are Mexican.
COUNTRY:
We are from Mexico.
OFFICIAL LANGUAGE:
We speak Spanish.

Laos : She

NATIONALITY:
She is Laotian.
COUNTRY:
She is from Laos.
OFFICIAL LANGUAGE:
She speaks Lao.

Botswana : I

NATIONALITY:
I am Motswana.*
COUNTRY:
I am from Botswana.
OFFICIAL LANGUAGE:
I speak English / Setswana.
* Motswana (singular), Batswana (plural)

Countries, Nationalities & Languages **GAME CARDS #5**

New Zealand : I

NATIONALITY:
I am a New Zealander.
COUNTRY:
I am from New Zealand.
OFFICIAL LANGUAGE:
I speak English / Maori.

Puerto Rico : I

NATIONALITY:
I am Puerto Rican.
COUNTRY:
I am from Puerto Rico.
OFFICIAL LANGUAGE:
I speak Spanish / English.

Norway : We

NATIONALITY:
We are Norwegian.
COUNTRY:
We are from Norway.
OFFICIAL LANGUAGE:
We speak Norwegian.

Romania : We

NATIONALITY:
We are Romanian.
COUNTRY:
We are from Romania.
OFFICIAL LANGUAGE:
We speak Romanian.

Philippines : We

NATIONALITY:
We are Philippine.
COUNTRY:
We are from the Philippines.
OFFICIAL LANGUAGE:
We speak Filipino (Tagalog) / English.

Russia : They

NATIONALITY:
They are Russian.
COUNTRY:
They are from Russia.
OFFICIAL LANGUAGE:
They speak Russian.

Poland : She

NATIONALITY:
She is Polish.
COUNTRY:
She is from Poland.
OFFICIAL LANGUAGE:
She speaks Polish.

Saudi Arabia : I

NATIONALITY:
I am Saudi (Arabian).
COUNTRY:
I am from Saudi Arabia.
OFFICIAL LANGUAGE:
I speak Arabic.

Countries, Nationalities & Languages GAME CARDS #6

Sweden : They

NATIONALITY:
They are Swedish.
COUNTRY:
They are from Sweden.
OFFICIAL LANGUAGE:
They speak Swedish.

Ukraine : He

NATIONALITY:
He is Ukrainian.
COUNTRY:
He is from Ukraine.
OFFICIAL LANGUAGE:
He speaks Ukrainian.

Switzerland : We

NATIONALITY:
We are Swiss.
COUNTRY:
We are from Switzerland.
OFFICIAL LANGUAGE:
We speak French / German / Italian / Romansch.

Uruguay : I

NATIONALITY:
I am Uruguayan.
COUNTRY:
I am from Uruguay.
OFFICIAL LANGUAGE:
I speak Spanish.

Taiwan : He

NATIONALITY:
He is Taiwanese.
COUNTRY:
He is from Taiwan.
OFFICIAL LANGUAGE:
He speaks Mandarin (Chinese).

Vietnam : I

NATIONALITY:
I am Vietnamese.
COUNTRY:
I am from Vietnam.
OFFICIAL LANGUAGE:
I speak Vietnamese.

Thailand : She

NATIONALITY:
She is Thai.
COUNTRY:
She is from Thailand.
OFFICIAL LANGUAGE:
She speaks Thai.

Wales : They

NATIONALITY:
They are Welsh.
COUNTRY:
They are from Wales.
OFFICIAL LANGUAGE:
They speak English / Welsh.

Countries, Nationalities & Languages **GAME CARDS #7**

Scotland : He

NATIONALITY:
He is Scottish.
COUNTRY:
He is from Scotland.
OFFICIAL LANGUAGE:
He speaks English.

Netherlands : He

NATIONALITY:
He is Dutch.
COUNTRY:
He is from the Netherlands (Holland).
OFFICIAL LANGUAGE:
He speaks Dutch.

Turkey : He

NATIONALITY:
He is Turkish.
COUNTRY:
He is from Turkey.
OFFICIAL LANGUAGE:
He speaks Turkish.

Latvia : He

NATIONALITY:
He is Latvian.
COUNTRY:
He is from Latvia.
OFFICIAL LANGUAGE:
He speaks Latvian.

Spain : She

NATIONALITY:
She is Spanish.
COUNTRY:
She is from Spain.
OFFICIAL LANGUAGE:
She speaks Spanish.

Israel : He

NATIONALITY:
He is Israeli.
COUNTRY:
He is from Israel.
OFFICIAL LANGUAGE:
He speaks Hebrew.

Portugal : He

NATIONALITY:
He is Portuguese.
COUNTRY:
He is from Portugal.
OFFICIAL LANGUAGE:
He speaks Portuguese / Mirandese.

Guatemala : He

NATIONALITY:
He is Guatemalan.
COUNTRY:
He is from Guatemala.
OFFICIAL LANGUAGE:
He speaks Spanish.

Countries, Nationalities & Languages GAME CARDS #8

Argentina : He

NATIONALITY:
He is Argentine.
(or Argentinian)
COUNTRY:
He is from Argentina.
OFFICIAL LANGUAGE:
He speaks Spanish.

Venezuela : I

NATIONALITY:
I am Venezuelan.
COUNTRY:
I am from Venezuela.
OFFICIAL LANGUAGE:
I speak Spanish.

Canada : He

NATIONALITY:
He is Canadian.
COUNTRY:
He is from Canada.
OFFICIAL LANGUAGE:
He speaks English / French.

Ecuador : I

NATIONALITY:
I am Ecuadorian.
COUNTRY:
I am from Ecuador.
OFFICIAL LANGUAGE:
I speak Spanish.

Cuba : She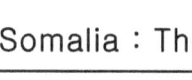

NATIONALITY:
She is Cuban.
COUNTRY:
She is from Cuba.
OFFICIAL LANGUAGE:
She speaks Spanish.

Somalia : They

NATIONALITY:
They are Somali.
COUNTRY:
They are from Somalia.
OFFICIAL LANGUAGE:
They speak Somali / Arabic.

Ethiopia : He

NATIONALITY:
He is Ethiopian.
COUNTRY:
He is from Ethiopia.
OFFICIAL LANGUAGE:
He speaks Amharic / Oromo.

Nigeria : She

NATIONALITY:
She is Nigerian.
COUNTRY:
She is from Nigeria.
OFFICIAL LANGUAGE:
She speaks English.

Questions & Negative Statements

PRE-INTERMEDIATE

LESSON PREPARATION:

Photocopy and cut out the GAME CARDS.

Divide the class into 2 teams or divide the class into groups of about 4 students and have each student play for themself.

A STUDY SHEET is provided (18).

BEGIN:

Stack the GAME CARDS, face down, on the table.

Student A takes the top card, reads the top sentence to Student B and then says **QUESTION** or **NEGATIVE**. Student B must correctly restate the sentence as a question or a negative statement to earn the card and thus the point.

If Student B says the sentence incorrectly, the card is put off to the side and no point is earned.

Student B then chooses a new card and reads to Student C, and so on until there are no more GAME CARDS left.

The student or team that earns the most GAME CARDS at the end of the game wins.

OBJECTIVE:

To learn how to ask questions and make negative statements in the simple present tense.

Upon completion of this lesson, students should know:

1. How to use *do* and *does* when asking questions.

2. How to use *don't* and *doesn't* when making negative statements.

PRIVATE LESSONS:

These GAME CARDS can also be used as flash cards for an enjoyable and effective way to review grammar with your one-to-one students.

The children **hate** peas.

 **QUESTION**

Do the children **hate** peas?

18 Simple Present: Questions & Negative Statements **STUDY SHEET**

VERB: EAT

he, she, it   **eats**
we, they, you, I   **eat**

STATEMENT

I *eat* breakfast.
We *eat* cereal.

QUESTION

we, they, you, I   **Do**

Do they *eat* pancakes?
Do your parents *eat* eggs?

NEGATIVE STATEMENT

we, they, you, I   **don't (= do not)**

We *don't eat* sweets.
Our neighbors *don't eat* meat.

VERB: DRINK

he, she, it   **drinks**
we, they, you, I   **drink**

STATEMENT

He *drinks* milk.
The cat (it) *drinks* water.

QUESTION

he, she, it   **Does**

Does Joe *drink* coffee?
Does your uncle *drink* tea?

NEGATIVE STATEMENT

he, she it   **doesn't (= does not)**

Mary *doesn't drink* soda.
My aunt *doesn't drink* lemonade.

PRACTICE: Complete these sentences.

I **talk** too fast.

1. (Do / Does) _____ I **talk** too fast?   (QUESTION)

2. I (don't / doesn't) _____ **talk** too fast.   (NEGATIVE)

He **walks** to school.

3. _____ he _____ to school?   (QUESTION)

4. He _____ _____ to school.   (NEGATIVE)

Bill and Sue **work** hard.

5. _____?   (QUESTION)

6. _____.   (NEGATIVE)

GRAMMAR GAMES FOR TEACHERS OF ADULT ESL

Questions & Negative Statements GAME CARDS #1

The children **hate** peas. **QUESTION** **Do** the children **hate** peas?	Mr. Wong **paints** houses. **QUESTION** **Does** Mr. Wong **paint** houses?	My camera **takes** bad pictures. **NEGATIVE** My camera **doesn't take** bad pictures.
Bees **make** honey. **QUESTION** **Do** bees **make** honey?	Children **learn** in school. **QUESTION** **Do** children **learn** in school?	My dog **stays** outside. **NEGATIVE** My dog **doesn't stay** outside.
I **use** a computer. **NEGATIVE** I **don't use** a computer.	Birds **fly** south for the winter. **QUESTION** **Do** birds **fly** south for the winter?	She **combs** her hair at night. **NEGATIVE** She **doesn't comb** her hair at night.
The painting **hangs** on the wall. **QUESTION** **Does** the painting **hang** on the wall?	Oranges **grow** in California. **QUESTION** **Do** oranges **grow** in California?	It **snows** in the winter. **NEGATIVE** It **doesn't snow** in the winter.
I **polish** the silver. **NEGATIVE** I **don't polish** the silver.	Tom **brushes** his teeth everyday. **QUESTION** **Does** Tom **brush** his teeth everyday?	She **sees** the bird. **QUESTION** **Does** she **see** the bird?

Questions & Negative Statements **GAME CARDS #2**

Mrs. Jones **loves** jazz music. **NEGATIVE** Mrs. Jones **doesn't love** jazz music.	They **sing** in the church choir. **QUESTION** **Do** they **sing** in the church choir?	He **washes** the dishes. **NEGATIVE** He **doesn't wash** the dishes.
I **jog** in the morning. **NEGATIVE** I **don't jog** in the morning.	Mary **takes** the train to work. **QUESTION** **Does** Mary **take** the train to work?	Our family **watches** a lot of TV. **NEGATIVE** Our family **doesn't watch** a lot of TV.
They **travel** in the summer. **NEGATIVE** They **don't travel** in the summer.	The cat **sleeps** in the chair. **QUESTION** **Does** the cat **sleep** in the chair?	Steve **wears** a necktie. **QUESTION** **Does** Steve **wear** a necktie?
Our client **speaks** French. **NEGATIVE** Our client **doesn't speak** French.	Water **boils** at 100 degrees Celsius. **QUESTION** **Does** water **boil** at 100 degrees Celsius?	The Nile **flows** into the Atlantic. **NEGATIVE** The Nile **doesn't flow** into the Atlantic.
He **cooks** dinner. **QUESTION** **Does** he **cook** dinner?	The Earth **goes** around the Sun. **QUESTION** **Does** the Earth **go** around the Sun?	Their kids **play** soccer. **QUESTION** **Do** their kids **play** soccer?

Questions & Negative Statements GAME CARDS #3

The baby **cries** all night. **QUESTION** **Does** the baby **cry** all night?	My parents **go** to bed early. **NEGATIVE** My parents **don't go** to bed early.	My boss **works** very hard. **NEGATIVE** My boss **doesn't work** very hard.
I **drive** too fast. **QUESTION** **Do** I **drive** too fast?	The children **need** new shoes. **QUESTION** **Do** the children **need** new shoes?	The store **opens** at 10 AM. **NEGATIVE** The store **doesn't open** at 10 AM.
I **eat** cereal for breakfast. **NEGATIVE** I **don't eat** cereal for breakfast.	Your hair **grows** fast. **QUESTION** **Does** your hair **grow** fast?	He **stays** up late every night. **NEGATIVE** He **doesn't stay** up late every night.
Maria and Mike **like** ice cream. **QUESTION** **Do** Maria and Mike **like** ice cream?	The computer **crashes** a lot. **QUESTION** **Does** the computer **crash** a lot?	My niece **likes** horror movies. **NEGATIVE** My niece **doesn't like** horror movies.
The bank **closes** at 5 PM. **QUESTION** **Does** the bank **close** at 5 PM?	The soup **tastes** good. **QUESTION** **Does** the soup **taste** good?	The roses **smell** nice. **QUESTION** **Do** the roses **smell** nice?

Questions & Negative Statements **GAME CARDS #4**

Flowers **bloom** in autumn. **NEGATIVE** Flowers **don't bloom** in autumn.	He **falls** asleep on the sofa. **QUESTION** **Does** he **fall** asleep on the sofa?	Tony **brings** donuts to work. **NEGATIVE** Tony **doesn't bring** donuts to work.
James **likes** to wash his car. **NEGATIVE** James **doesn't like** to wash his car.	I **understand** what you're saying. **NEGATIVE** I **don't understand** what you're saying.	Birds **build** nests in trees. **QUESTION** **Do** birds **build** nests in trees?
Kim and Ed **swim** at the beach. **NEGATIVE** Kim and Ed **don't swim** at the beach.	They **dance** very gracefully. **NEGATIVE** They **don't dance** very gracefully.	I **buy** candy at the movies. **NEGATIVE** I **don't buy** candy at the movies.
Our cousins **live** in China. **QUESTION** **Do** our cousins **live** in China?	Kim **spends** too much money. **QUESTION** **Does** Kim **spend** too much money?	He **catches** a cold every winter. **QUESTION** **Does** he **catch** a cold every winter?
Bill **hopes** he can retire soon. **QUESTION** **Does** Bill **hope** he can retire soon?	That dog **bites** people. **QUESTION** **Does** that dog **bite** people?	Mary **comes** home after school. **NEGATIVE** Mary **doesn't come** home after school.

Questions & Negative Statements GAME CARDS #5

That artist **draws** portraits. **QUESTION** **Does** that artist **draw** portraits?	The cat **meows** in the morning. **QUESTION** **Does** the cat **meow** in the morning?	I **give** my kids chores. **NEGATIVE** I **don't give** my kids chores.
The class **does** their homework. **QUESTION** **Does** the class **do** their homework?	Those dogs **bark** all night. **QUESTION** **Do** those dogs **bark** all night?	We **listen** to country music. **NEGATIVE** We **don't listen** to country music.
Jill **drinks** tea for breakfast. **NEGATIVE** Jill **doesn't drink** tea for breakfast.	Ted **finishes** his work everyday. **QUESTION** **Does** Ted **finish** his work everyday?	The mouse **hides** from the cat. **NEGATIVE** The mouse **doesn't hide** from the cat.
The cat **fights** with the dog. **NEGATIVE** The cat **doesn't fight** with the dog.	The kids **listen** to their teacher. **NEGATIVE** The kids **don't listen** to their teacher.	Kelly **keeps** food in her desk. **QUESTION** **Does** Kelly **keep** food in her desk?
Jim **gets** good grades in school. **QUESTION** **Does** Jim **get** good grades in school?	I **invite** my boss out for lunch. **NEGATIVE** I **don't invite** my boss out for lunch.	Will **makes** dinner on Fridays. **NEGATIVE** Will **doesn't make** dinner on Fridays.

Questions & Negative Statements GAME CARDS #6

My sister **wakes up** early. **NEGATIVE** My sister **doesn't wake up** early.	The sun **rises** in the East. **QUESTION** **Does** the sun **rise** in the East?	Our team **meets** at the park. **NEGATIVE** Our team **doesn't meet** at the park.
My brother **has** a cold. **NEGATIVE** My brother **doesn't have** a cold.	The sun **sets** in the West. **QUESTION** **Does** the sun **set** in the West?	My wife **pays** the phone bill. **NEGATIVE** My wife **doesn't pay** the phone bill.
Pam **leaves** her shoes outside. **QUESTION** **Does** Pam **leave** her shoes outside?	Mr. Smith **teaches** math. **NEGATIVE** Mr. Smith **doesn't teach** math.	Wendy **puts** jam on her toast. **NEGATIVE** Wendy **doesn't put** jam on her toast.
My kids **earn** a lot of money. **NEGATIVE** My kids **don't earn** a lot of money.	My aunt **sends** me cookies. **NEGATIVE** My aunt **doesn't send** me cookies.	My uncle **reads** the paper. **NEGATIVE** My uncle **doesn't read** the paper.
I **bake** pies for Christmas. **NEGATIVE** I **don't bake** pies for Christmas.	That bakery **sells** cookies. **QUESTION** **Does** that bakery **sell** cookies?	Jeff **rides** his bike to work. **QUESTION** **Does** Jeff **ride** his bike to work?

Word Scramble: Simple Present + Adjective

PRE-INTERMEDIATE

LESSON PREPARATION:

Photocopy and cut out the GAME CARDS.

Divide the class into 2 teams or divide the class into groups of about 4 students and have each student play for themselves.

A STUDY SHEET is provided (26).

BEGIN:

Stack the GAME CARDS, face down, on the table.

Student A takes the top card and reads the top sentence to Student B. Student B must unscramble the words to make a grammatically correct sentence to earn the card and thus the point. Student B may ask Student A to repeat the scrambled sentence only once.

If Student B says the sentence incorrectly, the card is put off to the side and no point is earned.

Student B then chooses a new card and reads to Student C, and so on until there are no more GAME CARDS left.

The student or team that earns the most GAME CARDS at the end of the game wins.

OBJECTIVE:

To learn how to use adjectives in simple present tense statements. Upon completion of this lesson, students should:

1. Expand their adjective vocabulary.

2. Better understand the syntax of simple present statements with adjectives.

CHEATER ALERT!

This is a listening exercise. Make sure your students are not writing the words down before unscrambling them.

PRIVATE LESSONS:

These GAME CARDS can also be used as flash cards for an enjoyable and effective way to review grammar with your one-to-one students.

---

to music He jazz listens.

ADJECTIVES: UNSCRAMBLE

He listens to *jazz* music.

26 Word Scramble: Simple Present + Adjective **STUDY SHEET**

VERB: MAKE	**VERB: LIKE**

he, she, it   **makes**   he, she, it   **likes**
we, they, you, I   **make**   we, they, you, I   **like**

NOUN: soup	**NOUN: milk**

I make **soup**.   She likes **milk**.

ADJECTIVE: delicious / terrible	**ADJECTIVE: warm / cold**

They make *delicious* **soup**.   You like *warm* **milk**.
I make *terrible* **soup**.   We like *cold* **milk**.

ADJECTIVE: spicy / healthy	**ADJECTIVE: chocolate / soy**

We make *spicy* **soup**.   He likes *chocolate* **milk**.
He makes *healthy* **soup**.   They like *soy* **milk**.

ADJECTIVE: vegetable / tomato	**ADJECTIVE: fresh / skim**

You make *vegetable* **soup**.   The dog (it) likes *fresh* **milk**.
She makes *tomato* **soup**.   I like *skim* **milk**.

PRACTICE: Complete these sentences.

a car sports drives He.

1. _____ _____ _____ _____ _____.

roses grow I red.

2. _____ _____ _____ _____.

have fresh We bread.

3. _____.

They a house in small live.

4. _____.

GRAMMAR GAMES FOR TEACHERS OF ADULT ESL

Word Scramble: Simple Present + Adjective GAME CARDS #1

---

to music He jazz listens.

ADJECTIVES: UNSCRAMBLE

He listens to *jazz* music.

You neighbors nice have.

ADJECTIVES: UNSCRAMBLE

You have *nice* neighbors.

---

delicious They pizza make.

ADJECTIVES: UNSCRAMBLE

They make *delicious* pizza.

She cake likes chocolate.

ADJECTIVES: UNSCRAMBLE

She likes *chocolate* cake.

---

pretty paints pictures She.

ADJECTIVES: UNSCRAMBLE

She paints *pretty* pictures.

---

black drinks He coffee.

ADJECTIVES: UNSCRAMBLE

He drinks *black* coffee.

I scary watch movies.

ADJECTIVES: UNSCRAMBLE

I watch *scary* movies.

---

shoes sell expensive They.

ADJECTIVES: UNSCRAMBLE

They sell *expensive* shoes.

---

wheat He bread buys.

ADJECTIVES: UNSCRAMBLE

He buys *wheat* bread.

---

mystery She novels reads.

ADJECTIVES: UNSCRAMBLE

She reads *mystery* novels.

---

jokes tell They funny.

ADJECTIVES: UNSCRAMBLE

They tell *funny* jokes.

---

wear clothes They trendy.

ADJECTIVES: UNSCRAMBLE

They wear *trendy* clothes.

Word Scramble: Simple Present + Adjective **GAME CARDS #2**

use soap We liquid. *ADJECTIVES: UNSCRAMBLE* We use **liquid** soap.	want house big a We. *ADJECTIVES: UNSCRAMBLE* We want a **big** house.
wild They tame horses. *ADJECTIVES: UNSCRAMBLE* They tame **wild** horses.	the dishes wash dirty I. *ADJECTIVES: UNSCRAMBLE* I wash the **dirty** dishes.
to islands I tropical travel. *ADJECTIVES: UNSCRAMBLE* I travel to **tropical** islands.	planes flies cargo She. *ADJECTIVES: UNSCRAMBLE* She flies **cargo** planes.
shop We stores discount at. *ADJECTIVES: UNSCRAMBLE* We shop at **discount** stores.	eat food They organic. *ADJECTIVES: UNSCRAMBLE* They eat **organic** food.
I change small save. *ADJECTIVES: UNSCRAMBLE* I save **small** change.	make You mistakes silly. *ADJECTIVES: UNSCRAMBLE* You make **silly** mistakes.
eggs We a need dozen. *ADJECTIVES: UNSCRAMBLE* We need a **dozen** eggs.	She classes math teaches. *ADJECTIVES: UNSCRAMBLE* She teaches **math** classes.

Word Scramble: Simple Present + Adjective **GAME CARDS #3**

seasonal sell produce We.	They cookies sugar bake.
ADJECTIVES: UNSCRAMBLE	**ADJECTIVES: UNSCRAMBLE**
We sell **seasonal** produce.	They bake **sugar** cookies.
cars He broken fixes.	in sauna a hot We sit.
ADJECTIVES: UNSCRAMBLE	**ADJECTIVES: UNSCRAMBLE**
He fixes **broken** cars.	We sit in a **hot** sauna.
She employees lazy fires.	the floor kitchen mop I.
ADJECTIVES: UNSCRAMBLE	**ADJECTIVES: UNSCRAMBLE**
She fires **lazy** employees.	I mop the **kitchen** floor.
people He sick heals.	want I air fresh some.
ADJECTIVES: UNSCRAMBLE	**ADJECTIVES: UNSCRAMBLE**
He heals **sick** people.	I want some **fresh** air.
ignores people She rude.	a area live in safe We.
ADJECTIVES: UNSCRAMBLE	**ADJECTIVES: UNSCRAMBLE**
She ignores **rude** people.	We live in a **safe** area.
about things absurd joke I.	firm work large We a for.
ADJECTIVES: UNSCRAMBLE	**ADJECTIVES: UNSCRAMBLE**
I joke about **absurd** things.	We work for a **large** firm.

Word Scramble: Simple Present + Adjective — GAME CARDS #4

---

homes rob wealthy They.

ADJECTIVES: UNSCRAMBLE

They rob **wealthy** homes.

---

a That good was meal.

ADJECTIVES: UNSCRAMBLE

That was a **good** meal.

We data gather classified.

ADJECTIVES: UNSCRAMBLE

We gather **classified** data.

---

support politicians I liberal.

ADJECTIVES: UNSCRAMBLE

I support **liberal** politicians.

---

food They spicy dislike.

ADJECTIVES: UNSCRAMBLE

They dislike **spicy** food.

---

percent He fifteen tips.

ADJECTIVES: UNSCRAMBLE

He tips **fifteen** percent.

---

develop software I audio.

ADJECTIVES: UNSCRAMBLE

I develop **audio** software.

---

a street busy live on They.

ADJECTIVES: UNSCRAMBLE

They live on a **busy** street.

---

during movies cry sad I.

ADJECTIVES: UNSCRAMBLE

I cry during **sad** movies.

---

says He things interesting.

ADJECTIVES: UNSCRAMBLE

He says **interesting** things.

---

people famous know They.

ADJECTIVES: UNSCRAMBLE

They know **famous** people.

---

lessons piano takes She.

ADJECTIVES: UNSCRAMBLE

She takes **piano** lessons.

Word Scramble: Simple Present + Adjective GAME CARDS #5

---

fears hairy He spiders.

ADJECTIVES: UNSCRAMBLE

He fears **hairy** spiders.

---

letters She long writes.

ADJECTIVES: UNSCRAMBLE

She writes **long** letters.

---

sales file reports They.

ADJECTIVES: UNSCRAMBLE

They file **sales** reports.

---

sends He emails pointless.

ADJECTIVES: UNSCRAMBLE

He sends **pointless** emails.

---

groups He tour leads.

ADJECTIVES: UNSCRAMBLE

He leads **tour** groups.

---

give advice They useful.

ADJECTIVES: UNSCRAMBLE

They give **useful** advice.

---

junk hides food She.

ADJECTIVES: UNSCRAMBLE

She hides **junk** food.

---

glamorous I events attend.

ADJECTIVES: UNSCRAMBLE

I attend **glamorous** events.

---

retirement I early of dream.

ADJECTIVES: UNSCRAMBLE

I dream of **early** retirement.

---

green We issues about care.

ADJECTIVES: UNSCRAMBLE

We care about **green** issues.

---

torches flaming juggles He.

ADJECTIVES: UNSCRAMBLE

He juggles **flaming** torches.

---

films dislike violent They.

ADJECTIVES: UNSCRAMBLE

They dislike **violent** films.

Word Scramble: Simple Present + Adjective GAME CARDS #6

on bed sleep I lumpy a.	vacations enjoy relaxing I.
ADJECTIVES: UNSCRAMBLE	**ADJECTIVES: UNSCRAMBLE**
I sleep on a **lumpy** bed.	I enjoy **relaxing** vacations.
people We intelligent are.	prices offer best the We.
ADJECTIVES: UNSCRAMBLE	**ADJECTIVES: UNSCRAMBLE**
We are **intelligent** people.	We offer the **best** prices.
good He manners has.	know people important I.
ADJECTIVES: UNSCRAMBLE	**ADJECTIVES: UNSCRAMBLE**
He has **good** manners.	I know **important** people.
books She library borrows.	a life happy lives She.
ADJECTIVES: UNSCRAMBLE	**ADJECTIVES: UNSCRAMBLE**
She borrows **library** books.	She lives a **happy** life.
music dance We polka to.	his He door front locks.
ADJECTIVES: UNSCRAMBLE	**ADJECTIVES: UNSCRAMBLE**
We dance to **polka** music.	He locks his **front** door.
at gym exercise I the local.	company import an own I.
ADJECTIVES: UNSCRAMBLE	**ADJECTIVES: UNSCRAMBLE**
I exercise at the **local** gym.	I own an **import** company.

Word Scramble: Simple Present + Adjective GAME CARDS #7

grow They roses beautiful. **ADJECTIVES: UNSCRAMBLE** They grow **beautiful** roses.	knits She sweaters warm. **ADJECTIVES: UNSCRAMBLE** She knits **warm** sweaters.
drive They cars vintage. **ADJECTIVES: UNSCRAMBLE** They drive **vintage** cars.	on a trail hike We peaceful. **ADJECTIVES: UNSCRAMBLE** We hike on a **peaceful** trail.
bags recycle We plastic. **ADJECTIVES: UNSCRAMBLE** We recycle **plastic** bags.	recent hire graduates We. **ADJECTIVES: UNSCRAMBLE** We hire **recent** graduates.
silver He dollars collects. **ADJECTIVES: UNSCRAMBLE** He collects **silver** dollars.	has She hair curly. **ADJECTIVES: UNSCRAMBLE** She has **curly** hair.
clothes used donate They **ADJECTIVES: UNSCRAMBLE** They donate **used** clothes.	rare He books owns. **ADJECTIVES: UNSCRAMBLE** He owns **rare** books.
hold elections We annual. **ADJECTIVES: UNSCRAMBLE** We hold **annual** elections.	salespeople I pushy avoid. **ADJECTIVES: UNSCRAMBLE** I avoid **pushy** salespeople.

Word Scramble: Simple Present + Adjective GAME CARDS #8

client meets She every.

ADJECTIVES: UNSCRAMBLE

She meets **every** client.

---

at They jokes laugh silly.

ADJECTIVES: UNSCRAMBLE

They laugh at **silly** jokes.

---

families help We needy.

ADJECTIVES: UNSCRAMBLE

We help **needy** families.

---

discounts daily offer We.

ADJECTIVES: UNSCRAMBLE

We offer **daily** discounts.

---

prefers tea strong She.

ADJECTIVES: UNSCRAMBLE

She prefers **strong** tea.

---

high They earn salaries.

ADJECTIVES: UNSCRAMBLE

They earn **high** salaries.

---

toys He unusual invents.

ADJECTIVES: UNSCRAMBLE

He invents **unusual** toys.

---

mountain own bike a I.

ADJECTIVES: UNSCRAMBLE

I own a **mountain** bike.

---

hate weather I muggy.

ADJECTIVES: UNSCRAMBLE

I hate **muggy** weather.

---

fancy They cakes bake.

ADJECTIVES: UNSCRAMBLE

They bake **fancy** cakes.

---

surprise loves parties She.

ADJECTIVES: UNSCRAMBLE

She loves **surprise** parties.

He cars antique repairs.

ADJECTIVES: UNSCRAMBLE

He repairs **antique** cars.

Word Scramble: Simple Present + Adjective GAME CARDS #9

shoes new need We. **ADJECTIVES: UNSCRAMBLE** We need **new** shoes.	cuckoo We clocks make. **ADJECTIVES: UNSCRAMBLE** We make **cuckoo** clocks.
climb trees They pine. **ADJECTIVES: UNSCRAMBLE** They climb **pine** trees.	tulips plant We pink. **ADJECTIVES: UNSCRAMBLE** We plant **pink** tulips.
fruit They dried sell. **ADJECTIVES: UNSCRAMBLE** They sell **dried** fruit.	cats She three has. **ADJECTIVES: UNSCRAMBLE** She has **three** cats.
show movies classic They. **ADJECTIVES: UNSCRAMBLE** They show **classic** movies.	raise hens free-range I. **ADJECTIVES: UNSCRAMBLE** I raise **free-range** hens.
parties wild throw They. **ADJECTIVES: UNSCRAMBLE** They throw **wild** parties.	taxes prepare I my income. **ADJECTIVES: UNSCRAMBLE** I prepare my **income** taxes.
a job has She part-time. **ADJECTIVES: UNSCRAMBLE** She has a **part-time** job.	a has He account savings. **ADJECTIVES: UNSCRAMBLE** He has a **savings** account.

BONUS! Could, Should, Would **GAME CARDS #1**

You ___ clean your yard. The neighbors are complaining. could **should** would	I was so surprised, you ___ have knocked me over with a feather. **could** should would	Your father ___ be home from work soon. It's getting late. could **should** would
You're in a library. You ___ be quiet. could **should** would	I think we ___ go to Spain for vacation. It's warmer there. could **should** would	I'm so hungry, I ___ eat a horse. **could** should would
The movie is starting. You ___ turn off your cell phone. could **should** would	You ___ not talk with your mouth full. It's impolite. could **should** would	Where ___ you like to go for dinner? could should **would**
She might be out to lunch, but she ___ also be in her office. **could** should would	You ___ call before coming over. I might be busy. could **should** would	I ___ like more information about this product. could should **would**
Please answer the phone. It ___ be an important call. **could** should would	He's lucky he fell into a pile of leaves. He ___ have hurt himself. **could** should would	___ you like to join us for dinner? Could Should **Would**

Present Continuous: Questions & Negative Statements

PRE-INTERMEDIATE

LESSON PREPARATION:

Photocopy and cut out the GAME CARDS.

Divide the class into 2 teams or divide the class into groups of about 4 students and have each student play for themselves.

A STUDY SHEET is provided (38).

BEGIN:

Stack the GAME CARDS, face down, on the table.

Student A takes the top card, reads the top sentence to Student B and then says **QUESTION** or **NEGATIVE**. Student B must correctly restate the sentence as a question or a negative statement to earn the card and thus the point.

If Student B says the sentence incorrectly, the card is put off to the side and no point is earned.

Student B then chooses a new card and reads to Student C, and so on until there are no more GAME CARDS left.

The student or team that earns the most GAME CARDS at the end of the game wins.

OBJECTIVE:

To learn how to ask questions and make negative statements in the present continuous tense. Upon completion of this lesson, students should:

1. Know how to conjugate the verb *be* for the present continuous tense.

2. Know the syntax of negative statements and questions in the present continuous tense.

PRIVATE LESSONS:

These GAME CARDS can also be used as flash cards for an enjoyable and effective way to review grammar with your one-to-one students.

She **is working** on a new project.

QUESTION

Is she **working** on a new project?

38 Present Continuous: Questions & Negative Statements **STUDY SHEET**

VERB: SLEEP

he, she, it	*is*	sleeping
we, they, you	*are*	sleeping
I	*am*	sleeping

STATEMENT

He *is* sleeping on the couch.

She *is* sleeping in a tent.

The dog (it) *is* sleeping in the yard.

QUESTION

Is he sleeping on the couch?

Is she sleeping in a tent?

Is the dog sleeping in the yard?

NEGATIVE STATEMENT

He *is* not sleeping on the couch.

She *is* not sleeping in a tent.

The dog *is* not sleeping in the yard.

VERB: BUY

he, she, it	*is*	buying
we, they, you	*are*	buying
I	*am*	buying

STATEMENT

They *are* buying groceries.

We *are* buying that house.

You *are* buying a new car.

I *am* buying dinner.

QUESTION

Are they buying groceries?

Are we buying that house?

Are you buying a new car?

Am I buying dinner?

NEGATIVE STATEMENT

They *are not* buying groceries.

We *are not* buying that house.

You *are not* buying a new car.

I *am not* buying dinner.

PRACTICE: Complete these sentences.

She *is* walking to school.

1. _____ she **walking** to school?   (Question)

2. She _____ _____ **walking** to school.   (Negative)

I *am* talking too fast.

3. _____?   (Question)

4. _____.   (Negative)

GRAMMAR GAMES FOR TEACHERS OF ADULT ESL

Pres. Cont.: Questions & Negative Statements GAME CARDS #1

She **is working** on a new project. **QUESTION** *Is she working on a new project?*	They **are waiting** for the train. **QUESTION** *Are they waiting for the train?*	They **are skiing** in Colorado. **NEGATIVE** *They are not skiing in Colorado.*
They **are selling** their house. **NEGATIVE** *They are not selling their house.*	He **is baking** pies. **QUESTION** *Is he baking pies?*	The baby **is sleeping** in her crib. **NEGATIVE** *The baby is not sleeping in her crib.*
I **am staying** at home today. **NEGATIVE** *I am not staying at home today.*	She **is washing** her bicycle. **NEGATIVE** *She is not washing her bicycle.*	The class **is learning** English. **QUESTION** *Is the class learning English?*
I **am standing** in the right place. **QUESTION** *Am I standing in the right place?*	They **are cooking** dinner. **NEGATIVE** *They are not cooking dinner.*	She **is combing** her hair. **NEGATIVE** *She is not combing her hair.*
You **are reading** my newspaper. **QUESTION** *Are you reading my newspaper?*	I **am talking** too fast. **QUESTION** *Am I talking too fast?*	He **is brushing** his teeth. **QUESTION** *Is he brushing his teeth?*

Pres. Cont.: Questions & Negative Statements GAME CARDS #2

They **are listening** to music. **NEGATIVE** They **are not listening** to music.	We **are sitting** together. **QUESTION** **Are** we **sitting** together?	We **are playing** baseball. **NEGATIVE** We **are not playing** baseball.
I **am working** on the reports. **QUESTION** **Am** I **working** on the reports?	They **are taking** the bus to work. **QUESTION** **Are** they **taking** the bus to work?	You **are wearing** a new coat. **QUESTION** **Are** you **wearing** a new coat?
Mary **is painting** a picture. **NEGATIVE** Mary **is not painting** a picture.	The dog **is barking** at the cars. **QUESTION** **Is** the dog **barking** at the cars?	You **are driving** too slowly. **NEGATIVE** You **are not driving** too slowly.
They **are singing** a song. **NEGATIVE** They **are not singing** a song.	The sun **is shining**. **QUESTION** **Is** the sun **shining**?	He **is whistling** while he works. **NEGATIVE** He **is not whistling** while he works.
Bill **is writing** a letter. **QUESTION** **Is** Bill **writing** a letter?	She **is thinking** about retiring. **NEGATIVE** She **is not thinking** about retiring.	They **are surfing** at the beach. **QUESTION** **Are** they **surfing** at the beach?

Pres. Cont.: Questions & Negative Statements **GAME CARDS #3**

You **are laughing** at me. **QUESTION** *Are you laughing at me?*	I **am listening** to the radio. **NEGATIVE** *I am not listening to the radio.*	The students **are buying** textbooks. **NEGATIVE** *The students are not buying textbooks.*
The refrigerator **is making** noise. **QUESTION** *Is the refrigerator making noise?*	He **is volunteering** at the hospital. **QUESTION** *Is he volunteering at the hospital?*	My mother **is sending** a package. **NEGATIVE** *My mother is not sending a package.*
Our boat **is sinking**. **NEGATIVE** *Our boat is not sinking.*	My sister **is helping** her friends move. **QUESTION** *Is my sister helping her friends move?*	We **are throwing** a party. **NEGATIVE** *We are not throwing a party.*
My phone **is ringing**. **NEGATIVE** *My phone is not ringing.*	The baby **is crying** again. **QUESTION** *Is the baby crying again?*	The roses **are blooming**. **NEGATIVE** *The roses are not blooming.*
They **are opening** the door. **QUESTION** *Are they opening the door?*	He **is holding** her hand. **NEGATIVE** *He is not holding her hand.*	The trees **are growing** quickly. **QUESTION** *Are the trees growing quickly?*

Pres. Cont.: Questions & Negative Statements **GAME CARDS #4**

You **are lying** to me. **QUESTION** *Are* you *lying* to me?	They **are sitting** on the bus. **QUESTION** *Are* they *sitting* on the bus?	The clerk **is putting** files on the table. **QUESTION** *Is* the clerk *putting* files on the table?
He **is trying** to fix his computer. **NEGATIVE** *He is not trying to fix his computer.*	Our team **is losing**. **NEGATIVE** *Our team is not losing.*	Leaves **are falling** from the trees. **QUESTION** *Are leaves falling from the trees?*
I **am swimming** in the pool. **NEGATIVE** *I am not swimming in the pool.*	We **are sewing** a quilt for Christmas. **NEGATIVE** *We are not sewing a quilt for Christmas.*	Your dog **is digging** up my flowers. **QUESTION** *Is your dog digging up my flowers?*
My brother **is feeding** the dogs. **NEGATIVE** *My brother is not feeding the dogs.*	She **is teaching** them how to swim. **QUESTION** *Is she teaching them how to swim?*	The baker **is slicing** the bread. **NEGATIVE** *The baker is not slicing the bread.*
Grandma **is knitting** a sweater. **QUESTION** *Is Grandma knitting a sweater?*	He **is shaving** in the bathroom. **QUESTION** *Is he shaving in the bathroom?*	The sun **is beginning** to rise. **QUESTION** *Is the sun beginning to rise?*

Pres. Cont.: Questions & Negative Statements GAME CARDS #5

The wind **is blowing** very hard. **NEGATIVE** *The wind **is not blowing** very hard.*	That dog **is following** me. **QUESTION** ***Is** that dog **following** me?*	The salesperson **is calling** the client. **NEGATIVE** *The salesperson **is not calling** the client.*
The artist **is drawing** a picture. **QUESTION** ***Is** the artist **drawing** a picture?*	The clerk **is filing** the papers. **QUESTION** ***Is** the clerk **filing** the papers?*	We **are shopping** for food. **NEGATIVE** *We **are not shopping** for food.*
The gardener **is raking** the leaves. **QUESTION** ***Is** the gardener **raking** the leaves?*	They **are moving** to a new apartment. **QUESTION** ***Are** they **moving** to a new apartment?*	They **are sailing** to Greece. **NEGATIVE** *They **are not sailing** to Greece.*
I **am shoveling** snow today. **NEGATIVE** *I **am not shoveling** snow today.*	They **are yelling** at the umpire. **QUESTION** ***Are** they **yelling** at the umpire?*	The farmers **are picking** potatoes. **NEGATIVE** *The farmers **are not picking** potatoes.*
The mailman **is delivering** the mail. **NEGATIVE** *The mailman **is not delivering** the mail.*	I **am watering** the garden. **NEGATIVE** *I **am not watering** the garden.*	He **is knocking** at the door. **QUESTION** ***Is** he **knocking** at the door?*

I **am walking** too slowly. **QUESTION** *Am I walking* too slowly?	It **is snowing** outside. **NEGATIVE** It *is not snowing* outside.	The kids **are cleaning** their room. **QUESTION** *Are* the kids *cleaning* their room?
Bill **is visiting** his parents. **NEGATIVE** Bill *is not visiting* his parents.	It **is raining**. **NEGATIVE** It *is not raining*.	The guests **are enjoying** the party. **QUESTION** *Are* the guests *enjoying* the party?
I **am building** a birdhouse. **NEGATIVE** *I am not building* a birdhouse.	The pond **is freezing**. **NEGATIVE** The pond *is not freezing*.	They **are frying** some fish. **NEGATIVE** They *are not frying* some fish.
My sister **is riding** her bike. **NEGATIVE** My sister *is not riding* her bike.	They **are boarding** the plane. **QUESTION** *Are* they *boarding* the plane?	She **is frosting** the cake. **NEGATIVE** She *is not frosting* the cake.
The cat **is purring**. **QUESTION** *Is* the cat *purring*?	He **is closing** the window. **QUESTION** *Is* he *closing* the window?	They **are decorating** the room. **QUESTION** *Are* they *decorating* the room?

Present Continuous vs. Present Simple

PRE-INTERMEDIATE

LESSON PREPARATION:

Photocopy and cut out the GAME CARDS.

Divide the class into 2 teams or divide the class into groups of about 4 students and have each student play for themself.

A STUDY SHEET is provided (46).

BEGIN:

Stack the GAME CARDS, face down, on the table.

Student A takes the top card and reads the top sentence to Student B. Student B must say whether the sentence is grammatically **CORRECT** or **INCORRECT**.

If the sentence is **INCORRECT**, Student B must say the sentence correctly to earn the card and thus the point. If the sentence is **CORRECT**, Student B must say so. If Student B gives the wrong answer, the card is put off to the side and no point is earned.

Student B then chooses a new card and reads to Student C, and so on until there are no more GAME CARDS left.

The student or team that earns the most GAME CARDS at the end of the game wins.

OBJECTIVE:

To know when to use the simple present tense and the present continuous tense. Upon completion of this lesson, students should:

1. Understand the rules for using each tense.

2. Understand the syntax of each tense.

PRIVATE LESSONS:

These GAME CARDS can also be used as flash cards for an enjoyable and effective way to review grammar with your one-to-one students.

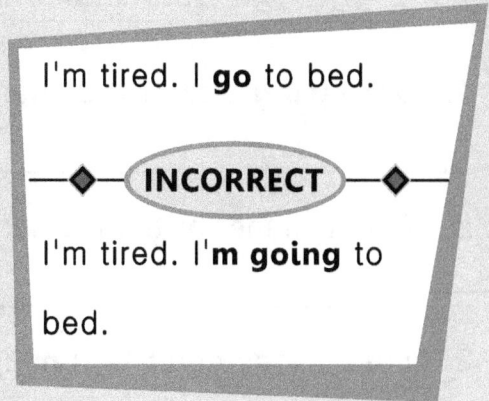

I'm tired. I **go** to bed.

◆ INCORRECT ◆

I'm tired. I**'m going** to bed.

Present Continuous vs. Simple Present — STUDY SHEET

PRESENT CONTINUOUS		SIMPLE PRESENT	
he, she, it	*is* eating	he, she, it	**eats**
we, they, you	*are* eating	we, they, you, I	**eat**
I	*am* eating		

TEMPORARY SITUATIONS	**FACTS**
I**'m reading** a good book.	Water **boils** at 100 degrees Celsius.
He**'s looking** for a new job.	The earth **goes** around the sun.

FUTURE PLANS	**GENERAL TRUTHS**
I**'m going** on vacation next week.	He **works** for ABC Company.
We**'re throwing** a dinner party.	We **speak** Spanish at home.

NOW OR AROUND NOW	**HABITS** (never, sometimes, usually, often, always)
The phone is **ringing**.	I *usually* **have** pizza for lunch.
She**'s studying** for a test today.	I *never* **watch** TV in the morning.

NON-CONTINUOUS VERBS:

be, believe, belong, concern, consist, contain, cost, depend, deserve, dislike, doubt, fit, hate, imagine, include, involve, know, lack, like, love, matter, mean, need, owe, own, prefer, possess, realize, recognize, remember, seem, suppose, understand, want, wish

PRACTICE: Are the following sentences correct? If not, rewrite them.

1. I **am eating** pizza for dinner every night.

   _____

2. We **eat** dinner at the moment.

   _____

3. These shoes don't fit. I**'m needing** a new pair.

   _____

GRAMMAR GAMES FOR TEACHERS OF ADULT ESL

Present Continuous vs. Present Simple **GAME CARDS #1**

I'm tired. I **go** to bed. — **INCORRECT** — I'm tired. I **'m going** to bed.	**Are** you **knowing** how to drive? — **INCORRECT** — **Do** you **know** how to drive?	Let's finish this meeting. It **gets** late. — **INCORRECT** — Let's finish this meeting. It**'s getting** late.
The earth **is going** around the sun. — **INCORRECT** — The earth **goes** around the sun.	She *usually* **is eating** breakfast before work. — **INCORRECT** — She *usually* **eats** breakfast before work.	The wind **blows** very hard. Let's go in. — **INCORRECT** — The wind **is blowing** very hard. Let's go in.
I'm a nurse. What **are** you **doing** for a living? — **INCORRECT** — I'm a nurse. What **do** you **do** for a living?	He **works** very hard today. — **INCORRECT** — He **is working** very hard today.	We **stay** at the hotel until Friday. — **INCORRECT** — We **are staying** at the hotel until Friday.
Every Sunday morning I **am going** to church. — **INCORRECT** — *Every* Sunday morning I **go** to church.	I **wear** my new dress to the party. — **INCORRECT** — I**'m wearing** my new dress to the party.	**Do** you **wear** that shirt today? — **INCORRECT** — **Are** you **wearing** that shirt today?
I *usually* **am watching** the news at 5:00 PM. — **INCORRECT** — I *usually* **watch** the news at 5:00 PM.	They **water** the plants this morning. — **INCORRECT** — They **are watering** the plants this morning.	Why **do** you **cry**? Here's a tissue. — **INCORRECT** — Why **are** you **crying**? Here's a tissue.

 Present Continuous vs. Present Simple **GAME CARDS #2**

They **surf** in Hawaii this week. ◆─ INCORRECT ─◆ They **are surfing** in Hawaii this week.	The score is 10 to 12. Our team **loses**. ◆─ INCORRECT ─◆ The score is 10 to 12. Our team **is losing**.	**Do** you **enjoy** this party? ◆─ INCORRECT ─◆ **Are** you **enjoying** this party?
The phone **rings**. Please answer it. ◆─ INCORRECT ─◆ The phone **is ringing**. Please answer it.	Please be quiet. The baby **sleeps**. ◆─ INCORRECT ─◆ Please be quiet. The baby **is sleeping**.	We **play** poker this Friday night. ◆─ INCORRECT ─◆ We**'re playing** poker this Friday night.
I **watch** a movie tonight. ◆─ INCORRECT ─◆ I**'m watching** a movie tonight.	I *never* **am drinking** tea in the morning. ◆─ INCORRECT ─◆ I *never* **drink** tea in the morning.	It **gets** dark. Let's turn on a light. ◆─ INCORRECT ─◆ It **is getting** dark. Let's turn on a light.
I **am working** for Telco. Who do you work for? ◆─ INCORRECT ─◆ I **work** for Telco. Who do you work for?	She **is teaching** Math every summer. ◆─ INCORRECT ─◆ She **teaches** Math every summer.	The dog **is barking** at the cars *every* night. ◆─ INCORRECT ─◆ The dog **barks** at the cars *every* night.
It **snows**. Let's make a snowman. ◆─ INCORRECT ─◆ It **is snowing**. Let's make a snowman.	Water **is boiling** at 100 Celsius? ◆─ INCORRECT ─◆ Water **boils** at 100 Celsius?	They **fish** tomorrow morning. ◆─ INCORRECT ─◆ They**'re fishing** tomorrow morning.

Present Continuous vs. Present Simple GAME CARDS #3

How **do** you **do** these days? ◆— INCORRECT —◆ How **are** you **doing** these days?	What **do** you **do** tomorrow? ◆— INCORRECT —◆ What **are** you **doing** tomorrow?	He **gets** a sled next Christmas. ◆— INCORRECT —◆ He **is getting** a sled next Christmas.
I can't go out tonight. I **study** for a test. ◆— INCORRECT —◆ I can't go out tonight. I **am studying** for a test.	I **am taking** piano lessons *every* week. ◆— INCORRECT —◆ I **take** piano lessons *every* week.	We **eat** dinner so I'll call you back. ◆— INCORRECT —◆ We **are eating** dinner so I'll call you back.
How often **are** you **going** to the doctor? ◆— INCORRECT —◆ How often **do** you **go** to the doctor?	They **move** to a new apartment today. ◆— INCORRECT —◆ They **are moving** to a new apartment today.	They **sail** to Greece in a week. ◆— INCORRECT —◆ They **are sailing** to Greece in a week.
Money **is** not **growing** on trees. ◆— INCORRECT —◆ Money **does** not **grow** on trees.	Hurry up! The bus **comes**. ◆— INCORRECT —◆ Hurry up! The bus **is coming**.	This is a fun party! I **have** a great time. ◆— INCORRECT —◆ This is a fun party! I **am having** a great time.
When **do** you **have** the baby? ◆— INCORRECT —◆ When **are** you **having** the baby?	They **are knowing** how to ride a horse. ◆— INCORRECT —◆ They **know** how to ride a horse.	I think someone **knocks** at the door. ◆— INCORRECT —◆ I think someone **is knocking** at the door.

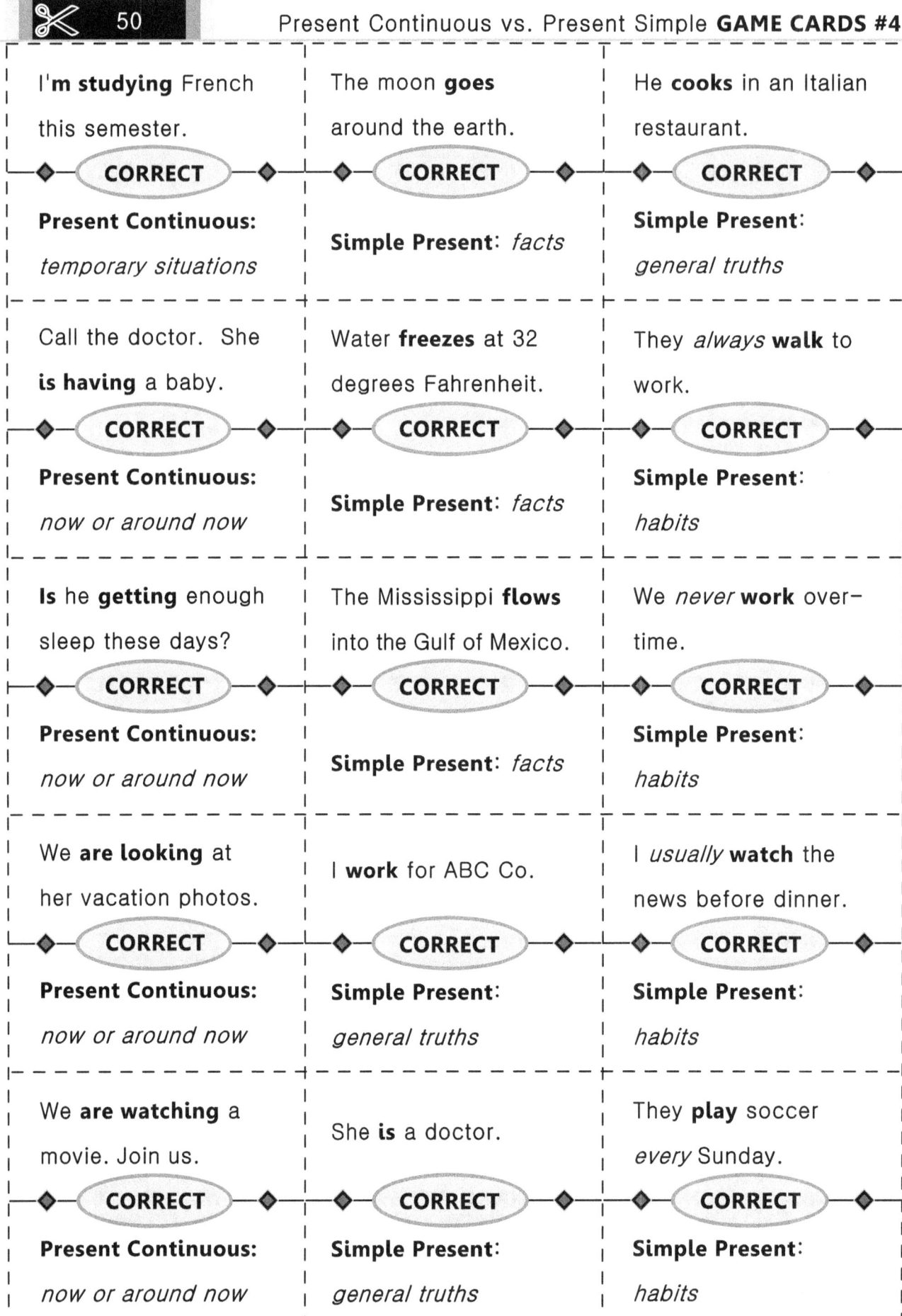

Present Continuous vs. Present Simple GAME CARDS #5   51

When **are** you **coming** over?	You**'re talking** too fast. I can't understand you.	My dinner **is burning**. I'll call you later.
CORRECT	**CORRECT**	**CORRECT**
Present Continuous: *future plans*	**Present Continuous:** *now or around now*	**Present Continuous:** *now or around now*
I **am studying** for a test next week.	I**'m moving** at the end of the month.	We**'re painting** the house next weekend.
CORRECT	**CORRECT**	**CORRECT**
Present Continuous: *future plans*	**Present Continuous:** *future plans*	**Present Continuous:** *future plans*
I**'m playing** tennis tomorrow.	He **is staying** with us until he finds a job.	I **am thinking** about taking a vacation.
CORRECT	**CORRECT**	**CORRECT**
Present Continuous: *future plans*	**Present Continuous:** *temporary situations*	**Present Continuous:** *temporary situations*
We**'re buying** a new house.	Wash up. I**'m putting** dinner on the table.	I**'m taking** a bath. Use the other bathroom.
CORRECT	**CORRECT**	**CORRECT**
Present Continuous: *future plans*	**Present Continuous:** *now or around now*	**Present Continuous:** *now or around now*
Is anyone **watching** TV or can I turn it off?	We**'re winning** but the game isn't over yet.	She**'s leaving** on Thursday.
CORRECT	**CORRECT**	**CORRECT**
Present Continuous: *now or around now*	**Present Continuous:** *temporary situations*	**Present Continuous:** *future plans*

Present Continuous vs. Present Simple **GAME CARDS #6**

My wallet **is missing**. Have you seen it?

CORRECT

Present Continuous: *now or around now*

Flowers **bloom** in the spring.

CORRECT

Simple Present: *facts*

Look! It**'s snowing** outside.

CORRECT

Present Continuous: *now or around now*

I**'m folding** the laundry at the moment.

CORRECT

Present Continuous: *now or around now*

I**'m staying** with a friend until I find a job.

CORRECT

Present Continuous: *temporary situations*

Penguins **live** in Antarctica.

CORRECT

Simple Present: *facts*

We **like** Italian food.

CORRECT

Simple Present: *general truths*

What **do** you **do**?

CORRECT

Simple Present: *general truths*

Prices **increase** *every* year.

CORRECT

Simple Present: *habits*

I **get** sick *every* winter.

CORRECT

Simple Present: *habits*

My sister **lives** in Boston.

CORRECT

Simple Present: *general truths*

My dog *often* **sleeps** on the couch.

CORRECT

Simple Present: *habits*

I**'m having** a soda. Would you like one?

CORRECT

Present Continuous: *now or around now*

I *usually* **wake** up at 8 AM.

CORRECT

Simple Present: *habits*

The pancreas **produces** insulin.

CORRECT

Simple Present: *facts*

Simple Past: Irregular Verbs

PRE-INTERMEDIATE

LESSON PREPARATION:

Photocopy and cut out the GAME CARDS.

Divide the class into 2 teams or divide the class into groups of about 4 students and have each student play for themself.

A STUDY SHEET is provided (54).

BEGIN:

Stack the GAME CARDS, face down, on the table.

Student A takes the top card and reads the present tense verb on top. Student B must correctly say the simple past tense form of that verb to earn the card and thus the point.

If Student B says the verb incorrectly, the card is put off to the side and no point is earned.

Student B then chooses a new card and reads to Student C, and so on until there are no more GAME CARDS left.

The student or team that earns the most GAME CARDS at the end of the game wins.

OBJECTIVE:

To become familiar with irregular verbs in the simple past tense.

CHEATER ALERT!

If you're not sure if the student really knows the verb or is just guessing, have them spell the verb to get the point.

PRIVATE LESSONS:

These GAME CARDS can also be used as flash cards for an enjoyable and effective way to review grammar with your one-to-one students.

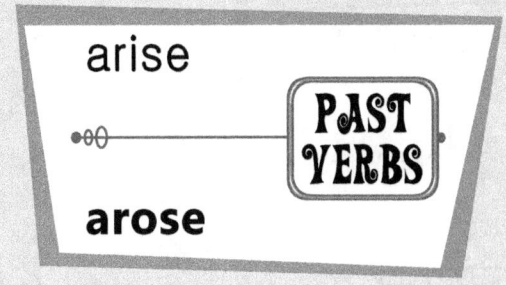

54 Simple Past: Irregular Verbs STUDY SHEET

REGULAR PAST TENSE VERBS
Add 'ed':

(walk) He walk**ed** to the store.
(talk) They talk**ed** to her.
(start) I start**ed** a new book.
(work) We work**ed** on a farm.

REGULAR PAST TENSE VERBS
with a vowel before the final 'y' add 'ed':

(play) She play**ed** tennis.
(stay) We stay**ed** in a hotel.
(enjoy) I enjoy**ed** my meal.

REGULAR PAST TENSE VERBS
with a vowel before the final consonant, double the final consonant and add 'ed':

(stop) He stop**ped** the car.
(drop) I drop**ped** my pen.

REGULAR PAST TENSE VERBS
with a consonant before the final 'y' drop the 'y' and add 'ied':

(study) I stud**ied** for the test.
(worry) You worr**ied** for nothing.

IRREGULAR PAST TENSE VERBS
have no set spelling rules and therefore must be memorized:

(eat)   He **ate** some pizza.
(drink) She **drank** a soda.
(write) I **wrote** a report.
(sit)   We **sat** in the park.

PRACTICE: Write the past tense for each verb. Which verbs are irregular? Circle the irregular verbs.

1. call = _____
2. carry = _____
3. copy = _____
4. say   = _____

5. sleep = _____
6. try   = _____
7. chop = _____
8. grab = _____

9. visit = _____
10. travel = _____
11. buy   = _____
12. put   = _____

GRAMMAR GAMES FOR TEACHERS OF ADULT ESL

Simple Past: Irregular Verbs **GAME CARDS #1**

arise / **arose**	begin / **began**	break / **broke**
babysit / **babysat**	bet / **bet**	breed / **bred**
win / **won**	bind / **bound**	bring / **brought**
wear / **wore**	bite / **bit**	wake / **woke**
beat / **beat**	bleed / **bled**	build / **built**
bend / **bent**	blow / **blew**	buy / **bought**

Simple Past: Irregular Verbs **GAME CARDS #2**

catch / caught	dig / dug	fall / fell
choose / chose	do / did	feed / fed
come / came	draw / drew	feel / felt
cost / cost	drink / drank	fight / fought
cut / cut	drive / drove	find / found
deal / dealt	eat / ate	fly / flew

Simple Past: Irregular Verbs **GAME CARDS #3**

write / **wrote**	hang / **hung**	hurt / **hurt**
forget / **forgot**	have / **had**	keep / **kept**
forgive / **forgave**	hear / **heard**	know / **knew**
freeze / **froze**	hide / **hid**	lay / **laid**
get / **got**	hit / **hit**	lead / **led**
grow / **grew**	hold / **held**	leave / **left**

Simple Past: Irregular Verbs **GAME CARDS #4**

lend / **lent**	meet / **met**	ring / **rang**
let / **let**	pay / **paid**	rise / **rose**
light / **lit**	put / **put**	run / **ran**
lose / **lost**	quit / **quit**	say / **said**
make / **made**	forbid / **forbade**	see / **saw**
mean / **meant**	ride / **rode**	sell / **sold**

Simple Past: Irregular Verbs **GAME CARDS #5**

send / sent	sing / sang	spend / spent
set / set	sink / sank	spin / spun
shake / shook	sit / sat	spread / spread
stink / stunk	sleep / slept	stand / stood
shoot / shot	slide / slid	steal / stole
shut / shut	speak / spoke	stick / stuck

Simple Past: Irregular Verbs **GAME CARDS #6**

sting / **stung**	take / **took**	understand / **understood**
strike / **struck**	teach / **taught**	broadcast / **broadcast**
swear / **swore**	tear / **tore**	become / **became**
sweep / **swept**	tell / **told**	be / **was/were**
swim / **swam**	think / **thought**	withdraw / **withdrew**
swing / **swung**	throw / **threw**	read (pronounced 'reed') / **read** (pronounced 'red')

Simple Present to Simple Past: Irregular Verbs

PRE-INTERMEDIATE

OBJECTIVE:

To become more fluent using irregular verbs in the simple past tense.

PRIVATE LESSONS:

These GAME CARDS can also be used as flash cards for an enjoyable and effective way to review grammar with your one-to-one students.

LESSON PREPARATION:

Photocopy and cut out the GAME CARDS.

Divide the class into 2 teams or divide the class into groups of about 4 students and have each student play for themselves.

A STUDY SHEET is provided (62).

BEGIN:

Stack the GAME CARDS, face down, on the table.

Student A takes the top card and reads the top sentence to Student B. Student B must correctly say the simple past tense form of that sentence to earn the card and thus the point.

If Student B says the sentence incorrectly, the card is put off to the side and no point is earned.

Student B then chooses a new card and reads to Student C, and so on until there are no more GAME CARDS left.

The student or team that earns the most GAME CARDS at the end of the game wins.

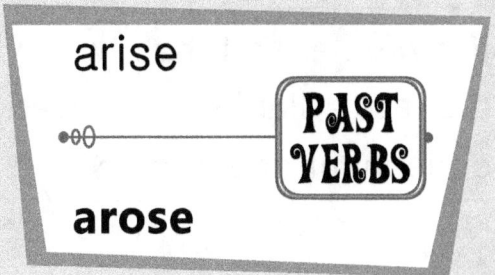

Spelling Regular Verbs **STUDY SHEET**

	PRESENT	PAST
Regular Verbs: add **ed**.	ask walk	ask**ed** walk**ed**
If a regular verb ends with an **e**, add **d**.	bake live	bake**d** live**d**
If a regular verb ends with a vowel (**a, e, i, o, u**) + **y**, add **ed**.	play enjoy	play**ed** enjoy**ed**
If a regular verb ends with a consonant + **y**, change the **y** to an **i** and add **ed**.	study try	stud**ied** tr**ied**
If a regular verb has one syllable and ends with a consonant + vowel, double the consonant and add **ed**. **	drop hug	drop**ped** hug**ged**
** don't double **w** or **x**.	mix follow	mix**ed** follow**ed**
If a regular verb has two syllables and the last syllable is stressed, double the consonant and add **ed**.	occur permit	occur**red** permit**ted**
If a regular verb has two syllables and the last syllable is *not* stressed, *don't* double the consonant.	visit travel	visit**ed** travel**ed**

GRAMMAR GAMES FOR TEACHERS OF ADULT ESL

Simple Present to Simple Past: Irregular Verbs GAME CARDS #1

I **pay** the bills. / *SIMPLE PAST* / I **paid** the bills.	She **is** at a meeting. / *SIMPLE PAST* / She **was** at a meeting.	The kids **grow** up so fast. / *SIMPLE PAST* / The kids **grew** up so fast.
I **run** 5 miles. / *SIMPLE PAST* / I **ran** 5 miles.	She **eats** lunch at noon. / *SIMPLE PAST* / She **ate** lunch at noon.	They **say** it's time to go. / *SIMPLE PAST* / They **said** it's time to go.
He **writes** the report. / *SIMPLE PAST* / He **wrote** the report.	The movie **begins** at 8 PM. / *SIMPLE PAST* / The movie **began** at 8 PM.	The ship **sinks** into the sea. / *SIMPLE PAST* / The ship **sank** into the sea.
We **drink** tea at noon. / *SIMPLE PAST* / We **drank** tea at noon.	She **throws** the ball. / *SIMPLE PAST* / She **threw** the ball.	They **come** to our house for Christmas. / *SIMPLE PAST* / They **came** to our house for Christmas.
We **set** the table. / *SIMPLE PAST* / We **set** the table.	He **catches** the ball. / *SIMPLE PAST* / He **caught** the ball.	She **takes** a walk. / *SIMPLE PAST* / She **took** a walk.

Simple Present to Simple Past: Irregular Verbs GAME CARDS #2

I **read** the newspaper. (Pronounced "**reed**".) **SIMPLE PAST** I **read** the newspaper. (Pronounced "**red**".)	We **give** gifts at Christmas. **SIMPLE PAST** We **gave** gifts at Christmas.	They **get** presents on their birthday. **SIMPLE PAST** They **got** presents on their birthday.
They **speak** Italian. **SIMPLE PAST** They **spoke** Italian.	I **make** the dinner. **SIMPLE PAST** I **made** the dinner.	She **brings** the dessert. **SIMPLE PAST** She **brought** the dessert.
We **meet** new people on vacation. **SIMPLE PAST** We **met** new people on vacation.	You **drive** a taxi. **SIMPLE PAST** You **drove** a taxi.	He **leads** the group. **SIMPLE PAST** He **led** the group.
We **sell** candy. **SIMPLE PAST** We **sold** candy.	You **win** many games. **SIMPLE PAST** You **won** many games.	You **see** a lot of people. **SIMPLE PAST** You **saw** a lot of people.
The sun **rises** early. **SIMPLE PAST** The sun **rose** early.	He **sleeps** in a hammock. **SIMPLE PAST** He **slept** in a hammock.	I **have** a cup of tea. **SIMPLE PAST** I **had** a cup of tea.

Simple Present to Simple Past: Irregular Verbs **GAME CARDS #3**

They **sing** in church.	They **tell** me everything.	The cat **tears** the furniture.
SIMPLE PAST	*SIMPLE PAST*	*SIMPLE PAST*
They **sang** in church.	They **told** me everything.	The cat **tore** the furniture.
We **fight** over money.	He **thinks** about retiring.	The player **swings** at the ball.
SIMPLE PAST	*SIMPLE PAST*	*SIMPLE PAST*
We **fought** over money.	He **thought** about retiring.	The player **swung** at the ball.
I **buy** new shoes.	They **understand** her.	I **fly** to London on business.
SIMPLE PAST	*SIMPLE PAST*	*SIMPLE PAST*
I **bought** new shoes.	They **understood** her.	I **flew** to London on business.
He **leaves** papers on his desk.	We **swim** in the pool.	We **lend** them our car.
SIMPLE PAST	*SIMPLE PAST*	*SIMPLE PAST*
He **left** papers on his desk.	We **swam** in the pool.	We **lent** them our car.
The phone **rings**.	He **sweeps** the floor.	He **teaches** history.
SIMPLE PAST	*SIMPLE PAST*	*SIMPLE PAST*
The phone **rang**.	He **swept** the floor.	He **taught** history.

Simple Present to Simple Past: Irregular Verbs GAME CARDS #4

We **shoot** many pictures. *SIMPLE PAST* We **shot** many pictures.	The trees **bend** in the wind. *SIMPLE PAST* The trees **bent** in the wind.	They **dig** holes with a shovel. *SIMPLE PAST* They **dug** holes with a shovel.
The basement **stinks**. *SIMPLE PAST* The basement **stunk**.	It **becomes** cold at night. *SIMPLE PAST* It **became** cold at night.	She **draws** pictures. *SIMPLE PAST* She **drew** pictures.
They **shake** hands. *SIMPLE PAST* They **shook** hands.	His heart **breaks** when he **sees** her. *SIMPLE PAST* His heart **broke** when he **saw** her.	Leaves **fall** from the trees. *SIMPLE PAST* Leaves **fell** from the trees.
I **lose** my keys. *SIMPLE PAST* I **lost** my keys.	We **go** out for dinner. *SIMPLE PAST* We **went** out for dinner.	She **bets** on that horse. *SIMPLE PAST* She **bet** on that horse.
The dog **bites** people. *SIMPLE PAST* The dog **bit** people.	They **cut** their prices in half. *SIMPLE PAST* They **cut** their prices in half.	They **choose** to work overtime. *SIMPLE PAST* They **chose** to work overtime.

Simple Present to Simple Past: Irregular Verbs GAME CARDS #5

They **feel** sick. **SIMPLE PAST** They **felt** sick.	We **hold** meetings on Thursday. **SIMPLE PAST** We **held** meetings on Thursday.	Your gift **means** a lot to me. **SIMPLE PAST** Your gift **meant** a lot to me.
They **keep** wine in the cellar. **SIMPLE PAST** They **kept** wine in the cellar.	They **light** the candles. **SIMPLE PAST** They **lit** the candles.	I **find** coins in the couch. **SIMPLE PAST** I **found** coins in the couch.
The water **freezes**. **SIMPLE PAST** The water **froze**.	The medicine **stings**. **SIMPLE PAST** The medicine **stung**.	They **do** the homework. **SIMPLE PAST** They **did** the homework.
They **hang** the pictures. **SIMPLE PAST** They **hung** the pictures.	They **swear** on the Bible. **SIMPLE PAST** They **swore** on the Bible.	He **deals** the cards for poker. **SIMPLE PAST** He **dealt** the cards for poker.
They **hear** crickets. **SIMPLE PAST** They **heard** crickets.	The toy **spins** on the floor. **SIMPLE PAST** The toy **spun** on the floor.	That baseball player **strikes** out a lot. **SIMPLE PAST** That baseball player **struck** out a lot.

I **know** the answer. **SIMPLE PAST** I **knew** the answer.	He **steals** jewelry. **SIMPLE PAST** He **stole** jewelry.	We **ride** the bus to work. **SIMPLE PAST** We **rode** the bus to work.
We **go** out for dinner. **SIMPLE PAST** We **went** out for dinner.	She **speeds** on the freeway. **SIMPLE PAST** She **sped** on the freeway.	I **send** the letters. **SIMPLE PAST** I **sent** the letters.
She **babysits** for us. **SIMPLE PAST** She **babysat** for us.	I **withdraw** money from the ATM. **SIMPLE PAST** I **withdrew** money from the ATM.	We **sit** on the porch. **SIMPLE PAST** We **sat** on the porch.
The car **slides** in the snow. **SIMPLE PAST** The car **slid** in the snow.	The wind **blows** hard. **SIMPLE PAST** The wind **blew** hard.	We **shut** the doors. **SIMPLE PAST** We **shut** the doors.
They **feed** the kids. **SIMPLE PAST** They **fed** the kids.	The mouse **hides** from the cat. **SIMPLE PAST** The mouse **hid** from the cat.	We **spend** a lot of money. **SIMPLE PAST** We **spent** a lot of money.

Simple Past Tense: Questions & Negative Statements

PRE-INTERMEDIATE

LESSON PREPARATION:

Photocopy and cut out the GAME CARDS.

Divide the class into 2 teams or divide the class into groups of about 4 students and have each student play for themselves.

A STUDY SHEET is provided (70).

BEGIN:

Stack the GAME CARDS, face down, on the table.

Student A takes the top card, reads the top sentence to Student B and then says **QUESTION** or **NEGATIVE**. Student B must correctly restate the sentence as a question or a negative statement to earn the card and thus the point.

If Student B says the sentence incorrectly, the card is put off to the side and no point is earned.

Student B then chooses a new card and reads to Student C, and so on until there are no more GAME CARDS left.

The student or team that earns the most GAME CARDS at the end of the game wins.

OBJECTIVE:

To gain fluency in making negative statements and asking questions in the past tense. Upon completion of this lesson, students should:

1. Know the syntax for the verb *be* in questions and negative statements in the past tense.

2. Have greater fluency when using irregular simple past tense verbs.

PRIVATE LESSONS:

These GAME CARDS can also be used as flash cards for an enjoyable and effective way to review grammar with your one-to-one students.

She **went** to the bank.

QUESTION

Did she **go** to the bank?

Simple Past: Questions & Negative Statements **STUDY SHEET**

VERB: GO	**VERB: BE**
Past Tense = **went**	Past Tense = **was / were**
STATEMENT	**STATEMENT**
He **went** to the store.	He **was** at the bank.
She **went** to the store.	She **was** at the bank.
I **went** to the store.	I **was** at the bank.
We **went** to the store.	We **were** at the bank.
They **went** to the store.	They **were** at the bank.
You **went** to the store.	You **were** at the bank.
QUESTION	**QUESTION**
Did he **go** to the store?	**Was** he at the bank?
Did she **go** to the store?	**Was** she at the bank?
Did I **go** to the store?	**Was** I at the bank?
Did we **go** to the store?	**Were** we at the bank?
Did they **go** to the store?	**Were** they at the bank?
Did you **go** to the store?	**Were** you at the bank?
NEGATIVE	**NEGATIVE**
He **didn't go** to the store.	He **wasn't** at the bank.
She **didn't go** to the store.	She **wasn't** at the bank.
I **didn't go** to the store.	I **wasn't** at the bank.
We **didn't go** to the store.	We **weren't** at the bank.
They **didn't go** to the store.	They **weren't** at the bank.
You **didn't go** to the store.	You **weren't** at the bank.

PRACTICE: Complete these sentences.

They ate pizza.

1. _____ they _____ pizza?   (Question)
2. They _____ _____ pizza.   (Negative)

I was late.

3. _____ ?   (Question)
4. _____ .   (Negative)

GRAMMAR GAMES FOR TEACHERS OF ADULT ESL

Simple Past: Questions & Negative Statements GAME CARDS #1

She **went** to the bank.	We **bet** a lot of money on the game.	They **built** a doghouse.
QUESTION	**NEGATIVE**	**QUESTION**
Did she **go** to the bank?	We **didn't bet** a lot of money on the game.	**Did** they **build** a doghouse?
He **did** his homework.	Your dog **bit** me on the leg.	The coffee **burned** my tongue.
NEGATIVE	**NEGATIVE**	**NEGATIVE**
He **didn't do** his homework.	Your dog **didn't bite** me on the leg.	The coffee **didn't burn** my tongue.
She **was** at the concert.	The wind **blew** papers everywhere.	He **bought** a new jacket.
QUESTION	**QUESTION**	**QUESTION**
Was she at the concert?	**Did** the wind **blow** papers everywhere?	**Did** he **buy** a new jacket?
The play **began** on time.	I **broke** your lamp.	She **caught** a cold.
NEGATIVE	**NEGATIVE**	**NEGATIVE**
The play **didn't begin** on time.	I **didn't break** your lamp.	She **didn't catch** a cold.
The trees **bent** in the wind.	He **brought** the potato chips.	He **chose** to work overtime.
QUESTION	**QUESTION**	**QUESTION**
Did the trees **bend** in the wind?	**Did** he **bring** the potato chips?	**Did** he **choose** to work overtime?

Simple Past: Questions & Negative Statements GAME CARDS #2

She **drew** a beautiful picture.	I **came** over to get some eggs.	I **felt** sick after eating a pizza.
NEGATIVE	**NEGATIVE**	**NEGATIVE**
She **didn't draw** a beautiful picture.	I **didn't come** over to get some eggs.	I **didn't feel** sick after eating a pizza.
We **drove** to the movie theater.	Our house **cost** a lot of money.	They always **fought** over money.
NEGATIVE	**NEGATIVE**	**NEGATIVE**
We **didn't drive** to the movie theater.	Our house **didn't cost** a lot of money.	They **didn't** always **fight** over money.
You **drank** all of the juice.	You **cut** your finger.	She **found** a wallet in the parking lot.
QUESTION	**QUESTION**	**QUESTION**
Did you **drink** all of the juice?	**Did** you **cut** your finger?	**Did** she **find** a wallet in the parking lot?
We **ate** a big dinner last night.	I **dug** a hole in the ground.	We **flew** from Paris to Chicago.
NEGATIVE	**NEGATIVE**	**NEGATIVE**
We **didn't eat** a big dinner last night.	I **didn't dig** a hole in the ground.	We **didn't fly** from Paris to Chicago.
The boy **fell** in the lake.	They **did** their homework.	They **forgot** the tickets.
QUESTION	**QUESTION**	**QUESTION**
Did the boy **fall** in the lake?	**Did** they **do** their homework?	**Did** they **forget** the tickets?

Simple Past: Questions & Negative Statements GAME CARDS #3

I **forgave** them for lying.	The pear tree **grew** quickly.	He **hit** a home run.
NEGATIVE	**NEGATIVE**	**NEGATIVE**
I **didn't forgive** them for lying.	The pear tree **didn't grow** quickly.	He **didn't hit** a home run.
The pond **froze** last winter.	I **hung** up the phone.	They **held** an election for mayor.
NEGATIVE	**NEGATIVE**	**QUESTION**
The pond **didn't freeze** last winter.	I **didn't hang** up the phone.	**Did** they **hold** an election for mayor?
She **got** a promotion at work.	They **had** a party.	He **hurt** his arm playing tennis.
QUESTION	**QUESTION**	**QUESTION**
Did she **get** a promotion at work?	**Did** they **have** a party?	**Did** he **hurt** his arm playing tennis?
We **gave** them candy.	She **heard** a sound in the attic.	I **kept** a pie in the freezer.
NEGATIVE	**NEGATIVE**	**NEGATIVE**
We **didn't give** them candy.	She **didn't hear** a sound in the attic.	I **didn't keep** a pie in the freezer.
They **went** to Paris for vacation.	He **hid** junk food in his desk.	You **knew** the answer.
QUESTION	**QUESTION**	**QUESTION**
Did they **go** to Paris for vacation?	**Did** he **hide** junk food in his desk?	**Did** you **know** the answer?

Simple Past: Questions & Negative Statements GAME CARDS #4

She **led** a tour group.	I **made** a salad for dinner.	He **read** the novel.
NEGATIVE	**NEGATIVE**	**NEGATIVE**
She **didn't lead** a tour group.	I **didn't make** a salad for dinner.	He **didn't read** the novel.
I **left** my keys in the car.	He **meant** what he said.	I **rode** my bicycle to work.
NEGATIVE	**NEGATIVE**	**NEGATIVE**
I **didn't leave** my keys in the car.	He **didn't mean** what he said.	I **didn't ride** my bicycle to work.
He **lent** her his textbook.	They **met** her at the station.	The phone **rang**.
QUESTION	**QUESTION**	**QUESTION**
Did he **lend** her his textbook?	**Did** they **meet** her at the station?	**Did** the phone **ring**?
She **let** me borrow her textbook.	I **paid** the phone bill.	The cake **rose** in the oven.
NEGATIVE	**NEGATIVE**	**NEGATIVE**
She **didn't let** me borrow her textbook.	I **didn't pay** the phone bill.	The cake **didn't rise** in the oven.
They **lost** the championship.	He **put** the files on my desk.	She **ran** 5 miles after work.
QUESTION	**QUESTION**	**QUESTION**
Did they **lose** the championship?	**Did** he **put** the files on my desk?	**Did** she **run** 5 miles after work?

Simple Past: Questions & Negative Statements GAME CARDS #5

They **said** the party was dull.	We **sang** our national anthem.	We **stood** at the bus stop.
NEGATIVE	**NEGATIVE**	**NEGATIVE**
They **didn't say** the party was dull.	We **didn't sing** our national anthem.	We **didn't stand** at the bus stop.
She **saw** a friend yesterday.	He **sat** in the park and **fed** the birds.	We **swam** in the lake.
NEGATIVE	**QUESTION**	**NEGATIVE**
She **didn't see** a friend yesterday.	**Did** he **sit** in the park and **feed** the birds?	We **didn't swim** in the lake.
They **sold** their house.	They **slept** in a tent.	She **took** the train to work.
QUESTION	**QUESTION**	**QUESTION**
Did they **sell** their house?	**Did** they **sleep** in a tent?	**Did** she **take** the train to work?
I **sent** them the contract.	I **spoke** too fast.	He **taught** them how to ski.
NEGATIVE	**QUESTION**	**QUESTION**
I **didn't send** them the contract.	**Did** I **speak** too fast?	**Did** he **teach** them how to ski?
He **shut** the door when he left.	He **spent** too much time at work.	You **tore** your shirt.
QUESTION	**QUESTION**	**QUESTION**
Did he **shut** the door when he left?	**Did** he **spend** too much time at work?	**Did** you **tear** your shirt?

Simple Past: Questions & Negative Statements GAME CARDS #6

I **told** her about my vacation.	I **wore** a hat to the beach.	The oranges **were** delicious.
NEGATIVE	**NEGATIVE**	**NEGATIVE**
I **didn't tell** her about my vacation.	I **didn't wear** a hat to the beach.	The oranges **weren't** delicious.
I **thought** about retiring.	They **won** the lottery.	She **was** in her office.
NEGATIVE	**QUESTION**	**NEGATIVE**
I **didn't think** about retiring.	**Did** they **win** the lottery?	She **wasn't** in her office.
She **threw** a party last night.	He **wrote** a report for class.	They **were** on vacation last week.
QUESTION	**QUESTION**	**QUESTION**
Did she **throw** a party last night?	**Did** he **write** a report for class?	**Were** they on vacation last week?
I **understood** what they said.	The weather **was** nice in Spain.	They **went** to the basketball game.
NEGATIVE	**QUESTION**	**QUESTION**
I **didn't understand** what they said.	**Was** the weather nice in Spain?	**Did** they **go** to the basketball game?
They **woke** up before dawn.	He **was** happy to see us.	They **were** late for the meeting.
QUESTION	**QUESTION**	**QUESTION**
Did they **wake** up before dawn?	**Was** he happy to see us?	**Were** they late for the meeting?

Present Perfect: Irregular Verbs

INTERMEDIATE

OBJECTIVE:

To learn the irregular verbs in the present perfect tense.

PRIVATE LESSONS:

These GAME CARDS can also be used as flash cards for an enjoyable and effective way to review grammar with your one-to-one students.

LESSON PREPARATION:

Photocopy and cut out the GAME CARDS.

Divide the class into 2 teams or divide the class into groups of about 4 students and have each student play for themselves.

BEGIN:

Stack the GAME CARDS, face down, on the table.

Student A takes the top card and reads the top, simple present verb to Student B. Student B must correctly say that verb in the present perfect tense to earn the card and thus the point.

If Student B says the verb incorrectly, the card is put off to the side and no point is earned.

Student B then chooses a new card and reads to Student C, and so on until there are no more GAME CARDS left.

The student or team that earns the most GAME CARDS at the end of the game wins.

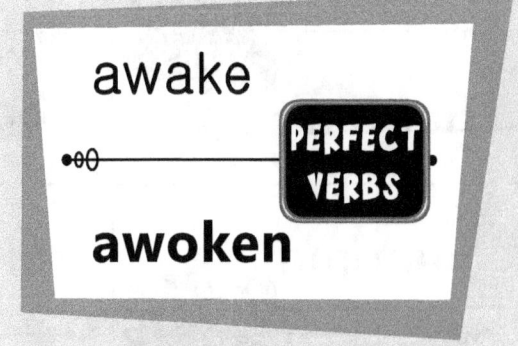

Present Perfect: Irregular Verbs **GAME CARDS #1**

base	past participle
awake	**awoken**
bend	**bent**
blow	**blown**
be	**been**
bet	**bet**
break	**broken**
bear	**born**
bid	**bid**
breed	**bred**
beat	**beaten**
bind	**bound**
bring	**brought**
become	**become**
bite	**bitten**
wear	**worn**
begin	**begun**
bleed	**bled**
build	**built**

Present Perfect: Irregular Verbs GAME CARDS #2

burst — burst	cost — cost	drive — driven
buy — bought	creep — crept	drink — drunk
catch — caught	cut — cut	eat — eaten
choose — chosen	dig — dug	fall — fallen
cling — clung	do — done	feed — fed
come — come	draw — drawn	feel — felt

Present Perfect: Irregular Verbs **GAME CARDS #3**

fight / fought	freeze / frozen	hang / hung
find / found	get / gotten	have / had
fit / fit	give / given	hear / heard
fly / flown	go / gone	hide / hidden
forget / forgotten	grind / ground	hit / hit
forgive / forgiven	grow / grown	hold / held

Present Perfect: Irregular Verbs **GAME CARDS #4**

hurt — **hurt**	leave — **left**	mean — **meant**
keep — **kept**	lend — **lent**	meet — **met**
knit — **knit**	let — **let**	thrust — **thrust**
know — **known**	lie — **lain**	upset — **upset**
lay — **laid**	lose — **lost**	wake — **woken**
lead — **led**	make — **made**	pay — **paid**

Present Perfect: Irregular Verbs **GAME CARDS #5**

prove / **proven**	rise / **risen**	send / **sent**
put / **put**	run / **run**	sew / **sewn**
quit / **quit**	say / **said**	shake / **shaken**
read / **read**	see / **seen**	shave / **shaven**
ride / **ridden**	seek / **sought**	shear / **shorn**
ring / **rung**	sell / **sold**	shine / **shone**

Present Perfect: Irregular Verbs **GAME CARDS #6**

shoot — **shot**	sit — **sat**	spin — **spun**
show — **shown**	slay — **slain**	stand — **stood**
shrink — **shrunk**	sleep — **slept**	sting — **stung**
shut — **shut**	speak — **spoken**	stink — **stunk**
sing — **sung**	speed — **sped**	swim — **swum**
sink — **sunk**	spend — **spent**	take — **taken**

Present Perfect: Irregular Verbs GAME CARDS #7

teach / **taught**	mistake / **mistaken**	weave / **woven**
tear / **torn**	understand / **understood**	wed / **wed**
tell / **told**	withhold / **withheld**	weep / **wept**
think / **thought**	broadcast / **broadcast**	win / **won**
tread / **trodden**	overcome / **overcome**	write / **written**
throw / **thrown**	overthrow / **overthrown**	uphold / **upheld**

Simple Past to Present Perfect

INTERMEDIATE

LESSON PREPARATION:

Photocopy and cut out the GAME CARDS.

Divide the class into 2 teams or divide the class into groups of about 4 students and have each student play for themselves.

A STUDY SHEET is provided (86).

BEGIN:

Stack the GAME CARDS, face down, on the table.

Student A takes the top card and reads the top sentence to Student B. Student B must correctly restate the sentence in the present perfect tense to earn the card and thus the point.

If Student B says the sentence incorrectly, the card is put off to the side and no point is earned.

Student B then chooses a new card and reads to Student C, and so on until there are no more GAME CARDS left.

The student or team that earns the most GAME CARDS at the end of the game wins.

OBJECTIVE:

To gain fluency in conjugating verbs from the simple past tense to the present perfect tense.

PRIVATE LESSONS:

These GAME CARDS can also be used as flash cards for an enjoyable and effective way to review grammar with your one-to-one students.

Did she **pay** the bill?

PRESENT PERFECT

Has she **paid** the bill?

Simple Past to Present Perfect STUDY SHEET

PAST TENSE VERBS

he, she, it **ate** pizza.

we, they, you, I **ate** pizza.

STATEMENT

He **went** to the store.

I **went** to the store.

QUESTION

Did you **buy** a pizza?

Did she **buy** a pizza?

NEGATIVE STATEMENT

They **didn't take** the train.

He **didn't take** the train.

I **didn't take** the train.

PRESENT PERFECT VERBS

he, she, it **has eaten** dinner.

we, they, you, I **have eaten** dinner.

STATEMENT

He **has been** to the store.

I **have been** to the store.

QUESTION

Have you **bought** a pizza?

Has she **bought** a pizza?

NEGATIVE STATEMENT

They **haven't taken** the train.

He **hasn't taken** the train.

I **haven't taken** the train.

PRACTICE: Write these sentences in the present perfect tense.

1. We **ate** dinner.

   We _____ _____ dinner.

2. She **didn't eat** dinner.

   She _____ _____ dinner.

3. **Did** you **eat** dinner?

   _____ you _____ dinner?

4. **Did** he **eat** dinner?

   _____ ?

GRAMMAR GAMES FOR TEACHERS OF ADULT ESL

Simple Past to Present Perfect GAME CARDS #1

Did she pay the bill?	We didn't pay the bill.	I paid the bill.
PRESENT PERFECT	**PRESENT PERFECT**	**PRESENT PERFECT**
Has she paid the bill?	We haven't paid the bill.	I have paid the bill.
Did we run 5 miles?	Chris didn't run 5 miles.	I ran 5 miles.
PRESENT PERFECT	**PRESENT PERFECT**	**PRESENT PERFECT**
Have we run 5 miles?	Chris hasn't run 5 miles.	I have run 5 miles.
Did you write the report?	I didn't write the report.	Ed wrote the report.
PRESENT PERFECT	**PRESENT PERFECT**	**PRESENT PERFECT**
Have you written the report?	I haven't written the report.	Ed has written the report.
Did the trees grow fast?	The tree didn't grow fast.	The trees grew fast.
PRESENT PERFECT	**PRESENT PERFECT**	**PRESENT PERFECT**
Have the trees grown fast?	The tree hasn't grown fast.	The trees have grown fast.
Did they take a walk?	I didn't take a walk.	Jill and Fay took a walk.
PRESENT PERFECT	**PRESENT PERFECT**	**PRESENT PERFECT**
Have they taken a walk?	I haven't taken a walk.	Jill and Fay have taken a walk.

Simple Past to Present Perfect GAME CARDS #2

You **threw** a party.	**Did** John **throw** a party?	I **didn't throw** a party.
PRESENT PERFECT	**PRESENT PERFECT**	**PRESENT PERFECT**
You **have thrown** a party.	**Has** John **thrown** a party?	I **haven't thrown** a party.
They **ate** the apples.	**Did** you **eat** the apples?	Kim **didn't eat** the apples.
PRESENT PERFECT	**PRESENT PERFECT**	**PRESENT PERFECT**
They **have eaten** the apples.	**Have** you **eaten** the apples?	Kim **hasn't eaten** the apples.
They **went** to the store.	**Did** Steve **go** to the store?	We **didn't go** to the store.
PRESENT PERFECT	**PRESENT PERFECT**	**PRESENT PERFECT**
They **have gone** to the store.	**Has** Steve **gone** to the store?	We **haven't gone** to the store.
Mary **drove** the car.	**Did** your friends **drive** the car?	Tom **didn't drive** the car.
PRESENT PERFECT	**PRESENT PERFECT**	**PRESENT PERFECT**
Mary **has driven** the car.	**Have** your friends **driven** the car?	Tom **hasn't driven** the car.
Sue **blew** out the candles.	**Did** you **blow** out the candles?	I **didn't blow** out the candles.
PRESENT PERFECT	**PRESENT PERFECT**	**PRESENT PERFECT**
Sue **has blown** out the candles.	**Have** you **blown** out the candles?	I **haven't blown** out the candles.

Simple Past to Present Perfect GAME CARDS #3

I **swam** in the lake.	**Did** the kids **swim** in the lake?	Jim **swam** in the lake.
PRESENT PERFECT	**PRESENT PERFECT**	**PRESENT PERFECT**
I **have swum** in the lake.	**Have** the kids **swum** in the lake?	Jim **has swum** in the lake.
I **spoke** to them.	**Did** you **speak** to them?	We **didn't speak** to them.
PRESENT PERFECT	**PRESENT PERFECT**	**PRESENT PERFECT**
I **have spoken** to them.	**Have** you **spoken** to them?	We **haven't spoken** to them.
They **stole** the money.	**Did** you **steal** the money?	He **didn't steal** the money.
PRESENT PERFECT	**PRESENT PERFECT**	**PRESENT PERFECT**
They **have stolen** the money.	**Have** you **stolen** the money?	He **hasn't stolen** the money.
Shelly **sang** in a choir.	**Did** he **sing** in a choir?	They **didn't sing** in a choir.
PRESENT PERFECT	**PRESENT PERFECT**	**PRESENT PERFECT**
Shelly **has sung** in a choir.	**Has** he **sung** in a choir?	They **haven't sung** in a choir.
The students **read** the book.	**Did** Angie **read** the book?	I **didn't read** the book.
PRESENT PERFECT	**PRESENT PERFECT**	**PRESENT PERFECT**
The students **have read** the book.	**Has** Angie **read** the book?	I **haven't read** the book.

Simple Past to Present Perfect GAME CARDS #4

I **wore** the coat.	**Did** he **wear** the coat?	Sherry **didn't wear** the coat.
PRESENT PERFECT	**PRESENT PERFECT**	**PRESENT PERFECT**
I **have worn** the coat.	**Has** he **worn** the coat?	Sherry **hasn't worn** the coat.
Ted **drank** the tea.	**Did** they **drink** some tea?	I **didn't drink** any tea.
PRESENT PERFECT	**PRESENT PERFECT**	**PRESENT PERFECT**
Ted **has drunk** the tea.	**Have** they **drunk** some tea?	I **haven't drunk** any tea.
I **forgot** the milk.	**Did** Uncle Bill **forget** the milk?	We **didn't forget** the milk.
PRESENT PERFECT	**PRESENT PERFECT**	**PRESENT PERFECT**
I **have forgotten** the milk.	**Has** Uncle Bill **forgotten** the milk?	We **haven't forgotten** the milk.
The twins **broke** the lamp.	**Did** Ken **break** the lamp?	I **didn't break** the lamp.
PRESENT PERFECT	**PRESENT PERFECT**	**PRESENT PERFECT**
The twins **have broken** the lamp.	**Has** Ken **broken** the lamp?	I **haven't broken** the lamp.
The pond **froze**.	The pond **didn't freeze**.	**Did** the pond **freeze**?
PRESENT PERFECT	**PRESENT PERFECT**	**PRESENT PERFECT**
The pond **has frozen**.	The pond **hasn't frozen**.	**Has** the pond **frozen**?

Simple Past to Present Perfect GAME CARDS #5

They **did** the homework.	**Did** you **do** the homework?	He **didn't do** the homework.
PRESENT PERFECT	**PRESENT PERFECT**	**PRESENT PERFECT**
They **have done** the homework.	**Have** you **done** the homework?	He **hasn't done** the homework.
The children **woke** up.	**Did** the baby **wake** up?	I **didn't wake** up.
PRESENT PERFECT	**PRESENT PERFECT**	**PRESENT PERFECT**
The children **have woken** up.	**Has** the baby **woken** up?	I **haven't woken** up.
Jeff **drew** a picture.	**Did** you **draw** a picture?	I **didn't draw** a picture.
PRESENT PERFECT	**PRESENT PERFECT**	**PRESENT PERFECT**
Jeff **has drawn** a picture.	**Have** you **drawn** a picture?	I **haven't drawn** a picture.
Our boss **chose** to retire.	**Did** they **choose** to retire?	Steve **didn't choose** to retire.
PRESENT PERFECT	**PRESENT PERFECT**	**PRESENT PERFECT**
Our boss **has chosen** to retire.	**Have** they **chosen** to retire?	Steve **hasn't chosen** to retire.
Our family **rode** in a limo.	**Did** Beth **ride** on a motorcycle?	You **didn't ride** on a mule.
PRESENT PERFECT	**PRESENT PERFECT**	**PRESENT PERFECT**
Our family **has ridden** in a limo.	**Has** Beth **ridden** on a motorcycle?	You **haven't ridden** on a mule.

Simple Past to Present Perfect **GAME CARDS #6**

We **swore** on the Bible.	**Did** they **swear** to tell the truth?	She **didn't swear** on the Bible.
PRESENT PERFECT	**PRESENT PERFECT**	**PRESENT PERFECT**
We **have sworn** on the Bible.	**Have** they **sworn** to tell the truth?	She **hasn't sworn** on the Bible.
The police **found** my wallet.	**Did** your mother **feel** sick?	We **didn't make** dinner.
PRESENT PERFECT	**PRESENT PERFECT**	**PRESENT PERFECT**
The police **have found** my wallet.	**Has** your mother **felt** sick?	We **haven't made** dinner.
They **shook** hands.	**Did** you **catch** a cold?	I **didn't sleep** in a tent.
PRESENT PERFECT	**PRESENT PERFECT**	**PRESENT PERFECT**
They **have shaken** hands.	**Have** you **caught** a cold?	I **haven't slept** in a tent.
Phil **showed** us the car.	**Did** the maid **sweep** the floor?	The client **didn't meet** my boss.
PRESENT PERFECT	**PRESENT PERFECT**	**PRESENT PERFECT**
Phil **has shown** us the car.	**Has** the maid **swept** the floor?	The client **hasn't met** my boss.
The dog **dug** a hole.	**Was** it a busy day?	I **didn't send** the letter.
PRESENT PERFECT	**PRESENT PERFECT**	**PRESENT PERFECT**
The dog **has dug** a hole.	**Has** it **been** a busy day?	I **haven't sent** the letter.

Simple Past vs. Present Perfect **GAME CARDS #7**

Our dog **came** home.	Our team **lost** the game.	The ship **didn't sink**.
PRESENT PERFECT	**PRESENT PERFECT**	**PRESENT PERFECT**
Our dog **has come** home.	Our team **has lost** the game.	The ship **hasn't sunk**.
We **forgave** them.	**Did** the cat **hide** in the tree?	I **didn't think** about retiring.
PRESENT PERFECT	**PRESENT PERFECT**	**PRESENT PERFECT**
We **have forgiven** them.	**Has** the cat **hidden** in the tree?	I **haven't thought** about retiring.
Karen **got** a raise.	My brother **quit** smoking.	He **didn't show** us his new car.
PRESENT PERFECT	**PRESENT PERFECT**	**PRESENT PERFECT**
Karen **has gotten** a raise.	My brother **has quit** smoking.	He **hasn't shown** us his new car.
Kelly **tore** her new jacket.	**Did** you **set** the table?	We **didn't shut** the doors.
PRESENT PERFECT	**PRESENT PERFECT**	**PRESENT PERFECT**
Kelly **has torn** her new jacket.	**Have** you **set** the table?	We **haven't shut** the doors.
The meeting **began**.	**Did** they **build** their new house?	She **didn't put** the books away.
PRESENT PERFECT	**PRESENT PERFECT**	**PRESENT PERFECT**
The meeting **has begun**.	**Have** they **built** their new house?	She **hasn't put** the books away.

Simple Past to Present Perfect **GAME CARDS #8**

Our family **flew** to Paris.	**Did** you **fly** to Paris?	Kate **didn't fly** to Paris.
PRESENT PERFECT	**PRESENT PERFECT**	**PRESENT PERFECT**
Our family **has flown** to Paris	**Have** you **flown** to Paris?	Kate **hasn't flown** to Paris.
The phone **rang**.	**Did** the phone **ring**?	The phone **didn't ring**.
PRESENT PERFECT	**PRESENT PERFECT**	**PRESENT PERFECT**
The phone **has rung**.	**Has** the phone **rung**?	The phone **hasn't rung**.
They **won** the tournament.	**Did** they **win** the tournament?	We **didn't win** the tournament.
PRESENT PERFECT	**PRESENT PERFECT**	**PRESENT PERFECT**
They **have won** the tournament.	**Have** they **won** the tournament?	We **haven't won** the tournament.
The temperature **rose**.	**Did** Dave's temperature **rise**?	Her temperature **didn't rise**.
PRESENT PERFECT	**PRESENT PERFECT**	**PRESENT PERFECT**
The temperature **has risen**.	**Has** Dave's temperature **risen**?	Her temperature **hasn't risen**.
We **didn't say** where it is.	**Did** Jane **say** where it is?	Bob **said** where it is.
PRESENT PERFECT	**PRESENT PERFECT**	**PRESENT PERFECT**
We **haven't said** where it is.	**Has** Jane **said** where it is?	Bob **has said** where it is.

Prepositions of Time

PRE-INTERMEDIATE

LESSON PREPARATION:

Photocopy and cut out the GAME CARDS.

Divide the class into 2 teams or divide the class into groups of about 4 students and have each student play for themselves.

A STUDY SHEET is provided (96).

BEGIN:

Stack the GAME CARDS, face down, on the table.

Student A takes the top card and reads the top sentence to Student B. Student B must say whether the sentence is grammatically **CORRECT** or **INCORRECT**.

If the sentence is **INCORRECT**, Student B must say the sentence correctly to earn the card and thus the point. If the sentence is **CORRECT**, Student B must say so. If Student B gives the wrong answer, the card is put off to the side and no point is earned.

Student B then chooses a new card and reads to Student C, and so on until there are no more GAME CARDS left.

The student or team that earns the most GAME CARDS at the end of the game wins.

OBJECTIVE:

To know how to use the prepositions of time:

1. at
2. in
3. on
4. for
5. since

PRIVATE LESSONS:

These GAME CARDS can also be used as flash cards for an enjoyable and effective way to review grammar with your one-to-one students.

The movie starts **on** 8:30.

•—[**INCORRECT**]—•

The movie starts **at** 8:30.

Prepositions of Time — STUDY SHEET

TIME OF DAY: at	**DAYS OF THE WEEK: on**
The movie starts **at** 8 PM.	I have English class **on** Monday.
I went to lunch **at** noon.	I go jogging **on** Sunday mornings.
DATE: on	**SPECIFIC DAYS: on**
I was born **on** May 15, 1965.	We had a party **on** my birthday.
Valentine's Day is **on** February 14th.	We took a cruise **on** our anniversary.
PUNCTUAL = on time	**HAVE ENOUGH TIME = in time**
My bus is never **on time**.	I arrived **in time** for the meeting.
LONGER PERIODS OF TIME: in	**DURATIONS OF TIME: in**
I was born **in** 1965.	Dinner will be ready **in** 10 minutes.
Valentine's Day is **in** February.	I ran the marathon **in** 6 hours.
HOW LONG: for	**FROM A POINT IN THE PAST: since**
I've lived in Atlanta **for** 3 years.	I've lived in Atlanta **since** 2008.
PERIODS OF THE DAY: in	**SOON = in a moment**
I get up early **in** the morning.	The doctor will see you **in a moment.**
I go to the gym **in** the afternoon.	**NOW = at the moment**
I watch the news **in** the evening.	She's on the phone **at the moment.**
PERIOD OF THE DAY: at night	**SIMULTANEOUSLY = at the same time**
I go to sleep late **at** night.	I can walk and eat **at the same time**.

There are no prepositions before the words: **This, Last, Next, Every.**

I have English class *every* Tuesday.
I went to the movies *last* Sunday.
I'm having pizza *this* afternoon.

PRACTICE: Replace any incorrect prepositions in the spaces provided.

1. I get up **in** 10 AM. _____

2. Please be **in** time for dinner. _____

3. I've worked on this project **since** 5 days. _____

4. I'm going to a party **on** next Saturday night. _____

GRAMMAR GAMES FOR TEACHERS OF ADULT ESL

Prepositions of Time GAME CARDS #1

The movie starts **on** 8:30. **INCORRECT** The movie starts **at** 8:30.	The festival is **on** October. **INCORRECT** The festival is **in** October.	The twins were born **on** 2005. **INCORRECT** The twins were born **in** 2005.
She's not at her desk **in** the moment. **INCORRECT** She's not at her desk **at** the moment.	I'll be home **on** two hours. **INCORRECT** I'll be home **in** two hours.	I never work **in** the weekend. **INCORRECT** I never work **on** the weekend.
The bus will leave **at** 20 minutes. **INCORRECT** The bus will leave **in** 20 minutes.	The wedding is **at** April. **INCORRECT** The wedding is **in** April.	She finished the report **on** an hour. **INCORRECT** She finished the report **in** an hour.
I like to read **in** night. **INCORRECT** I like to read **at** night.	I eat lunch **in** noon. **INCORRECT** I eat lunch **at** noon.	I was born **in** May 15, 1985. **INCORRECT** I was born **on** May 15, 1985.
I went out to dinner **at** my birthday. **INCORRECT** I went out to dinner **on** my birthday.	I'll be retiring **at** 6 months. **INCORRECT** I'll be retiring **in** 6 months.	The meeting is **on** 2 o'clock. **INCORRECT** The meeting is **at** 2 o'clock.

Prepositions of Time GAME CARDS #2

The movie will start **at** 15 minutes. **INCORRECT** The movie will start **in** 15 minutes.	She moved to Miami **on** 2005. **INCORRECT** She moved to Miami **in** 2005.	They get up early **at** the morning. **INCORRECT** They get up early **in** the morning.
Joe is never home **at** Friday nights. **INCORRECT** Joe is never home **on** Friday nights.	I've worked here **since** 10 years. **INCORRECT** I've worked here **for** 10 years.	We visited Italy **in** last winter. **INCORRECT** We visited Italy last winter. **(no prep)**
I'll meet you at home **at** an hour. **INCORRECT** I'll meet you at home **in** an hour.	Are you free **on** this evening? **INCORRECT** Are you free this evening? **(no prep)**	That dog always barks **in** midnight. **INCORRECT** That dog always barks **at** midnight.
I was born **on** May. **INCORRECT** I was born **in** May.	He has lived here **since** 5 years. **INCORRECT** He has lived here **for** 5 years.	I do all my chores **in** Sunday. **INCORRECT** I do all my chores **on** Sunday.
We went out to dinner **at** our anniversary. **INCORRECT** We went out to dinner **on** our anniversary.	I'm busy **in** the moment. **INCORRECT** I'm busy **at** the moment.	I sleep in **at** Sunday mornings. **INCORRECT** I sleep in **on** Sunday mornings.

Prepositions of Time GAME CARDS #3

I'll see you **in** Friday night. **INCORRECT** I'll see you **on** Friday night.	I cried **in** the end of the movie. **INCORRECT** I cried **at** the end of the movie.	He got married **on** this year. **INCORRECT** He got married this year. **(no prep)**
I'll be in India **in** next week. **INCORRECT** I'll be in India next week. **(no prep)**	I'll be there **on** an hour. **INCORRECT** I'll be there **in** an hour.	The doctor will see you **at** a moment. **INCORRECT** The doctor will see you **in** a moment.
Please be **in** time for class. **INCORRECT** Please be **on** time for class.	The buses don't run **at** Sundays. **INCORRECT** The buses don't run **on** Sundays.	Don't talk and eat **in** the same time. **INCORRECT** Don't talk and eat **at** the same time.
Disco music started **at** the 70s. **INCORRECT** Disco music started **in** the 70s.	We let the cat out **in** night. **INCORRECT** We let the cat out **at** night.	I'll call you **at** Tuesday. **INCORRECT** I'll call you **on** Tuesday.
I'll be home **at** three days. **INCORRECT** I'll be home **in** three days.	We're going to Paris **at** a week. **INCORRECT** We're going to Paris **in** a week.	Valentine's Day is **at** February 14th. **INCORRECT** Valentine's Day is **on** February 14th.

Prepositions of Time **GAME CARDS #4**

They both spoke **in** the same time. **INCORRECT** They both spoke **at** the same time.	My bus never arrives **at** time. **INCORRECT** My bus never arrives **on** time.	Let's have lunch **at** noon. **CORRECT** **At** *time of day*
I finished the race **on** 3 hours. **INCORRECT** I finished the race **in** 3 hours.	The meeting is at 9. Please be **in** time. **INCORRECT** The meeting is at 9. Please be **on** time.	I went to sleep **at** midnight. **CORRECT** **At** *time of day*
She's never at home **at** Friday nights. **INCORRECT** She's never at home **on** Friday nights.	I get paid **on** the end of the month. **INCORRECT** I get paid **at** the end of the month.	We go fishing **at** sunrise. **CORRECT** **At** *time of day*
They have been married **for** 1980. **INCORRECT** They have been married **since** 1980.	I'll be home **on** time for dinner. **INCORRECT** I'll be home **in** time for dinner.	I don't like to drive **at** night. **CORRECT** **At** *period of the day (night)*
We can't offer a discount **in** this time. **INCORRECT** We can't offer a discount **at** this time.	I paid the bill **at** last month. **INCORRECT** I paid the bill last month. **(No Prep)**	I'm not working **on** my birthday. **CORRECT** **On** *days & dates*

Prepositions of Time GAME CARDS #5

Our anniversary is **on** June 12th. **CORRECT** **On** *days & dates*	We have brunch *every* weekend. **CORRECT** *No prep before* **last, next, this, every**	I was born **in** the 70s. **CORRECT** **in** *longer periods of time*
I can work and talk **at** the same time. **CORRECT** **At** *the same time = simultaneously*	She went to Boston *last* winter. **CORRECT** *No prep before* **last, next, this, every**	I play tennis **on** Sunday afternoons. **CORRECT** **On** *day + night(s), morning(s), evening(s)*
I'm busy **at** the moment. **CORRECT** **At** *the moment = now*	I'll be at a seminar *next* week. **CORRECT** *No prep before* **last, next, this, every**	I go home early **on** Friday afternoons. **CORRECT** **On** *day + night(s), morning(s), evening(s)*
I'll take questions **at** this time. **CORRECT** **At** *this time = now*	We're leaving *this* Tuesday morning. **CORRECT** *No prep before* **last, next, this, every**	I'll be starting my new job **in** a week. **CORRECT** **in** *from now to a point in the future*
We're having breakfast **in** an hour. **CORRECT** **in** *from now to a point in the future*	I take Math classes **in** the evenings. **CORRECT** **in** *the morning(s), the afternoon(s), the evening(s)*	They'll be here **in** a minute. **CORRECT** **in** *from now to a point in the future*

Prepositions of Time GAME CARDS #6

They cleaned the house **in** an hour.	The card arrived **in time** for her birthday.	We will be home **at** 6:30.
CORRECT	**CORRECT**	**CORRECT**
in *how long something takes*	**in time** = *soon enough*	**At** *the time of day*

We sold the candy **in** two weeks.	We've been waiting **for** 2 hours.	He'll be starting classes **in** August.
CORRECT	**CORRECT**	**CORRECT**
in *how long something takes*	**for** *how long*	**in** *longer periods of time*

My flight left **on** time.	Stocks have been down **since** last May.	I have a test **in** the afternoon.
CORRECT	**CORRECT**	**CORRECT**
on time = *punctual or punctually*	**since** *from a point in the past to now*	**in** *the morning(s), afternoon(s), evening(s)*

Our meetings never start **on time**.	I can hold my breath **for** 5 minutes.	I hate getting up **on** Monday mornings.
CORRECT	**CORRECT**	**CORRECT**
on time = *punctual or punctually*	**for** *how long*	**On** *day + night(s), morning(s), evening(s)*

I'll be home **in time** for dinner.	We've been retired **since** 2011.	The sun will set **in** about an hour.
CORRECT	**CORRECT**	**CORRECT**
in time = *soon enough*	**since** *from a point in the past to now*	**in** *from now to a point in the future*

Prepositions of Place

PRE-INTERMEDIATE

LESSON PREPARATION:

Photocopy and cut out the GAME CARDS.

Divide the class into 2 teams or divide the class into groups of about 4 students and have each student play for themself.

A STUDY SHEET is provided (104).

BEGIN:

Stack the GAME CARDS, face down, on the table.

Student A takes the top card and reads the top sentence to Student B. Student B must say whether the sentence is grammatically **CORRECT** or **INCORRECT**.

If the sentence is **INCORRECT**, Student B must say the sentence correctly to earn the card and thus the point. If the sentence is **CORRECT**, Student B must say so. If Student B gives the wrong answer, the card is put off to the side and no point is earned.

Student B then chooses a new card and reads to Student C, and so on until there are no more GAME CARDS left.

The student or team that earns the most GAME CARDS at the end of the game wins.

OBJECTIVE:

To know how to use the prepositions of place:

1. at
2. in
3. on

PRIVATE LESSONS:

These GAME CARDS can also be used as flash cards for an enjoyable and effective way to review grammar with your one-to-one students.

She left her hat **in** the bus.

INCORRECT

She left her hat **on** the bus.

Prepositions of Place — STUDY SHEET

SURFACES: on

There is a sign **on** the door.

We played **on** the beach.

MOUNTAINS, WOODS, FOREST: in

She goes hiking **in** the mountains.

I like to camp **in** the woods.

A POINT: at

Turn left **at** the traffic light.

The office is **at** the end of the hall.

TRANSPORATION (CAR, TAXI): in

I left my keys **in** the car.

I read the report **in** the taxi.

GEOGRAPHIC LOCATIONS: in

She lives **in** Ireland.

The Sears Tower is **in** Chicago.

WHERE ACTIONS/EVENTS OCCUR: at

We ate dinner **at** the Smiths.

I stayed **at** a hotel.

TELEVISION, RADIO, PHONE: on

We saw the accident **on** TV.

I listen to the news **on** the radio.

ENCLOSURES: in

They had a picnic **in** the garden.

It's cold **in** this office.

DIRECTIONS: on

The bakery is **on** the left.

The bank is **on** the right.

DOCTOR, DENTIST, SALON: at

He's **at** the doctor's.

She's **at** the salon for a haircut.

SMALL ISLANDS: on

He vacationed **on** Maui.

They live **on** a deserted island.

WATER: in

There's a fly **in** my soup.

The kids are **in** the pool.

LINES: in

I hate waiting **in** lines.

Arrange these cups **in** a row.

TRANSPORATION (PLANE, BUS): on

It was crowded **on** the bus.

Smoking isn't allowed **on** the plane.

STREETS, ROADS, ETC.: on

He lives **on** Madison Ave.

The bakery is **on** MLK Blvd.

POINTS ALONG A ROUTE: at

We stopped **at** Grand Central Station.

The commuter ferry docks **at** 3 ports.

BOOK, NEWSPAPER, MAGAZINE: in

Please don't write **in** that book.

I read it **in** the newspaper.

HOME, SCHOOL, WORK: at

She's working **at** home today.

We had a Christmas party **at** work.

BED, JAIL: in

He's **in** bed with a fever.

She's **in** jail for stealing.

ADDRESS: at

We live **at** 1234 Main Street.

Our office is **at** 5678 North Avenue.

PRACTICE: Replace any incorrect prepositions in the spaces provided.

1. Jupiter is the largest planet **at** our solar system. _____

2. I live **at** Carter Blvd. _____

GRAMMAR GAMES FOR TEACHERS OF ADULT ESL

Prepositions of Place GAME CARDS #1

She left her hat **in** the bus. **INCORRECT** She left her hat **on** the bus.	I spent my vacation **in** a cruise ship. **INCORRECT** I spent my vacation **on** a cruise ship.	We have a pool table **at** our basement. **INCORRECT** We have a pool table **in** our basement.
I read the paper **in** the train. **INCORRECT** I read the paper **on** the train.	I was sleepy so I stayed **at** bed. **INCORRECT** I was sleepy so I stayed **in** bed.	The meeting is **at** Room 12. **INCORRECT** The meeting is **in** Room 12.
He sings **at** the shower. **INCORRECT** He sings **in** the shower.	Your shoes are **in** the stairs. **INCORRECT** Your shoes are **on** the stairs.	Your books are **on** the hallway. **INCORRECT** Your books are **in** the hallway.
They showed two movies **in** the plane. **INCORRECT** They showed two movies **on** the plane.	I must be **in** work at 8AM. **INCORRECT** I must be **at** work at 8AM.	We watched the tournament **in** Joe's. **INCORRECT** We watched the tournament **at** Joe's.
We stayed **at** Spain all summer. **INCORRECT** We stayed **in** Spain all summer.	I stayed **in** home for my vacation. **INCORRECT** I stayed **at** home for my vacation.	The supermarket is **at** 12th Avenue. **INCORRECT** The supermarket is **on** 12th Avenue.

Prepositions of Place GAME CARDS #2

I saw it **in** television. **INCORRECT** I saw it **on** television.	We have a cabin **at** the woods. **INCORRECT** We have a cabin **in** the woods.	He was waiting **on** the bus stop. **INCORRECT** He was waiting **at** the bus stop.
I read about it **on** a magazine. **INCORRECT** I read about it **in** a magazine.	Please hang that picture **at** the wall. **INCORRECT** Please hang that picture **on** the wall.	The bakery is **on** the end of the street. **INCORRECT** The bakery is **at** the end of the street.
She found it **in** the map. **INCORRECT** She found it **on** the map.	Someone's **in** the door. **INCORRECT** Someone's **at** the door.	He is **at** jail for stealing. **INCORRECT** He is **in** jail for stealing.
We live **at** Maple Avenue. **INCORRECT** We live **on** Maple Avenue.	She lives **in** the island of Hawaii. **INCORRECT** She lives **on** the island of Hawaii.	There are 20 rooms **at** this hotel. **INCORRECT** There are 20 rooms **in** this hotel.
Ms. Jones is talking **in** the phone. **INCORRECT** Ms. Jones is talking **on** the phone.	She's **in** the dentist for a check-up. **INCORRECT** She's **at** the dentist for a check-up.	I hate standing **on** long lines. **INCORRECT** I hate standing **in** long lines.

Prepositions of Place GAME CARDS #3

Is someone **at** the lobby? **INCORRECT** Is someone **in** the lobby?	Turn right **in** the next intersection. **INCORRECT** Turn right **at** the next intersection.	Please put the food **in** the table. **INCORRECT** Please put the food **on** the table.
She's working **in** her desk. **INCORRECT** She's working **at** her desk.	There's a spider **in** the ceiling. **INCORRECT** There's a spider **on** the ceiling.	The switch is **on** the top of the stairs. **INCORRECT** The switch is **at** the top of the stairs.
We played croquet **in** the lawn. **INCORRECT** We played croquet **on** the lawn.	There are bears **at** the forest. **INCORRECT** There are bears **in** the forest.	Buy your tickets **in** the next window. **INCORRECT** Buy your tickets **at** the next window.
We had a picnic **in** the grass. **INCORRECT** We had a picnic **on** the grass.	The office is **in** the end of the hall. **INCORRECT** The office is **at** the end of the hall.	Put the ice cream **on** the freezer. **INCORRECT** Put the ice cream **in** the freezer.
I got two books **in** the library. **INCORRECT** I got two books **at** the library.	We had dinner **in** a friend's house. **INCORRECT** We had dinner **at** a friend's house.	We live **on** 1234 Elm Street. **INCORRECT** We live **at** 1234 Elm Street.

Prepositions of Place GAME CARDS #4

I live **at** Australia. **INCORRECT** I live **in** Australia.	Grandma sits **on** her rocking chair. **INCORRECT** Grandma sits **in** her rocking chair.	Please put the bottles **in** a row. **CORRECT** *in* lines, rows
Smoking **in** the plane is prohibited. **INCORRECT** Smoking **on** the plane is prohibited.	The baby is crawling **at** the floor. **INCORRECT** The baby is crawling **on** the floor.	Is there any cereal **in** the kitchen? **CORRECT** *in* an enclosure
The water **on** the pool is warm. **INCORRECT** The water **in** the pool is warm.	I fell asleep **in** the couch. **INCORRECT** I fell asleep **on** the couch.	I'm a student **at** Stanford University. **CORRECT** *at* home, school, work
I'll be working **at** my garden tomorrow. **INCORRECT** I'll be working **in** my garden tomorrow.	She is sitting **in** a park bench. **INCORRECT** She is sitting **on** a park bench.	I sat **in** the Jacuzzi. **CORRECT** *in* water
There is a stain **in** your tie. **INCORRECT** There is a stain **on** your tie.	I like to lie **in** the beach. **INCORRECT** I like to lie **on** the beach.	I put the chairs **in** my truck. **CORRECT** *in* a car, taxi

Prepositions of Place GAME CARDS #5

We live **on** Maple Blvd. **CORRECT** **on** *roads, streets, etc.*	The prices aren't written **on** the menu. **CORRECT** **on** *surfaces*	The local bus stops **at** every station. **CORRECT** **at** *points or stations along a trip*
We went for a spin **in** my convertible. **CORRECT** **in** *a car, taxi*	The school is **at** 45 West Elm Circle. **CORRECT** **at** *a street address*	We had a bake sale **at** our school. **CORRECT** **at** *where an action or event happens*
My apartment is **on** the 5th floor. **CORRECT** **on** *surfaces*	I heard a great song **on** the radio. **CORRECT** **on** *television, radio, phone*	Please put these books **on** that shelf. **CORRECT** **on** *surfaces*
Please wipe your shoes **on** the mat. **CORRECT** **on** *surfaces*	We get our tax forms **at** the post office. **CORRECT** **at** *where an action or event happens*	What would you like **on** your pizza? **CORRECT** **on** *surfaces*
There's a pie **in** the oven. **CORRECT** **in** *an enclosure*	It was crowded **in** the bank today. **CORRECT** **in** *an enclosure*	We saw a play **at** the theater. **CORRECT** **at** *where an action or event happens*

Prepositions of Place GAME CARDS #6

The rooms **in** that hotel are too cold.	CORRECT	**in** *an enclosure*
I have an appointment **at** the hairdresser's.	CORRECT	**at** *doctor, dentist, salon*
We had a barbeque **in** the backyard.	CORRECT	**in** *an enclosure*
Write your answers **on** the yellow paper.	CORRECT	**on** *surfaces*
The Eiffel Tower is **in** Paris.	CORRECT	**in** *a geographic location*
The directions are **in** the manual.	CORRECT	**in** *a newspaper, book, magazine*
Please don't write **in** your textbook.	CORRECT	**in** *a newspaper, book, magazine*
Were you **at** the wedding?	CORRECT	**at** *where an action or event happens*
The train stops **in** New York and Boston.	CORRECT	**in** *a geographic location*
The party is **at** Mary's house.	CORRECT	**at** *where an action or event happens*
Did you leave your key **in** the door?	CORRECT	**in** *an enclosure*
The bathroom is **on** the left.	CORRECT	**on** *directions*
My dog is **at** the veterinarian.	CORRECT	**at** *doctor, dentist, salon*
I'm going to soak **in** the tub.	CORRECT	**in** *an enclosure*
I like to listen to music **on** the radio.	CORRECT	**on** *the radio, phone, television*

Phrasal Verbs with Prepositions

LESSON PREPARATION:

Photocopy and cut out the GAME CARDS.

Divide the class into 2 teams or divide the class into groups of about 4 students and have each student play for themselves.

BEGIN:

Stack the GAME CARDS, face down, on the table.

Student A takes the top card and reads the sentence and the 3 prepositions to Student B. Student B must choose the correct preposition that completes the phrasal verb to earn the card and thus the point. *A brief definition of the phrasal verb is included to help students make an informed choice.*

If Student B chooses the wrong preposition, the card is put off to the side and no point is earned.

Student B then chooses a new card and reads to Student C, and so on until there are no more GAME CARDS left.

The student or team that earns the most GAME CARDS at the end of the game wins.

ADVANCED

OBJECTIVE:

To learn how to use phrasal verbs with prepositions.

PRIVATE LESSONS:

These GAME CARDS can also be used as flash cards for an enjoyable and effective way to review grammar with your one-to-one students.

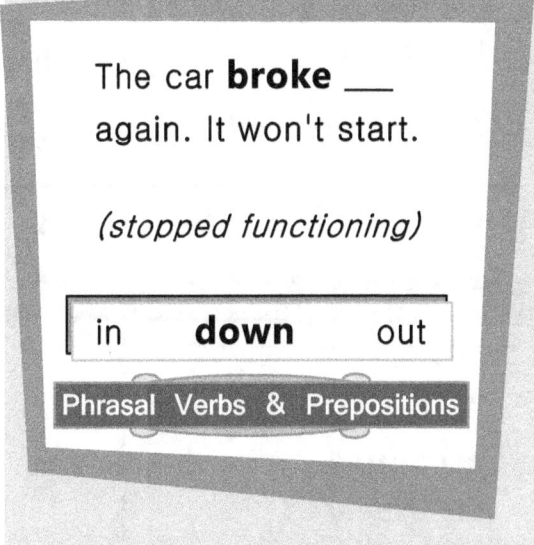

Phrasal Verbs with Prepositions **GAME CARDS #1**

The car **broke** ___ again. It won't start. (stopped functioning) in **down** out	Behave yourself and don't **talk** ___ to your mother! (a rude reply to an order or request) **back** up out	I **blacked** ___ when I fell and hit my head. (lost consciousness) off down **out**
Your explanation doesn't **add** ___. It doesn't make sense. (seem reasonable) **up** to in	He's **applying** ___ a new job. (submitting an application) at on **for**	Let's buy candles in case there is another **black** ___. (widespread power outage) **out** off under
You must **abide** ___ our rules if you want to live here. (agree to, accept) with for **by**	I should **avail** myself ___ the chance to retire early. (take advantage) **of** with to	The crime scene was **blocked** ___ by the police. (stopped access to, closed) out **off** in
We need to **account** ___ all of our expenses. (explain or justify) with **for** on	He slowly **backed** ___ from the big dog. (retreated or withdrew) out **away** up	The potato **blew** ___ in the microwave. (exploded) out away **up**

Phrasal Verbs with Prepositions GAME CARDS #2

Too many lies can **break** ___ a marriage. (end a relationship) **up** off out	The game has been **called** ___ due to rain. (cancelled) out away **off**	The child just **clammed** ___ and never said a word. (was quiet) back **up** away
It takes a lot of hard work to **bring** ___ a child. (raise a child) **up** on in	You should **calm** ___ and not get so excited. (relax) **down** away out	The shop **closed** ___ after only 1 year in business. (termination of operation) out off **down**
We **bumped** ___ our neighbors at the station. (met by chance) on **into** by	Sorry for the interruption. Please **carry** ___. (continue) away **on** into	I **came** ___ some old photos in the attic. (find unexpectedly) for to **across**
She's **burned** ___ from working too hard. (fatigue from being overworked) **out** away up	Evaluations will be **carried** ___ in each department. (put into effect, completed) **out** across up	The politician did not **come** ___ as honest. (leave an impression) out on **across**

Phrasal Verbs with Prepositions GAME CARDS #3

We can **count** ___ our new boss. She's very competent.

(depend or rely upon)

| across | **on** | of |

I must **draw** ___ a contract before we can do business.

(draft a legal document)

| on | in | **up** |

Our vacation plans **fell** ___ when our car broke down.

(came to nothing)

| off | away | **through** |

If you make a mistake on your test, just **cross** it ___.

(draw a line through)

| down | in | **out** |

I like to **dress** ___ for special events.

(wear fancy clothes)

| down | **up** | in |

I can't **figure** ___ how to put this toy together.

(understand, solve)

| **out** | on | up |

You should **cut** ___ snacks between meals.

(eliminate)

| around | into | **out** |

I always **drop** ___ the bakery on the way to work.

(a brief, unannounced visit)

| **by** | across | at |

Fill ___ this job application.

(complete a document)

| on | up | **out** |

I'll **deal** ___ the calls when I get back from vacation.

(take action)

| **with** | away | in |

I **dropped** the kids ___ at school this morning.

(delivered, unloaded)

| out | **off** | up |

I need to **find** ___ what time the train leaves.

(discover, confirm)

| **out** | in | through |

Phrasal Verbs with Prepositions GAME CARDS #4

I've been **getting** ___ with temporary work. (barely surviving financially)	I usually **get** ___ at 8 AM. (rise from bed)	I'm bored. Let's **hang** ___ at the mall. (idle one's time)
by up away	out back **up**	**out** away up

Push the button when you want to **get** ___ the bus. (disembark)	I feel better since I **gave** ___ smoking. (quit)	Please **hang** ___ the phone. (break a telephone connection)
on **off** out	out **up** back	**up** off down

Have your tickets ready before you **get** ___ the plane. (embark)	I **went** ___ a lot of red tape before buying my house. (endured)	If you don't **hurry** ___, we'll be late. (move faster)
in into **on**	into over **through**	on **up** off

I don't **get** ___ much anymore. (leave one's home, socialize)	We **grew** ___ in a strict household. (were raised, reared)	Try to **iron** ___ your differences. (resolve, clear up)
out by up	out on **up**	**out** away through

Phrasal Verbs with Prepositions GAME CARDS #5

We should **kick** ___ our promotion before Christmas.

(start, begin)

| **off** | on | in |

Our new neighbors are **moving** ___.

(occupy a living or working space)

| **in** | on | off |

He nearly **passed** ___ after running the marathon.

(lost consciousness)

| **out** | away | up |

Don't **leave** ___ the salt when you make the sauce.

(omit, exclude)

| away | off | **out** |

Our son has finally **moved** ___ of the house.

(vacated a living or working space)

| away | **out** | off |

When will you **pay** ___ the $10 I lent you?

(repay a loan)

| up | **back** | away |

The team is counting on you. Don't **let** them ___.

(disappoint)

| back | **down** | off |

My aunt often **nods** ___ in her chair.

(falls asleep)

| out | over | **off** |

We can't **put** ___ fixing the heater any longer.

(postpone, defer)

| out | down | **off** |

We hired a nanny to **look** ___ our kids.

(take care of)

| over | around | **after** |

We chose to **opt** ___ of the firm's savings plan.

(choose not to participate)

| **out** | down | off |

The firefighters were able to **put** ___ the fire.

(extinguish)

| **out** | away | down |

Phrasal Verbs with Prepositions GAME CARDS #6

Our teacher **pointed** ___ our errors on the test.

(to indicate, note)

| along | on | **out** |

Phrasal Verbs & Prepositions

He likes to **show** ___ his new sports car.

(seek attention by displaying one's attributes)

| around | up | **off** |

Phrasal Verbs & Prepositions

They **turned** ___ our first offer on the house.

(refuse, reject)

| **down** | away | out |

Phrasal Verbs & Prepositions

We have a new district manager we can **rely** ___.

(have trust in)

| **on** | from | in |

Phrasal Verbs & Prepositions

This meeting is important so please **show** ___ on time.

(arrive at a specified meeting)

| **up** | around | in |

Phrasal Verbs & Prepositions

Don't **use** ___ all the hot water. I need to take a bath.

(consume completely)

| **up** | out | down |

Phrasal Verbs & Prepositions

Let's not **rule** ___ changing our logo.

(reject for consideration)

| off | **out** | over |

Phrasal Verbs & Prepositions

Our flight is scheduled to **take** ___ at midnight.

(leave the ground)

| out | over | **off** |

Phrasal Verbs & Prepositions

I can **vouch** ___ Jim's honesty.

(support as being true, certain, etc.)

| from | **for** | by |

Phrasal Verbs & Prepositions

We can't **run** ___ from our responsibilities.

(flee, escape)

| back | **away** | out |

Phrasal Verbs & Prepositions

Our team cannot **take** ___ any more projects. We're busy.

(undertake, assume)

| along | **on** | in |

Phrasal Verbs & Prepositions

Watch ___! There's a dog in the road.

(be careful)

| **out** | up | away |

Phrasal Verbs & Prepositions

Phrasal Verbs with Prepositions **GAME CARDS #7**

I **agree** ___ what he says. I have the same opinion.

(have the same views)

| **with** | on | to |

Phrasal Verbs & Prepositions

I already **checked** ___ at the hotel.

(registered – i.e. at a hotel)

| out | around | **in** |

Phrasal Verbs & Prepositions

Try to **focus** ___ your goals and not get distracted.

(concentrate)

| in | to | **on** |

Phrasal Verbs & Prepositions

If we **back** ___ from this strike, we won't get better pay.

(withdraw, retreat)

| in | out | **down** |

Phrasal Verbs & Prepositions

Come ___ with any information you may have.

(volunteer)

| **forward** | down | up |

Phrasal Verbs & Prepositions

He never **got** ___ the loss of his mother.

(recovered from)

| around | behind | **over** |

Phrasal Verbs & Prepositions

The robber **broke** ___ our house with a crowbar.

(enter by force)

| down | around | **into** |

Phrasal Verbs & Prepositions

The party **died** ___ after the neighbors called the police.

(become calm or quiet)

| out | away | **down** |

Phrasal Verbs & Prepositions

Please **hand** ___ your reports before you leave.

(submit)

| up | around | **in** |

Phrasal Verbs & Prepositions

Please don't **butt** ___ on my personal affairs.

(interfere)

| on | up | **in** |

Phrasal Verbs & Prepositions

If you **drop** ___ of school you won't get a good job.

(stop attending school)

| **out** | down | away |

Phrasal Verbs & Prepositions

You're welcome to **join** ___ the game.

(participate)

| on | **in** | over |

Phrasal Verbs & Prepositions

Phrasal Verbs with Prepositions **GAME CARDS #8**

I need to **make** ___ an excuse for taking the day off.

(concoct or invent)

| **up** | over | in |

Phrasal Verbs & Prepositions

Let's **think** ___ our options before we make a decision.

(ponder)

| around | down | **over** |

Phrasal Verbs & Prepositions

She was so tired, she **conked** ___ on the plane.

(fell into a deep sleep)

| **out** | down | away |

Phrasal Verbs & Prepositions

She finally **owned** ___ to eating all the cake.

(admitted)

| in | **up** | on |

Phrasal Verbs & Prepositions

The brakes have **worn** ___ and need to be replaced.

(used beyond repair)

| back | over | **out** |

Phrasal Verbs & Prepositions

The speech was boring and seemed to **drag** ___ forever.

(proceed with tedious slowness)

| off | out | **on** |

Phrasal Verbs & Prepositions

Your Aunt can **put** you ___ while you're in Chicago.

(to house someone)

| in | on | **up** |

Phrasal Verbs & Prepositions

I need to **work** ___ exactly how much tax I owe.

(calculate)

| from | **out** | down |

Phrasal Verbs & Prepositions

The car slowed down when I **eased** ___ the gas pedal.

(reduce severity, pressure, tension)

| out | **off** | up |

Phrasal Verbs & Prepositions

I want to **set** ___ a bank account for my kids.

(create or enable)

| **up** | to | down |

Phrasal Verbs & Prepositions

I need to **shop** ___ for a new computer.

(look for the best bargain)

| **around** | out | away |

Phrasal Verbs & Prepositions

The burglar **got** ___ with all of our cash and jewelry.

(escaped)

| **away** | up | across |

Phrasal Verbs & Prepositions

Phrasal Verbs with Prepositions **GAME CARDS #9**

We should **allow** ___ extra guests and buy more food. (make concessions) about **for** around	We need to **check** ___ by 12 PM. (vacate and pay your bill at a hotel) **out** up off	Grandma **passed** ___ peacefully in her sleep. (died) out **away** down
Can you **back** ___ your statement with proof? (support) **up** in off	Water bottles will be **handed** ___ before the race. (distributed) **out** away in	Please **pick** ___ the laundry at the dry cleaners. (collect or gather) away **up** through
A riot **broke** ___ during the strike. (began abruptly) **out** down in	You should **jot** ___ a few notes during the meeting. (write quickly or briefly) away in **down**	I'll try to **work** ___ your schedule. (accommodate) in **around** from
Mr. Hill is not in at the moment. Can he **call** you ___? (return a phone call) out **back** in	There was a **mix** ___ at the hotel and I got the wrong key. (to confuse a person or a thing for another) around **up** in	It's time for our boss to **step** ___. (resign, relinquish control) **down** out away

Countable vs. Uncountable Nouns

LESSON PREPARATION:

Photocopy and cut out the GAME CARDS.

Divide the class into 2 teams or divide the class into groups of about 4 students and have each student play for themselves.

A STUDY SHEET is provided (122).

BEGIN:

Stack the GAME CARDS, face down, on the table.

Student A takes the top card and reads the top word to Student B. Student B must correctly say if the noun is countable or uncountable to earn the card and thus the point.

If Student B is incorrect, the card is put off to the side and no point is earned.

Student B then chooses a new card and reads to Student C, and so on until there are no more GAME CARDS left.

The student or team that earns the most GAME CARDS at the end of the game wins.

BEGINNER

OBJECTIVE:

To learn the proper usage of countable nouns versus uncountable nouns.

PRIVATE LESSONS:

These GAME CARDS can also be used as flash cards for an enjoyable and effective way to review grammar with your one-to-one students.

SUGGESTION:

To add more of a challenge, have the students give a sentence for each word to show that they really understand the countable vs. uncountable concept.

122 Countable vs. Uncountable Nouns **STUDY SHEET**

COUNTABLE NOUN:
A noun that can be counted.

For example:

UNCOUNTABLE NOUN:
A noun that can't be counted.

For example:

I have **one** apple.

They ate **a dozen** donuts.

We sang **three** songs.

He bought **four** shirts.

She read **two** books.

I have information. (correct)

I have some information. (correct)

We cannot say:

I have informations. (incorrect)

I have two informations. (incorrect)

I have some informations. (incorrect)

Countable nouns are usually made plural by adding an 's' at the end of the word. However, there are exceptions to this rule. For example:

Uncountable nouns cannot be made plural by adding an 's' at the end of the word. A noun quantifier is used instead. For example:

At the zoo I saw *three* **tigers**, *four* **bears**, *five* **sheep**, *eight* **deer**, *hundreds* of **fish**, *ten* **geese**, *two* **mice**, *nine* **elk**, and *six* **oxen**.

To make this cake you'll need **2** eggs, **3 cups of** flour, **2 cups of** sugar, **2 sticks of** butter, **1 teaspoon of** vanilla, **1 tablespoon of** baking soda and **a pinch of** salt.

PRACTICE: Are these nouns countable or uncountable?

1. bread _____
2. music _____
3. time _____

4. juice _____
5. car _____
6. hour _____

7. house _____
8. name _____
9. water _____

GRAMMAR GAMES FOR TEACHERS OF ADULT ESL

Countable vs. Uncountable Nouns **GAME CARDS #1**

air	information	pasta
UNCOUNTABLE	UNCOUNTABLE	UNCOUNTABLE
baggage	data	progress
UNCOUNTABLE	UNCOUNTABLE	UNCOUNTABLE
bread	knowledge	research
UNCOUNTABLE	UNCOUNTABLE	UNCOUNTABLE
equipment	luggage	travel
UNCOUNTABLE	UNCOUNTABLE	UNCOUNTABLE
furniture	money	work
UNCOUNTABLE	UNCOUNTABLE	UNCOUNTABLE
garbage	news	water
UNCOUNTABLE	UNCOUNTABLE	UNCOUNTABLE

Countable vs. Uncountable Nouns **GAME CARDS #2**

cheese UNCOUNTABLE	coffee UNCOUNTABLE	homework UNCOUNTABLE
makeup UNCOUNTABLE	education UNCOUNTABLE	ice UNCOUNTABLE
art UNCOUNTABLE	electricity UNCOUNTABLE	love UNCOUNTABLE
beef UNCOUNTABLE	entertainment UNCOUNTABLE	music UNCOUNTABLE
blood UNCOUNTABLE	food UNCOUNTABLE	rain UNCOUNTABLE
butter UNCOUNTABLE	gold UNCOUNTABLE	rice UNCOUNTABLE

Countable vs. Uncountable Nouns GAME CARDS #3

salt	traffic	flour
UNCOUNTABLE	UNCOUNTABLE	UNCOUNTABLE
sand	jewelry	grass
UNCOUNTABLE	UNCOUNTABLE	UNCOUNTABLE
snow	plastic	soup
UNCOUNTABLE	UNCOUNTABLE	UNCOUNTABLE
sugar	weather	cream
UNCOUNTABLE	UNCOUNTABLE	UNCOUNTABLE
tea	honey	luck
UNCOUNTABLE	UNCOUNTABLE	UNCOUNTABLE
toothpaste	shampoo	gas / petrol
UNCOUNTABLE	UNCOUNTABLE	UNCOUNTABLE

Countable vs. Uncountable Nouns **GAME CARDS #4**

house	door	ticket
COUNTABLE	COUNTABLE	COUNTABLE
car	window	movie
COUNTABLE	COUNTABLE	COUNTABLE
dog	poem	box
COUNTABLE	COUNTABLE	COUNTABLE
child	suitcase	bag
COUNTABLE	COUNTABLE	COUNTABLE
cat	dollar bill	toe
COUNTABLE	COUNTABLE	COUNTABLE
doctor	coin	cup
COUNTABLE	COUNTABLE	COUNTABLE

Countable vs. Uncountable Nouns **GAME CARDS #5**

word	address	towel
COUNTABLE	COUNTABLE	COUNTABLE
trip / journey	stamp	chair
COUNTABLE	COUNTABLE	COUNTABLE
banana	pencil	spoon
COUNTABLE	COUNTABLE	COUNTABLE
cake	jar	necklace
COUNTABLE	COUNTABLE	COUNTABLE
job	bottle	shirt
COUNTABLE	COUNTABLE	COUNTABLE
company	tube	leaf
COUNTABLE	COUNTABLE	COUNTABLE

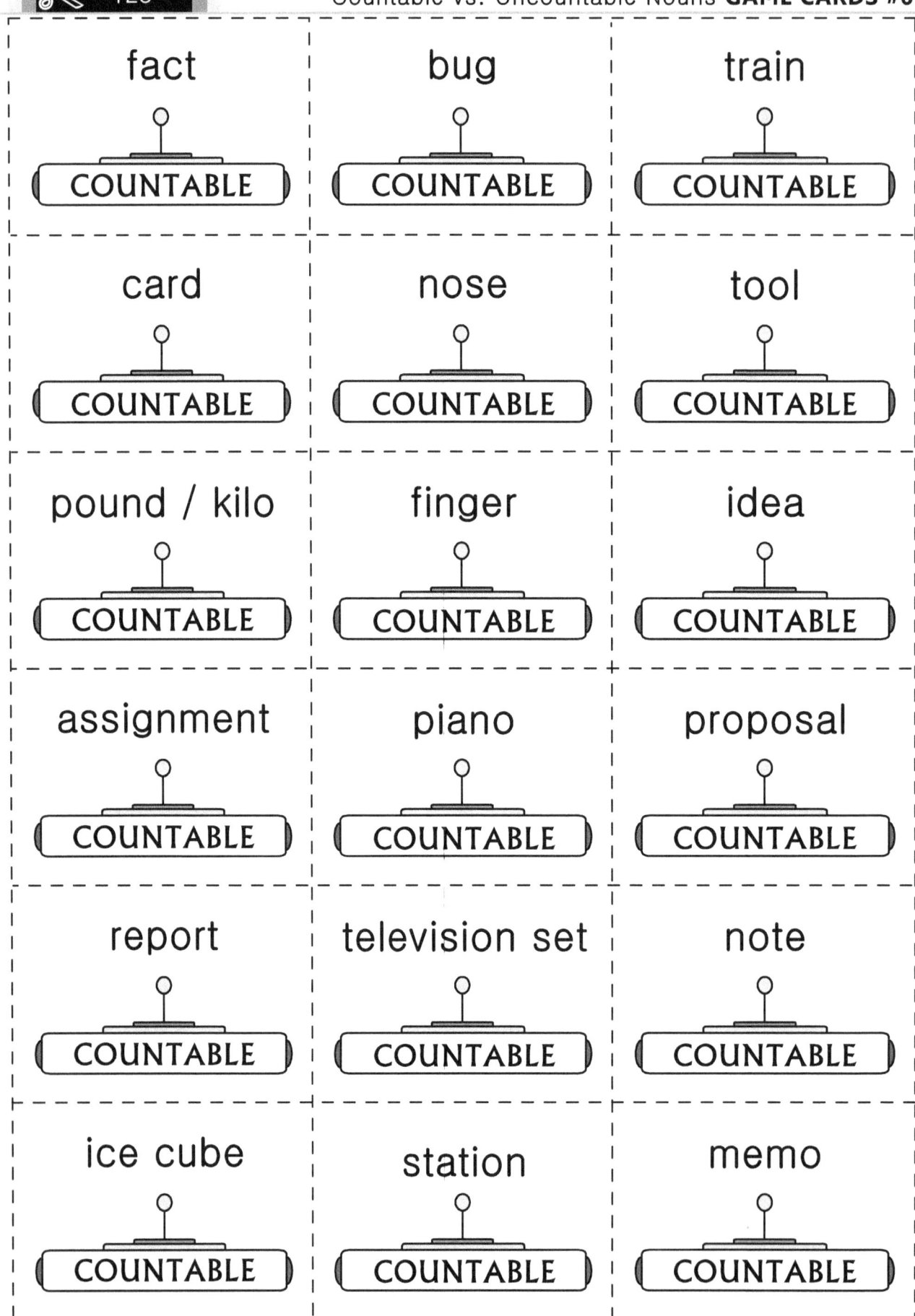

Noun Quantifiers

LESSON PREPARATION:

Photocopy and cut out the GAME CARDS.

Divide the class into 2 teams or divide the class into groups of about 4 students and have each student play for themselves.

A STUDY SHEET is provided (130).

BEGIN:

Stack the GAME CARDS, face down, on the table.

Student A takes the top card and reads the phrase and the 3 nouns to Student B. Student B must choose the correct noun to complete the phrase to earn the card and thus the point.

If Student B chooses incorrectly, the card is put off to the side and no point is earned.

Student B then chooses a new card and reads to Student C, and so on until there are no more GAME CARDS left.

The student or team that earns the most GAME CARDS at the end of the game wins.

BEGINNER

OBJECTIVE:

To become more fluent with quantifiers.

PRIVATE LESSONS:

These GAME CARDS can also be used as flash cards for an enjoyable and effective way to review grammar with your one-to-one students.

A *glass* of ____

a. apples
b. milk
c. butter

Noun Quantifiers

Noun Quantifiers STUDY SHEET

Quantifiers are words that precede and modify both countable and uncountable *nouns*. They tell us *how many* or *how much*.

Countable Noun: Puppies	**Uncountable Noun:** Salt
a *couple* of puppies	*some* salt
a *few* puppies	a *cup* of salt
a *litter* of puppies	a *pound* of salt
some puppies	a *teaspoon* of salt
several puppies	a *pinch* of salt
five puppies	a *grain* of salt

Countable Noun: Cookies	**Uncountable Noun:** Soda
a *box* of cookies	a *bottle* of soda
a *dozen* cookies	a *case* of soda
a *plate* of cookies	a *can* of soda
a *batch* of cookies	a *liter* of soda

PRACTICE: Which noun goes with each quantifier?

1. A *loaf* of ____.
   a. sugar
   b. butter
   c. bread

2. A *slice* of ____.
   a. ice cream
   b. cookies
   c. cake

3. A *cup* of ____.
   a. tea
   b. bagels
   c. pizza

4. A *dozen* ____.
   a. grapes
   b. donuts
   c. potatoes

5. A *head* of ____.
   a. lettuce
   b. cantaloupe
   c. watermelon

6. A *bar* of ____.
   a. bacon
   b. soap
   c. pie

GRAMMAR GAMES FOR TEACHERS OF ADULT ESL

Noun Quantifiers **GAME CARDS #1**

A *glass* of ___
a. apples
b. milk
c. butter
Noun Quantifiers

A *glass* of ___
a. juice
b. jam
c. sugar
Noun Quantifiers

A *glass* of ___
a. tea
b. coffee
c. water
Noun Quantifiers

A *stick* of ___
a. butter
b. cheese
c. carrot
Noun Quantifiers

A *dozen* ___
a. eggs
b. crackers
c. bananas
Noun Quantifiers

A *dozen* ___
a. ice cream
b. bread
c. donuts
Noun Quantifiers

A *slice* of ___
a. coffee
b. cookies
c. pizza
Noun Quantifiers

A *slice* of ___
a. cheese
b. lettuce
c. pasta
Noun Quantifiers

A *slice* of ___
a. chocolate
b. bread
c. potatoes
Noun Quantifiers

A *cup* of ___
a. coffee
b. spaghetti
c. steak
Noun Quantifiers

A *cup* of ___
a. eggs
b. tea
c. cereal
Noun Quantifiers

A *cup* of ___
a. potato chips
b. sausage
c. hot cocoa
Noun Quantifiers

A *carton* of ___
a. rice
b. honey
c. milk
Noun Quantifiers

A *gallon* of ___
a. apples
b. milk
c. sugar
Noun Quantifiers

A *bottle* of ___
a. aspirin
b. dental floss
c. bandages
Noun Quantifiers

Noun Quantifiers **GAME CARDS #2**

A *sheet* of ___
- **a. paper**
- b. towel
- c. napkin

Noun Quantifiers

A *piece* of ___
- a. pen
- **b. paper**
- c. rubber band

Noun Quantifiers

A *pinch* of ___
- a. tea
- **b. salt**
- c. water

Noun Quantifiers

A *piece* of ___
- a. butter
- b. eggs
- **c. cake**

Noun Quantifiers

A *bunch* of ___
- a. cherries
- b. apples
- **c. bananas**

Noun Quantifiers

A *bunch* of ___
- **a. grapes**
- b. plums
- c. pineapples

Noun Quantifiers

An *ear* of ___
- a. mushroom
- b. cucumber
- **c. corn**

Noun Quantifiers

A *head* of ___
- **a. lettuce**
- b. grapefruit
- c. coconut

Noun Quantifiers

A *head* of ___
- a. pumpkin
- **b. cabbage**
- c. eggplant

Noun Quantifiers

A *bowl* of ___
- a. hot dogs
- **b. soup**
- c. pizza

Noun Quantifiers

A *bowl* of ___
- **a. cereal**
- b. toast
- c. pancakes

Noun Quantifiers

A *glass* of ___
- a. soup
- b. ice cream
- **c. wine**

Noun Quantifiers

A *can* of ___
- **a. soda**
- b. honey
- c. water

Noun Quantifiers

A *bulb* of ___
- a. onion
- **b. garlic**
- c. radish

Noun Quantifiers

A *stalk* of ___
- a. cucumber
- b. carrot
- **c. celery**

Noun Quantifiers

Noun Quantifiers **GAME CARDS #3** 133

A *tube* of ___
a. toothpaste
b. sponges
c. toilet paper
Noun Quantifiers

A *roll* of ___
a. napkins
b. paper
c. film
Noun Quantifiers

A *roll* of ___
a. soap
b. toilet paper
c. towels
Noun Quantifiers

A *grain* of ___
a. sand
b. flour
c. tea
Noun Quantifiers

A *drop* of ___
a. eggs
b. water
c. jelly
Noun Quantifiers

A *strand* of ___
a. teeth
b. toes
c. hair
Noun Quantifiers

A *pair* of ___
a. pants
b. clothes
c. jewelry
Noun Quantifiers

A *roll* of ___
a. glue
b. tape
c. staples
Noun Quantifiers

A *tank* of ___
a. charcoal
b. wood
c. gas
Noun Quantifiers

A *jar* of ___
a. butter
b. peanut butter
c. cereal
Noun Quantifiers

A *pint* of ___
a. hair
b. bones
c. blood
Noun Quantifiers

A *bottle* of ___
a. perfume
b. deodorant
c. toothpaste
Noun Quantifiers

A *batch* of ___
a. cookies
b. pies
c. cakes
Noun Quantifiers

A *keg* of ___
a. wine
b. beer
c. whiskey
Noun Quantifiers

A *box* of ___
a. butter
b. eggs
c. cereal
Noun Quantifiers

Noun Quantifiers **GAME CARDS #4**

A *pitcher* of ___	A *gust* of ___	A *ray* of ___
a. beer	a. rain	a. snow
b. whiskey	**b. wind**	b. rain
c. wine	c. sunshine	**c. sunshine**
Noun Quantifiers	**Noun Quantifiers**	**Noun Quantifiers**

A *bolt* of ___	A *work* of ___	A *pair* of ___
a. lightning	a. pencil	a. umbrellas
b. thunder	**b. art**	b. hats
c. snow	c. painting	**c. shoes**
Noun Quantifiers	**Noun Quantifiers**	**Noun Quantifiers**

A *pair* of ___	A *yard* of ___	An *acre* of ___
a. eyeglasses	a. towels	a. snow
b. watches	**b. fabric**	b. plums
c. handkerchiefs	c. grass	**c. land**
Noun Quantifiers	**Noun Quantifiers**	**Noun Quantifiers**

A *breath* of ___	A *deck* of ___	A *herd* of ___
a. air	a. chips	a. butterflies
b. wind	**b. cards**	b. cats
c. leaves	c. coins	**c. elephants**
Noun Quantifiers	**Noun Quantifiers**	**Noun Quantifiers**

A *litter* of ___	A *litter* of ___	A *school* of ___
a. kittens	a. snakes	a. cows
b. bees	**b. puppies**	b. tigers
c. fish	c. birds	**c. fish**
Noun Quantifiers	**Noun Quantifiers**	**Noun Quantifiers**

Noun Quantifiers **GAME CARDS #5**

A *pot* of ___
- **a. coffee**
- b. vodka
- c. juice

Noun Quantifiers

A *pint* of ___
- a. wine
- **b. beer**
- c. water

Noun Quantifiers

A *mug* of ___
- a. milk
- b. wine
- **c. beer**

Noun Quantifiers

A *grain* of ___
- **a. rice**
- b. pasta
- c. bread

Noun Quantifiers

A *slice* of ___
- a. hot dog
- **b. ham**
- c. hamburger

Noun Quantifiers

A *pride* of ___
- a. alligators
- b. monkeys
- **c. lions**

Noun Quantifiers

A *can* of ___
- a. cereal
- b. jam
- **c. soup**

Noun Quantifiers

A *bar* of ___
- a. paper
- b. melon
- **c. soap**

Noun Quantifiers

A *loaf* of ___
- a. butter
- b. cheese
- **c. bread**

Noun Quantifiers

A *flock* of ___
- **a. birds**
- b. whales
- c. squirrels

Noun Quantifiers

A *piece* of ___
- **a. furniture**
- b. paint
- c. chair

Noun Quantifiers

A *stick* of ___
- **a. gum**
- b. candy
- c. chocolate

Noun Quantifiers

A *pack* of ___
- a. worms
- **b. wolves**
- c. whales

Noun Quantifiers

A *pad* of ___
- a. glue
- **b. paper**
- c. chairs

Noun Quantifiers

A *bar* of ___
- a. cheese
- **b. chocolate**
- c. butter

Noun Quantifiers

Could, Should, Would GAME CARDS #2

He spoke quickly but I ___ understand him. **could** should would	___ I have your name please? **Could** Should Would	The doctor says I ___ eat better. could **should** would
She was so smart, she ___ speak 3 languages as a child. **could** should would	What ___ you do if you won the lottery? could should **would**	Where is Peter? He ___ be here by now. could **should** would
After years of saving, they ___ finally buy a house. **could** should would	I wish you ___ be quiet. I'm studying. could should **would**	I wish it ___ stop raining. could should **would**
I ___ not go to the party last night because I had to work. **could** should would	You look sleepy. You ___ go to bed. could **should** would	We ___ prefer a room with a view. could should **would**
___ you mind if I smoke? Could Should **Would**	___ you like a cup of coffee? Could Should **Would**	I ___ like to see these shoes in blue please. could should **would**

Adjectives: Vocabulary Building

PRE-INTERMEDIATE

OBJECTIVE:

To expand the vocabulary for adjectives.

PRIVATE LESSONS:

These GAME CARDS can also be used as flash cards for an enjoyable and effective way to review grammar with your one-to-one students.

LESSON PREPARATION:

Photocopy and cut out the GAME CARDS.

Divide the class into 2 teams or divide the class into groups of about 4 students and have each student play for themself.

A STUDY SHEET is provided (138).

BEGIN:

Stack the GAME CARDS, face down, on the table.

Student A takes the top card and reads the sentence and the 3 possible adjectives to Student B. Student B must choose the correct word to earn the card and thus the point.

If Student B chooses incorrectly, the card is put off to the side and no point is earned.

Student B then chooses a new card and reads to Student C, and so on until there are no more GAME CARDS left.

The student or team that earns the most GAME CARDS at the end of the game wins.

Basketball players are usually very ___.

ADJECTIVES

a. tall
b. high
c. tallest

Adjectives: Vocabulary Building STUDY SHEET

> **Adjectives** describe a *noun* (person, place, or thing) or *pronoun* (he, she, it, we, they, you, I).

I saw a **cute** dog yesterday. '*Cute*' describes the noun '*dog*'.

She likes **yellow** roses. '*Yellow*' describes the noun '*roses*'.

> **Adjectives** almost always appear before nouns and after some verbs, especially the verbs '*be, become, feel, get, look, seem, smell, sound*'.

He is **funny**. '*Funny*' describes the pronoun '*He*'.

I feel **sick**. '*Sick*' describes the pronoun '*I*'.

You look **beautiful**. '*Beautiful*' describes the pronoun '*You*'.

Dinner smells **good**. '*Good*' describes the noun '*Dinner*'.

They seem **happy**. '*Happy*' describes the pronoun '*They*'.

PRACTICE: Choose the best adjective to complete these sentences.

1. The music is too ____. Please turn it down.

    a. loud
    b. high
    c. big

2. I feel ____. I'm going to bed.

    a. thirsty
    b. tired
    c. hungry

3. Your desk is always so ____. How do you find anything?

    a. dirty
    b. dusty
    c. cluttered

4. The weather is very ____. I'm always sweating.

    a. muggy
    b. dry
    c. chilly

Adjectives: Vocabulary Building GAME CARDS #1

Basketball players are usually very ___.

ADJECTIVES

a. tall
b. high
c. tallest

That movie star is ___.

ADJECTIVES

a. glamour
b. glamorous
c. glamorously

I just ran in the rain. Now, my boots are ___.

ADJECTIVES

a. dusty
b. muddy
c. dry

That sports car is very ___.

ADJECTIVES

a. fast
b. speed
c. quickly

My cat is ___.

ADJECTIVES

a. soft
b. sharp
c. scaly

He gets good grades because he's ___.

ADJECTIVES

a. smart
b. interesting
c. intelligence

Our teacher is ___.

ADJECTIVES

a. helps
b. helpful
c. helpfully

My dog is ___.

ADJECTIVES

a. friend
b. friendly
c. friendship

He got promoted because he's ___.

ADJECTIVES

a. dull
b. hard-working
c. ordinary

That book was ___.

ADJECTIVES

a. interested
b. interesting
c. interest

These prices are too ___ for me.

ADJECTIVES

a. rich
b. high
c. expensive

Your new clothes are very ___.

ADJECTIVES

a. cuddly
b. fashionable
c. successful

Adjectives: Vocabulary Building GAME CARDS #2

The sky is so ___ that I can see the stars.

ADJECTIVES

a. cloudy
b. sunny
c. clear

That light is too ___. It's hurting my eyes.

ADJECTIVES

a. dark
b. shiny
c. bright

My desk is ___. I can't find anything.

ADJECTIVES

a. spotless
b. organized
c. cluttered

She asks a lot of questions. She is ___.

ADJECTIVES

a. nosy
b. jealous
c. shy

Your music is too ___. Please turn it down.

ADJECTIVES

a. loud
b. early
c. soft

She is ___. You can't believe what she says.

ADJECTIVES

a. friendly
b. dishonest
c. optimistic

I stayed up late last night, so now I'm ___.

ADJECTIVES

a. dopey
b. sleepy
c. sneezy

My dessert is too ___.

ADJECTIVES

a. orange
b. sweet
c. fresh

That sofa is ___. No one is going to buy it.

ADJECTIVES

a. ugly
b. lovely
c. trendy

He never wastes his money. He's ___.

ADJECTIVES

a. thrifty
b. careless
c. generous

Her new phone is so ___.

ADJECTIVES

a. envious
b. quaint
c. high-tech

My shirt is ___. I'm going to iron it.

ADJECTIVES

a. silky
b. dirty
c. wrinkled

Adjectives: Vocabulary Building GAME CARDS #3

This food is ___. I'm sending it back.

ADJECTIVES

a. good
b. affordable
c. disgusting

That old man is always mean and ___.

ADJECTIVES

a. glad
b. happy
c. grumpy

We should fly a kite on a ___ day.

ADJECTIVES

a. rainy
b. sunny
c. windy

This bread is ___. I need a fresh one.

ADJECTIVES

a. stale
b. sweet
c. small

This sweater is ___ and uncomfortable.

ADJECTIVES

a. soft
b. light
c. itchy

I was very ___ with my low test scores.

ADJECTIVES

a. upset
b. sleepy
c. pleased

That was the ___ movie I've ever seen.

ADJECTIVES

a. best
b. good
c. better

Don't eat that cheese – it's ___.

ADJECTIVES

a. fresh
b. moldy
c. delicious

They are ___ musicians.

ADJECTIVES

a. timid
b. talented
c. tolerant

That was the ___ book I've ever read.

ADJECTIVES

a. bad
b. worst
c. worse

It is too ___ to go shopping.

ADJECTIVES

a. quiet
b. tired
c. early

He is tall, dark and ___.

ADJECTIVES

a. pretty
b. lovely
c. handsome

Adjectives: Vocabulary Building GAME CARDS #4

Their baby is ___.

ADJECTIVES

a. adorable
b. deplorable
c. affordable

That's a ___ bouquet of flowers.

ADJECTIVES

a. lively
b. lonely
c. lovely

Their honeymoon sounds very ___.

ADJECTIVES

a. stoic
b. logical
c. romantic

He got a ___ score on his test.

ADJECTIVES

a. small
b. perfect
c. winning

I think this painting is ___.

ADJECTIVES

a. attractive
b. confident
c. beautiful

It's too ___ to do my taxes myself.

ADJECTIVES

a. compassionate
b. compatible
c. complicated

They are ___ and always want the best.

ADJECTIVES

a. lazy
b. content
c. ambitious

The ocean is so ___, I can see the bottom.

ADJECTIVES

a. clear
b. cold
c. deep

Living in the country can be very ___.

ADJECTIVES

a. urban
b. peaceful
c. embarrassing

She was very ___ to try skydiving.

ADJECTIVES

a. dull
b. brave
c. successful

This coffee is ___; it has no flavor.

ADJECTIVES

a. weak
b. slim
c. strong

He's a responsible and ___ employee.

ADJECTIVES

a. absent
b. worthless
c. competent

Adjectives: Vocabulary Building GAME CARDS #5

She looks very ___. Is she sick?

ADJECTIVES

a. plump
b. petite
c. skinny

The championship was ___ to watch.

ADJECTIVES

a. excited
b. excitement
c. exciting

The toaster is ___. I want a refund.

ADJECTIVES

a. damage
b. damaging
c. damaged

The roads were ___ with ice and snow.

ADJECTIVES

a. slippery
b. slipping
c. slips

She's a ___ person. She gets a lot done.

ADJECTIVES

a. relaxed
b. forgetful
c. productive

The air in the city is gray and ___.

ADJECTIVES

a. clean
b. muddy
c. smoggy

His speech was ___ and concise.

ADJECTIVES

a. brief
b. endless
c. boring

I'm always dropping things. I'm ___.

ADJECTIVES

a. cold
b. clumsy
c. confident

He always tells jokes. He is a ___ person.

ADJECTIVES

a. witty
b. selfish
c. gentle

I was ___ to enter the haunted house.

ADJECTIVES

a. joyful
b. afraid
c. jealous

This is ___ and should be taken seriously.

ADJECTIVES

a. funny
b. strong
c. important

One end of the pool is deep, the other is ___.

ADJECTIVES

a. cold
b. empty
c. shallow

Adjectives: Vocabulary Building **GAME CARDS #6**

These oranges are fresh and ___.

ADJECTIVES

a. salty
b. juicy
c. greasy

This bathroom is ___. You should clean it.

ADJECTIVES

a. filthy
b. pristine
c. damaged

They say it's ___ to find a 4-leaf clover.

ADJECTIVES

a. silly
b. lucky
c. serious

These French fries are too ___.

ADJECTIVES

a. fuzzy
b. sticky
c. greasy

It was a ___ day with heavy rain and wind.

ADJECTIVES

a. snowy
b. calm
c. stormy

The quality of the recording was ___.

ADJECTIVES

a. poor
b. quaint
c. cloudy

They were ___ after playing in the mud.

ADJECTIVES

a. icy
b. pristine
c. grubby

Strong, ___ winds blew the trees around.

ADJECTIVES

a. gutsy
b. gusty
c. gory

The cake was ___ and delicious.

ADJECTIVES

a. moist
b. chewy
c. crunchy

The ___ witch flew on a broom.

ADJECTIVES

a. weary
b. wicked
c. worried

It's ___ today – very hot and humid.

ADJECTIVES

a. wet
b. muggy
c. musty

They are ___. They have lots of money.

ADJECTIVES

a. wimpy
b. wealthy
c. wholesome

Adjectives: Vocabulary Building GAME CARDS #7

That comedian is very ___.

ADJECTIVES

a. fun
b. funny
c. funnily

This desk is ___. Let's put it down.

ADJECTIVES

a. small
b. heavy
c. expensive

They were ___ of her success.

ADJECTIVES

a. sincere
b. envious
c. punctual

The soup is ___, so be careful.

ADJECTIVES

a. cold
b. wet
c. hot

That little puppy is so ___.

ADJECTIVES

a. cute
b. mature
c. dangerous

I don't like that store. The clerks are ___.

ADJECTIVES

a. rude
b. jovial
c. amiable

I haven't eaten yet, so I'm very ___.

ADJECTIVES

a. hunger
b. hungry
c. hungrily

Their new kitchen is very ___.

ADJECTIVES

a. tasty
b. eccentric
c. modern

I need a ___ cup of tea to wake up.

ADJECTIVES

a. strong
b. bland
c. watery

Has he been running? He's ___.

ADJECTIVES

a. clean
b. violent
c. sweaty

It's too ___ to go the park.

ADJECTIVES

a. late
b. breezy
c. pleasant

Our attic is dark and ___ at night.

ADJECTIVES

a. jolly
b. creepy
c. cheerful

Adjectives: Vocabulary Building **GAME CARDS #8**

Our new boss is very ___. He works hard.

ADJECTIVES

a. eager
b. apathetic
c. scatterbrained

My parents are ___ and have traditional values.

ADJECTIVES

a. liberal
b. trendy
c. conservative

That test was very ___.

ADJECTIVES

a. nervous
b. difficult
c. entertaining

She is a positive person. She's ___.

ADJECTIVES

a. pragmatic
b. pessimistic
c. optimistic

The flight is ___. There are no extra seats.

ADJECTIVES

a. full
b. empty
c. spacious

Teddy bears are ___ toys for kids.

ADJECTIVES

a. itchy
b. cuddly
c. complicated

My meal was ___ and tasteless.

ADJECTIVES

a. juicy
b. bland
c. spicy

Disneyland is a ___ place to visit.

ADJECTIVES

a. fun
b. funny
c. depressing

The basement is ___. Let's open a window.

ADJECTIVES

a. fresh
b. musty
c. clean

The vase is ___. Handle it carefully.

ADJECTIVES

a. light
b. fragile
c. square

This TV show is ___. Let's turn it off.

ADJECTIVES

a. entertaining
b. boring
c. interesting

This pie is ___. May I have some more?

ADJECTIVES

a. stale
b. delicious
c. terrible

Adjectives vs. Adverbs

PRE-INTERMEDIATE

LESSON PREPARATION:

Photocopy and cut out the GAME CARDS.

Divide the class into 2 teams or divide the class into groups of about 4 students and have each student play for themself.

A STUDY SHEET is provided (148).

BEGIN:

Stack the GAME CARDS, face down, on the table.

Student A takes the top card and reads the sentence and the 2 choices to Student B. Student B must correctly complete the sentence to earn the card and thus the point.

If Student B chooses incorrectly, the card is put off to the side and no point is earned.

Student B then chooses a new card and reads to Student C, and so on until there are no more GAME CARDS left.

The student or team that earns the most GAME CARDS at the end of the game wins.

OBJECTIVE:

To know the difference between an adverb and an adjective. Upon completion of this lesson, students should:

1. Know that an adjective modifies a noun and an adverb modifies a verb.

2. Have an expanded adverb and adjective vocabulary.

PRIVATE LESSONS:

These GAME CARDS can also be used as flash cards for an enjoyable and effective way to review grammar with your one-to-one students.

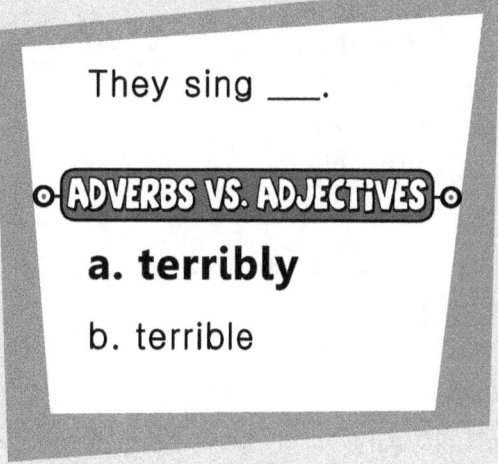

They sing ___.

ADVERBS VS. ADJECTIVES

a. terribly

b. terrible

Adjectives vs. Adverbs STUDY SHEET

ADJECTIVE
An adjective describes a noun or pronoun.

ADVERB
An adverb describes a verb.

Sherry is a **beautiful** dancer.
Bradley is a **careful** driver.

Sherry dances **beautifully**.
Bradley drives **carefully**.

Some words can be either an adjective or an adverb.

Many adverbs are made by adding 'ly' to the end of an adjective.

They are **fast** swimmers.
They swim **fast**.

We are **slow** eaters.
We eat **slowly**.

'Good' is an adjective.

'Well' is an adverb.

You are a **good** guitar player.

I play the guitar **well**.

PRACTICE: Choose the correct word to complete the sentence.

1. I speak 3 languages _____.

a. fluent
b. fluently

2. We are _____ students.

a. serious
b. seriously

3. Don't speak too _____ in the library.

a. loud
b. loudly

4. The food was _____.

a. terrible
b. terribly

5. The sky looks _____.

a. clear
b. clearly

6. Please pack this crystal _____.

a. careful
b. carefully

GRAMMAR GAMES FOR TEACHERS OF ADULT ESL

Adjectives vs. Adverbs GAME CARDS #1

They sing ___.	Don't eat too ___.	That comedian is ___.
ADVERBS VS. ADJECTIVES	**ADVERBS VS. ADJECTIVES**	**ADVERBS VS. ADJECTIVES**
a. terribly	a. quick	a. fun
b. terrible	**b. quickly**	**b. funny**

She paints ___.	I always drive ___.	This food tastes ___.
ADVERBS VS. ADJECTIVES	**ADVERBS VS. ADJECTIVES**	**ADVERBS VS. ADJECTIVES**
a. well	a. careful	**a. awful**
b. good	**b. carefully**	b. awfully

That test was ___.	Why are you ___?	They are ___ married.
ADVERBS VS. ADJECTIVES	**ADVERBS VS. ADJECTIVES**	**ADVERBS VS. ADJECTIVES**
a. hard	**a. sad**	a. happy
b. hardly	b. sadly	**b. happily**

He speaks ___.	That story is ___.	That movie was ___.
ADVERBS VS. ADJECTIVES	**ADVERBS VS. ADJECTIVES**	**ADVERBS VS. ADJECTIVES**
a. intelligent	**a. incredible**	a. terribly
b. intelligently	b. incredibly	**b. terrible**

Disneyland is ___.	I speak French ___.	He is very ___.
ADVERBS VS. ADJECTIVES	**ADVERBS VS. ADJECTIVES**	**ADVERBS VS. ADJECTIVES**
a. funny	**a. fluently**	**a. intelligent**
b. fun	b. fluent	b. intelligently

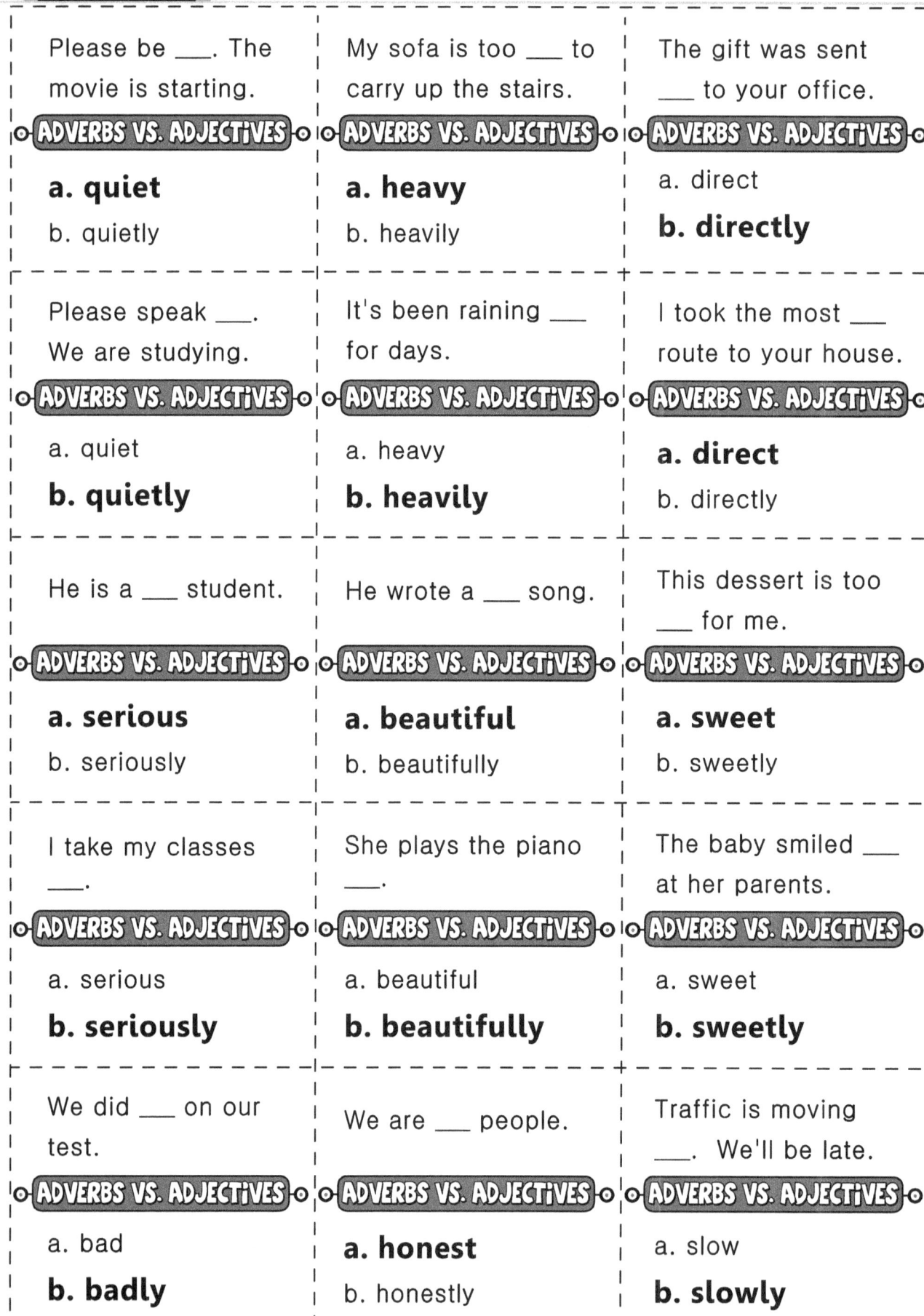

Adjectives vs. Adverbs GAME CARDS #3

I accepted the promotion ___. **ADVERBS VS. ADJECTIVES** **a. gladly** b. glad	That salesclerk is very ___. **ADVERBS VS. ADJECTIVES** **a. rude** b. rudely	We saw the ___ performance. **ADVERBS VS. ADJECTIVES** **a. final** b. finally
I was ___ to get the promotion. **ADVERBS VS. ADJECTIVES** a. gladly **b. glad**	That clerk treats customers ___. **ADVERBS VS. ADJECTIVES** a. rude **b. rudely**	After 3 days, it ___ stopped raining. **ADVERBS VS. ADJECTIVES** a. final **b. finally**
They are ___ business people. **ADVERBS VS. ADJECTIVES** **a. successful** b. successfully	The nurse spoke with a ___ voice. **ADVERBS VS. ADJECTIVES** **a. soft** b. softly	The plane ___ shook. **ADVERBS VS. ADJECTIVES** a. sudden **b. suddenly**
They completed the course ___. **ADVERBS VS. ADJECTIVES** a. successful **b. successfully**	We spoke ___ in the library. **ADVERBS VS. ADJECTIVES** a. soft **b. softly**	There was a ___ knock on the door. **ADVERBS VS. ADJECTIVES** **a. sudden** b. suddenly
We were ___ for the help. **ADVERBS VS. ADJECTIVES** **a. thankful** b. thankfully	They play their music ___. **ADVERBS VS. ADJECTIVES** a. loud **b. loudly**	I'm feeling too ___ to go to work. **ADVERBS VS. ADJECTIVES** **a. lazy** b. lazily

Adjectives vs. Adverbs GAME CARDS #4

He was ___ when he gave his speech. **ADVERBS VS. ADJECTIVES** **a. nervous** b. nervously	Our English teacher is very ___. **ADVERBS VS. ADJECTIVES** **a. strict** b. strictly	The people in line are getting ___. **ADVERBS VS. ADJECTIVES** **a. impatient** b. impatiently
She ___ gave her presentation. **ADVERBS VS. ADJECTIVES** a. nervous **b. nervously**	We ___ enforce the 'No Smoking' rule. **ADVERBS VS. ADJECTIVES** a. strict **b. strictly**	We ___ waited in line for an hour. **ADVERBS VS. ADJECTIVES** a. impatient **b. impatiently**
That test was ___. **ADVERBS VS. ADJECTIVES** **a. easy** b. easily	I need more ___ time. **ADVERBS VS. ADJECTIVES** **a. leisure** b. leisurely	The supermarket was ___ today. **ADVERBS VS. ADJECTIVES** **a. busy** b. busily
She ___ passed that test. **ADVERBS VS. ADJECTIVES** a. easy **b. easily**	We walked at a ___ pace. **ADVERBS VS. ADJECTIVES** a. leisure **b. leisurely**	I ___ began packing for my trip. **ADVERBS VS. ADJECTIVES** a. busy **b. busily**
Your table will be ready ___. **ADVERBS VS. ADJECTIVES** a. short **b. shortly**	This is a ___ addition to the plan. **ADVERBS VS. ADJECTIVES** **a. recent** b. recently	The weather is ___ hot today. **ADVERBS VS. ADJECTIVES** a. unbelievable **b. unbelievably**

Adjectives vs. Adverbs GAME CARDS #5

They apologized ___.	His English fluency has improved ___.	The old car was ___ fast.
ADVERBS VS. ADJECTIVES	**ADVERBS VS. ADJECTIVES**	**ADVERBS VS. ADJECTIVES**
a. sincere **b. sincerely**	a. gradual **b. gradually**	a. surprising **b. surprisingly**
My ___ apologies for being late.	His improvement in math has been ___.	The end of the movie was ___.
ADVERBS VS. ADJECTIVES	**ADVERBS VS. ADJECTIVES**	**ADVERBS VS. ADJECTIVES**
a. sincere b. sincerely	**a. gradual** b. gradually	**a. surprising** b. surprisingly
The afternoon sun was ___.	I ___ waited for the bus.	I made a ___ turn on 5th Avenue.
ADVERBS VS. ADJECTIVES	**ADVERBS VS. ADJECTIVES**	**ADVERBS VS. ADJECTIVES**
a. bright b. brightly	a. patient **b. patiently**	**a. sharp** b. sharply
The sun shone ___ through the trees.	Our teacher is always ___ with us.	I turned ___ on 5th Avenue.
ADVERBS VS. ADJECTIVES	**ADVERBS VS. ADJECTIVES**	**ADVERBS VS. ADJECTIVES**
a. bright **b. brightly**	**a. patient** b. patiently	a. sharp **b. sharply**
We were ___ to get to the beach.	I ___ locked my keys in my car.	We need an ___ answer from you.
ADVERBS VS. ADJECTIVES	**ADVERBS VS. ADJECTIVES**	**ADVERBS VS. ADJECTIVES**
a. eager b. eagerly	a. stupid **b. stupidly**	**a. immediate** b. immediately

Adjectives vs. Adverbs GAME CARDS #6

My neighborhood is very ___. **ADVERBS VS. ADJECTIVES** **a. safe** b. safety	Please write your answers ___. **ADVERBS VS. ADJECTIVES** a. neat **b. neatly**	It's an ___ replica of a Ming vase. **ADVERBS VS. ADJECTIVES** **a. exact** b. exactly
My jewelry is ___ locked in a vault. **ADVERBS VS. ADJECTIVES** a. safety **b. safely**	I keep my desk ___ at all times. **ADVERBS VS. ADJECTIVES** **a. neat** b. neatly	The bank is ___ one mile from here. **ADVERBS VS. ADJECTIVES** a. exact **b. exactly**
She spoke with a ___ voice. **ADVERBS VS. ADJECTIVES** **a. clear** b. clearly	Please be ___ for your interview. **ADVERBS VS. ADJECTIVES** **a. punctual** b. punctually	I received a ___ welcome at home. **ADVERBS VS. ADJECTIVES** **a. warm** b. warmly
Please speak ___. **ADVERBS VS. ADJECTIVES** a. clear **b. clearly**	The meeting will start ___ at 10 AM. **ADVERBS VS. ADJECTIVES** a. punctual **b. punctually**	I was welcomed ___ by our hosts. **ADVERBS VS. ADJECTIVES** a. warm **b. warmly**
I lost 10 lbs. Now, my clothes are ___. **ADVERBS VS. ADJECTIVES** **a. loose** b. loosely	I was ___ to my wife's folks. **ADVERBS VS. ADJECTIVES** **a. polite** b. politely	Don't handle my dog ___. He's old. **ADVERBS VS. ADJECTIVES** a. rough **b. roughly**

Adjectives vs. Adverbs GAME CARDS #7

That movie is too ___ for kids.	I made many ___ errors on my test.	I ___ got out of bed.
ADVERBS VS. ADJECTIVES	**ADVERBS VS. ADJECTIVES**	**ADVERBS VS. ADJECTIVES**
a. violent b. violently	**a. stupid** b. stupidly	a. lazy **b. lazily**

He speaks ___ French.	He responded to my email ___.	There was a ___ line at the bank.
ADVERBS VS. ADJECTIVES	**ADVERBS VS. ADJECTIVES**	**ADVERBS VS. ADJECTIVES**
a. fluent b. fluently	a. immediate **b. immediately**	**a. short** b. shortly

The wind is blowing ___.	These jeans fit ___.	He ___ had surgery.
ADVERBS VS. ADJECTIVES	**ADVERBS VS. ADJECTIVES**	**ADVERBS VS. ADJECTIVES**
a. violent **b. violently**	a. loose **b. loosely**	a. recent **b. recently**

That movie was really ___.	I spoke ___ to our customers.	Your story is ___.
ADVERBS VS. ADJECTIVES	**ADVERBS VS. ADJECTIVES**	**ADVERBS VS. ADJECTIVES**
a. bad b. badly	a. polite **b. politely**	**a. unbelievable** b. unbelievably

We gave our opinion ___.	He had a ___ time finding a new job.	We ___ ran to the beach.
ADVERBS VS. ADJECTIVES	**ADVERBS VS. ADJECTIVES**	**ADVERBS VS. ADJECTIVES**
a. honest **b. honestly**	**a. rough** b. roughly	a. eager **b. eagerly**

Adjectives vs. Adverbs **GAME CARDS #8**

The local bus is too ___.	She is a ___ dancer.	The doctor spoke ___ on the phone.
ADVERBS VS. ADJECTIVES	**ADVERBS VS. ADJECTIVES**	**ADVERBS VS. ADJECTIVES**
a. slow b. slowly	a. graceful b. gracefully	a. urgent **b. urgently**

We accepted her help ___.	He dances ___.	She learns ___.
ADVERBS VS. ADJECTIVES	**ADVERBS VS. ADJECTIVES**	**ADVERBS VS. ADJECTIVES**
a. thankful **b. thankfully**	a. graceful **b. gracefully**	a. quick **b. quickly**

She has a ___ voice.	He is a ___ driver.	He is a ___ learner.
ADVERBS VS. ADJECTIVES	**ADVERBS VS. ADJECTIVES**	**ADVERBS VS. ADJECTIVES**
a. loud b. loudly	**a. reckless** b. recklessly	**a. quick** b. quickly

I answered the questions ___.	You drive ___.	That test was ___ difficult.
ADVERBS VS. ADJECTIVES	**ADVERBS VS. ADJECTIVES**	**ADVERBS VS. ADJECTIVES**
a. correct **b. correctly**	a. reckless **b. recklessly**	a. real **b. really**

This answer is not ___.	We got an ___ call from the hospital.	This is a ___ antique.
ADVERBS VS. ADJECTIVES	**ADVERBS VS. ADJECTIVES**	**ADVERBS VS. ADJECTIVES**
a. correct b. correctly	**a. urgent** b. urgently	**a. real** b. really

Question Words

LESSON PREPARATION:

Photocopy and cut out the GAME CARDS.

Divide the class into 2 teams or divide the class into groups of about 4 students and have each student play for themself.

A STUDY SHEET is provided (158).

BEGIN:

Stack the GAME CARDS, face down, on the table.

Student A takes the top card and reads the sentence and the 3 choices to Student B. Student B must correctly complete the sentence using one of the three choices to earn the card and thus the point.

If Student B chooses incorrectly, the card is put off to the side and no point is earned.

Student B then chooses a new card and reads to Student C, and so on until there are no more GAME CARDS left.

The student or team that earns the most GAME CARDS at the end of the game wins.

BEGINNER

OBJECTIVE:

To gain fluency in using the questions words:

1. Who
2. What
3. When
4. Where
5. Why
6. How
7. Which

PRIVATE LESSONS:

These GAME CARDS can also be used as flash cards for an enjoyable and effective way to review grammar with your one-to-one students.

Question Words STUDY SHEET

WHO = PEOPLE

Who is on the phone?

It's your mother.

Who are you?

My name is Bob.

WHEN = TIME / DURATION

When does the meeting start?

At 10 AM.

When are we leaving?

In about 5 minutes.

WHERE = LOCATION / PLACE

Where are you?

I'm at the airport.

Where are my glasses?

On the kitchen table.

WHY = REASON

Why are you late?

I missed my train.

Why isn't Bob at work?

He called in sick today.

WHAT = VARIOUS

What are you doing?

I'm studying for a test.

What does she do?

She's a teacher.

What are your store hours?

We are open from 9 AM to 5 PM.

What time is it?

It's 2 o'clock.

What's your shoe size?

I'm a size 8.

What's the matter?

I feel sick.

HOW = CONDITION / MANNER

How are you?

I'm fine, thanks.

How much does this cost?

It's 5 dollars.

How do I get to the bank?

Turn left at the next light.

How long is the movie?

It's about 90 minutes long.

WHICH = CHOICE

Which movie should we watch?

Let's watch Star Wars.

Which way is the bank?

Go straight and turn left.

GRAMMAR GAMES FOR TEACHERS OF ADULT ESL

Question Words GAME CARDS #1

___ is my hat?
a. **Where**
b. Who
c. When

___ is the meeting?
a. Who
b. **When**
c. Which

___ are you from?
a. **Where**
b. What
c. Which

___ time is it?
a. When
b. Where
c. **What**

___ is your name?
a. Where
b. When
c. **What**

___ is your job?
a. Which
b. **What**
c. Why

___ will the bus arrive?
a. Which
b. **When**
c. What

___ are you?
a. When
b. Why
c. **Who**

___ do you start work?
a. **When**
b. What
c. Which

___ is the bathroom?
a. What
b. Who
c. **Where**

___ does the movie start?
a. Who
b. Which
c. **When**

___ time do you start work?
a. When
b. **What**
c. How

___ much is the bill?
a. **How**
b. Which
c. Why

___ do I get to the station?
a. **How**
b. Where
c. Which

___ old are you?
a. What
b. Where
c. **How**

Question Words GAME CARDS #2

___ were you born?

a. **Where**
b. Who
c. What

___ are you studying in school?

a. **What**
b. How
c. Which

___ much do you weigh?

a. **How**
b. What
c. Which

___ are your hobbies?

a. When
b. Why
c. **What**

___ do you go to school?

a. **Where**
b. Which
c. What

___ tall are you?

a. Which
b. **How**
c. What

___ many children do you have?

a. Who
b. **How**
c. Which

___ company do you work for?

a. Where
b. Who
c. **What**

___ is my book?

a. When
b. Why
c. **Where**

___ is the station?

a. When
b. Why
c. **Where**

___ many apples do you want?

a. **How**
b. Which
c. When

___ are my shoes?

a. When
b. **Where**
c. Who

___ is your marital status?

a. Which
b. **What**
c. Why

___ much does this cost?

a. **How**
b. Where
c. Which

___ are you here?

a. What
b. Who
c. **Why**

Question Words GAME CARDS #3

___ is the traffic so slow?
a. Who
b. Why
c. What

___ are you going on vacation?
a. What
b. When
c. Which

___ was your vacation?
a. When
b. Who
c. Which

___ are you laughing?
a. Why
b. When
c. What

___ did you go on your vacation?
a. Where
b. Which
c. What

___ long have you been married?
a. Which
b. How
c. What

___ are you staring at me?
a. Who
b. How
c. Why

___ did you do on your vacation?
a. When
b. Where
c. What

___ did you graduate?
a. When
b. Which
c. Who

___ tie do you want, red or blue?
a. Which
b. Where
c. Why

___ did you meet on your vacation?
a. What
b. Which
c. Who

___ do you like your job?
a. When
b. Where
c. How

___ meal would you like, pasta or fish?
a. How
b. Why
c. Which

___ was your vacation?
a. How
b. Why
c. Which

___ are you late?
a. What
b. Where
c. Why

Question Words GAME CARDS #4

___ are you sad?
a. Where
b. Why
c. What

___ would you like to speak to?
a. What
b. Who
c. Which

___ many kids do you have?
a. How
b. Who
c. Which

___ is your appointment?
a. When
b. Why
c. Who

___ are you meeting for lunch?
a. Who
b. Which
c. What

___ are you responsible for?
a. When
b. How
c. What

___ time is your appointment?
a. When
b. How
c. What

___ is your new boss?
a. When
b. Why
c. Who

___ are you in charge of?
a. What
b. Why
c. When

___ was your job interview?
a. Who
b. What
c. How

___ is your English class?
a. How
b. Why
c. Who

___ did you start working here?
a. When
b. Which
c. Who

___ was at the door?
a. How
b. Who
c. Which

___ department do you work in?
a. How
b. What
c. Where

___ will you retire?
a. What
b. Who
c. When

Question Words GAME CARDS #5

___ will this class end?
a. Who
b. When
c. What

___ do you do?
a. What
b. Where
c. When

___ don't you quit smoking?
a. Why
b. Who
c. Which

___ is your company?
a. When
b. Where
c. Why

___ are you free for lunch?
a. Who
b. When
c. What

___ do you always work over-time?
a. Which
b. Who
c. Why

___ was your company founded?
a. Who
b. Which
c. When

___ is your house?
a. Why
b. Where
c. Who

___ do you prefer, coffee or tea?
a. Which
b. How
c. Where

___ is the president of your company?
a. When
b. What
c. Who

___ do I register for my classes?
a. Where
b. Which
c. Who

___ is cheaper, the bus or the train?
a. How
b. Where
c. Which

___ do you spell your last name?
a. How
b. Who
c. Which

___ is the nearest coffee shop?
a. How
b. Why
c. Where

___ way is the library?
a. Which
b. Who
c. When

Question Words GAME CARDS #6

___ is your favorite singer?
a. **Who**
b. When
c. What

___ are the towels?
a. Who
b. **Where**
c. When

___ will it snow?
a. **When**
b. Who
c. Which

___ is your favorite actress?
a. Why
b. **Who**
c. When

___ is your flight?
a. Who
b. **When**
c. Why

___ are my keys?
a. **Where**
b. When
c. Why

___ is the CEO of this company?
a. **Who**
b. Why
c. When

___ is our next break?
a. **When**
b. Which
c. Who

___ are you going?
a. Which
b. Who
c. **Where**

___ is our hotel?
a. When
b. What
c. **Where**

___ do you want to leave?
a. Where
b. Which
c. **When**

___ is the library?
a. Who
b. **Where**
c. When

___ much does this cost?
a. **How**
b. Who
c. Which

___ does class start?
a. Who
b. What
c. **When**

___ way is the bus stop?
a. **Which**
b. Who
c. When

Question Words GAME CARDS #7

___ do you buy your clothes?	___ are you angry?	___ is today's date?
a. **Where** b. Which c. What	a. What b. **Why** c. Which	a. **What** b. Where c. Why

___ are you today?	___ is calling?	___ size are you?
a. **How** b. Why c. When	a. What b. How c. **Who**	a. **How** b. Who c. What

___ many days will you be staying?	___ do you like your job?	___ are you laughing?
a. **How** b. Which c. When	a. Where b. **Why** c. What	a. What b. **Why** c. Which

___ will you get home?	___ are we going to the movies?	___ were you born?
a. Where b. **How** c. What	a. What b. **When** c. Which	a. What b. **When** c. Which

___ are my reports?	___ do you do?	___ long was your vacation?
a. **Where** b. What c. Who	a. **How** b. Which c. Where	a. Where b. **How** c. What

Still, Yet, Already **GAME CARDS #1**

Our company isn't profitable ___. **yet** still already	Did you finish that report ___? We're waiting for it. **yet** still already	I've ___ had 5 cups of coffee today. yet still **already**
I haven't been paid ___. **yet** still already	We ___ haven't received your letter. yet **still** already	Have you ___ eaten dinner? yet still **already**
She hasn't quit smoking ___. **yet** still already	That music is ___ too loud. Please turn it down. yet **still** already	I can't believe our vacation is over ___. yet still **already**
It hasn't stopped raining ___. **yet** still already	Although it's cloudy, I ___ want to have a picnic. yet **still** already	You're late. The meeting has ___ started. yet still **already**
I haven't finished my lunch ___. **yet** still already	I can't leave now. I ___ have more work to do. yet **still** already	I've ___ been to the store. I'm not going again. yet still **already**

Simple Present vs. Present Continuous

LESSON PREPARATION:

Photocopy and cut out the GAME CARDS.

Divide the class into 2 teams or divide the class into groups of about 4 students and have each student play for themselves.

A STUDY SHEET is provided (168).

BEGIN:

Stack the GAME CARDS, face down, on the table.

Student A takes the top card and reads the question and the 3 choices to Student B. Student B must correctly complete the question to earn the card and thus the point.

If Student B chooses incorrectly, the card is put off to the side and no point is earned.

Student B then chooses a new card and reads to Student C, and so on until there are no more GAME CARDS left.

The student or team that earns the most GAME CARDS at the end of the game wins.

BEGINNER

OBJECTIVE:

To review the difference in syntax between questions in the present simple tense and questions in the present continuous tense.

PRIVATE LESSONS:

These GAME CARDS can also be used as flash cards for an enjoyable and effective way to review grammar with your one-to-one students.

___ you going to the party?

a. Is
b. Do
c. Are

Simple Present vs. Present Continuous — STUDY SHEET

SIMPLE PRESENT KNOW

he, she, it	*knows*
we, they, you, I	*know*

PRESENT CONTINUOUS SLEEP

he, she, it	*is* sleeping
we, they, you	*are* sleeping
I	*am* sleeping

SIMPLE PRESENT QUESTION

we, they, you, I   Do

PRESENT CONTINUOUS QUESTION

we, they, you   Are

Do we know the password?

Do they know the answer?

Do I know you?

Do you know your blood type?

Are you **sleeping** on the couch?

Are they **sleeping** in a tent?

Are we **sleeping** in a hotel?

SIMPLE PRESENT QUESTION

he, she, it   Does

PRESENT CONTINUOUS QUESTION

he, she, it   Is

Does he know the rules?

Does she know karate?

Does the dog (it) know it's name?

Is he **sleeping** in the hammock?

Is she **sleeping** in the den?

Is the cat (it) **sleeping** inside?

PRESENT CONTINUOUS QUESTION

I   Am

Am I sleeping in the guest room?

PRACTICE: Complete the sentences below.

1. _____ you going to the store?   (Is, Does, Are)

2. _____ we have the sandwiches?   (Do, Am, Are)

3. _____ she like ice cream?   (Is, Does, Do)

4. _____ I driving too fast?   (Do, Am, Is)

Simple Present vs. Present Continuous GAME CARDS #1

___ you going to the party?
a. Is
b. Do
c. Are

___ the light on?
a. Do
b. Is
c. Are

___ the house big?
a. Do
b. Is
c. Are

___ you like soccer?
a. Does
b. Do
c. Are

___ your name John?
a. Is
b. Are
c. Am

___ we leaving soon?
a. Are
b. Is
c. Do

___ you work for ABC Inc.?
a. Am
b. Do
c. Are

___ she tall?
a. Are
b. Do
c. Is

___ they work here?
a. Does
b. Do
c. Are

___ you an accountant?
a. Is
b. Do
c. Are

___ I too loud?
a. Is
b. Am
c. Are

___ she live here?
a. Does
b. Do
c. Is

___ it raining?
a. Does
b. Are
c. Is

___ the library quiet?
a. Is
b. Am
c. Do

___ they work hard?
a. Is
b. Are
c. Do

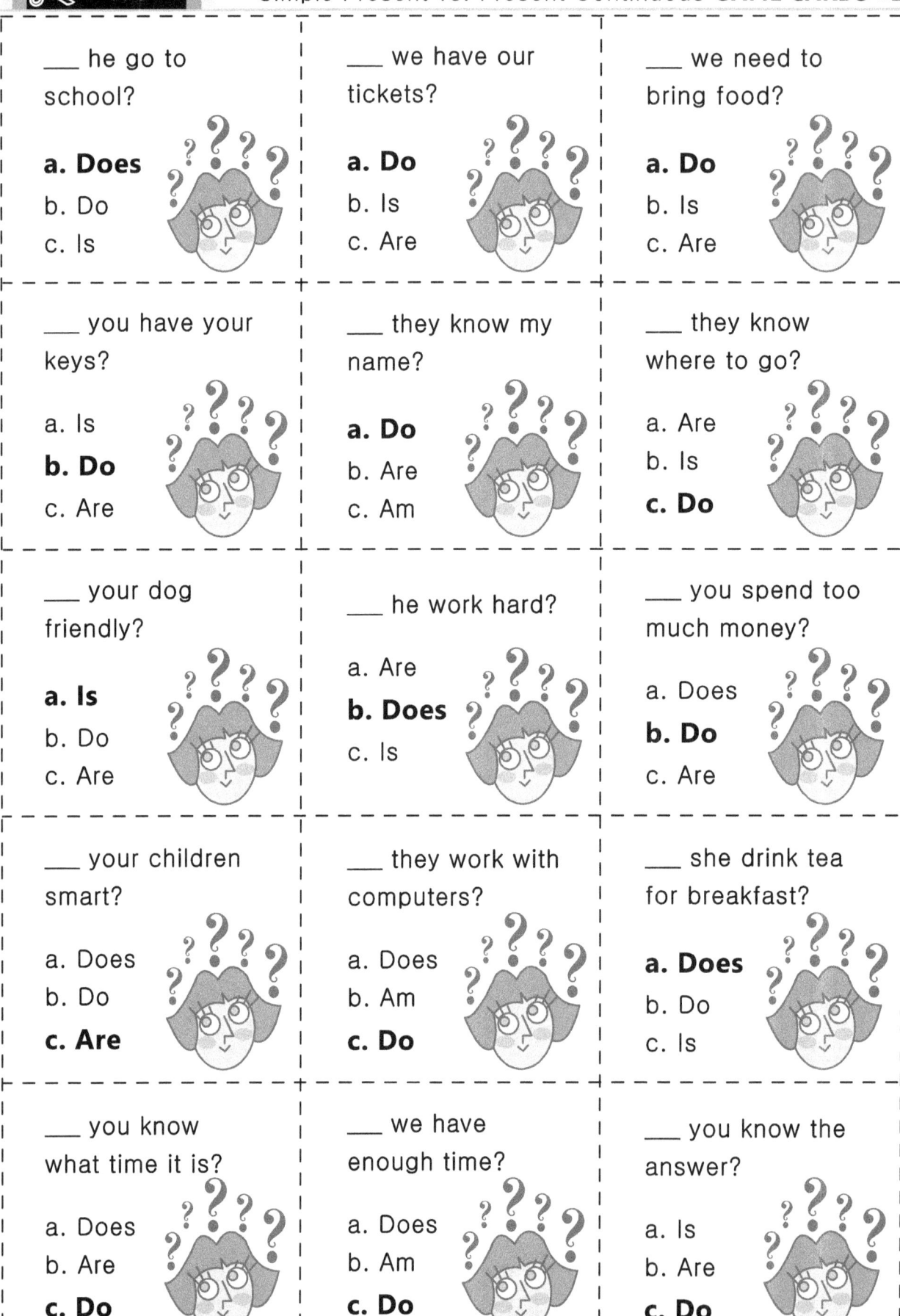

Simple Present vs. Present Continuous GAME CARDS #3

___ you athletic?
a. Does
b. Do
c. Are

___ he Australian?
a. Do
b. Is
c. Are

___ we finished yet?
a. Do
b. Is
c. Are

___ he married?
a. Is
b. Do
c. Are

___ they engineers?
a. Do
b. Are
c. Am

___ we there yet?
a. Are
b. Is
c. Do

___ she single?
a. Is
b. Do
c. Are

___ he a teacher?
a. Are
b. Does
c. Is

___ they nice?
a. Does
b. Do
c. Are

___ they American?
a. Does
b. Do
c. Are

___ she a doctor?
a. Is
b. Am
c. Does

___ I very sick?
a. Am
b. Do
c. Is

___ you British?
a. Does
b. Are
c. Do

___ I late?
a. Is
b. Am
c. Do

___ I know you?
a. Is
b. Are
c. Do

Simple Present vs. Present Continuous **GAME CARDS #4**

___ you read a lot?
a. Does
b. Do
c. Are

___ I have any mail today?
a. Do
b. Is
c. Are

___ he have a cold?
a. Do
b. Is
c. Does

___ she play the piano?
a. Is
b. Do
c. Does

___ we getting a raise?
a. Do
b. Are
c. Am

___ you have any picture ID?
a. Are
b. Is
c. Do

___ he cook dinner?
a. Is
b. Does
c. Are

___ we having a Christmas Party?
a. Are
b. Does
c. Do

___ he have a high school diploma?
a. Does
b. Do
c. Is

___ she a good cook?
a. Does
b. Do
c. Is

___ today your birthday?
a. Is
b. Am
c. Does

___ she have a college degree?
a. Am
b. Do
c. Does

___ they buying a new house?
a. Does
b. Are
c. Do

___ I need a ticket?
a. Is
b. Am
c. Do

___ he have a savings account?
a. Is
b. Does
c. Do

Simple Present vs. Present Continuous GAME CARDS #5

___ you have any pets? a. Does **b. Do** c. Is	___ he a widower? a. Does **b. Is** c. Are	___ they need some water? **a. Do** b. Is c. Does
___ they getting married? a. Is b. Do **c. Are**	___ I getting the kids? a. Do b. Are **c. Am**	___ your head hurt? a. Are b. Is **c. Does**
___ they getting divorced? a. Is b. Does **c. Are**	___ you sick? **a. Are** b. Does c. Do	___ your job interesting? a. Does b. Do **c. Is**
___ they getting engaged? a. Does **b. Are** c. Is	___ you feel sick? **a. Do** b. Am c. Does	___ the movie funny? a. Am **b. Is** c. Does
___ they getting separated? a. Does **b. Are** c. Do	___ she need an aspirin? a. Is b. Am **c. Does**	___ the food too spicy? **a. Is** b. Does c. Do

Simple Present vs. Present Continuous **GAME CARDS #6**

___ you going to school today?
a. Does
b. Do
c. Are

___ her hair short?
a. Do
b. Is
c. Are

___ her blouse blue?
a. Do
b. Is
c. Does

___ she going to the dentist?
a. Is
b. Do
c. Are

___ he have brown eyes?
a. Does
b. Are
c. Am

___ he wearing brown shoes?
a. Are
b. Is
c. Does

___ we going to the opera?
a. Is
b. Does
c. Are

___ your eyes brown?
a. Are
b. Does
c. Do

___ his shoes brown?
a. Does
b. Are
c. Is

___ I babysitting the kids tonight?
a. Do
b. Are
c. Am

___ they have black hair?
a. Do
b. Am
c. Does

___ they wearing red hats?
a. Am
b. Are
c. Does

___ he working late tonight?
a. Does
b. Is
c. Do

___ their hair red?
a. Is
b. Am
c. Does

___ her hat green?
a. Is
b. Does
c. Are

Simple Present vs. Present Continuous **GAME CARDS #7**   175

___ he need a Band-Aid?
a. Do
b. Does
c. Is

___ I hired?
a. Is
b. Are
c. Am

___ they take the train to work?
a. Am
b. Do
c. Are

___ the flowers blooming?
a. Does
b. Are
c. Do

___ we moving to a new apartment?
a. Do
b. Is
c. Are

___ I have enough money?
a. Am
b. Does
c. Do

___ she have long hair?
a. Does
b. Is
c. Are

___ you have a credit card?
a. Do
b. Does
c. Are

___ they have a car?
a. Is
b. Are
c. Do

___ she wearing a blue blouse?
a. Do
b. Does
c. Is

___ we have a library card?
a. Does
b. Are
c. Do

___ your wife Canadian?
a. Am
b. Is
c. Are

___ your cat gray?
a. Does
b. Are
c. Is

___ she a widow?
a. Do
b. Is
c. Are

___ we ready?
a. Am
b. Does
c. Are

  Still, Yet, Already **GAME CARDS #2**

| Ms. Smith has ___ gone home for the day. | He's ___ not in his office. | We haven't seen the doctor ___. |
| yet still **already** | yet **still** already | **yet** still already |

| You've cleaned your room ___? That was fast. | Do you ___ work for the same company? | I haven't found my keys ___. |
| yet still **already** | yet **still** already | **yet** still already |

| I ___ got your letter weeks ago. | I ___ don't know the answer. | I haven't been to the store ___. |
| yet still **already** | yet **still** already | **yet** still already |

| Someone has ___ fixed your computer. | I filled the gas tank but the car ___ won't start. | We haven't sold the house ___. |
| yet still **already** | yet **still** already | **yet** still already |

| He's ___ visited Cuba several times. | I took the medicine but I ___ feel sick. | The movie isn't over ___. |
| yet still **already** | yet **still** already | **yet** still already |

Word Scramble: Common Questions

PRE-INTERMEDIATE

LESSON PREPARATION:

Photocopy and cut out the GAME CARDS.

Divide the class into 2 teams or divide the class into groups of about 4 students and have each student play for themselves.

A STUDY SHEET is provided (178).

BEGIN:

Stack the GAME CARDS, face down, on the table.

Student A takes the top card and reads the top 'scrambled' sentence to Student B. Student B must unscramble the words to make a grammatically correct sentence to earn the card and thus the point. Student B may ask Student A to repeat the scrambled sentence.

If Student B says the sentence incorrectly, the card is put off to the side and no point is earned.

Student B then chooses a new card and reads to Student C, and so on until there are no more GAME CARDS left.

The student or team that earns the most GAME CARDS at the end of the game wins.

OBJECTIVE:

To improve fluency in asking common questions. To review the syntax for using question words.

CHEATER ALERT!

This is a listening exercise. Make sure your students are not writing the words down before unscrambling them.

PRIVATE LESSONS:

These GAME CARDS can also be used as flash cards for an enjoyable and effective way to review grammar with your one-to-one students.

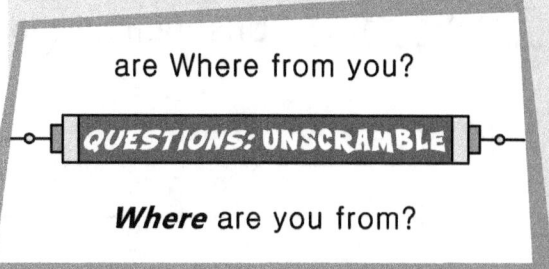

are Where from you?

QUESTIONS: UNSCRAMBLE

Where are you from?

Word Scramble: Common Questions — STUDY SHEET

DO we, they, you, I	**DOES** he, she, it

They study every day.
Do they study every day?

She studies every day.
Does she study every day?

ARE we, they, you	**IS** he, she, it	**AM** I

You **are** tired.
Are you tired?

He **is** tired.
Is he tired?

I **am** late.
Am I late?

We **are** leaving.
Are we leaving?

The dog (it) **is** leaving.
Is the dog (it) leaving?

I **am** staying.
Am I staying?

DID we, they, you, I, she, he, it	**HAVE** you, we, they, I	**HAS** he, she, it

They went home.
Did they go home?

You have been sick.
Have you been sick?

He has eaten.
Has he eaten?

MAY = asking permission	**HOW** = condition, manner	**CAN** = ability

May I sit down?

How are you?

Can you drive?

WHO = people	**WHEN** = time, duration	**WHERE** = place

Who is at the door?

When is dinner?

Where is the store?

WHY = reason	**WHICH** = choice	**WHAT** = various

Why are you tired?

Which way is the bank?

What is your name?

PRACTICE: Unscramble these sentences.

1. name is your What?

   _____?

2. my are Where shoes?

   _____?

3. this How is much?

   _____?

4. I help Can you?

   _____?

GRAMMAR GAMES FOR TEACHERS OF ADULT ESL

Word Scramble: Common Questions GAME CARDS #1

are Where from you?	is When the party?
QUESTIONS: UNSCRAMBLE	**QUESTIONS: UNSCRAMBLE**
Where are you from?	*When* is the party?
speak you English Can?	name your is What?
QUESTIONS: UNSCRAMBLE	**QUESTIONS: UNSCRAMBLE**
Can you speak English?	*What* is your name?
you are Where going?	live do Where you?
QUESTIONS: UNSCRAMBLE	**QUESTIONS: UNSCRAMBLE**
Where are you going?	*Where* do you live?
is time it What?	you Where born were?
QUESTIONS: UNSCRAMBLE	**QUESTIONS: UNSCRAMBLE**
What time is it?	*Where* were you born?
open time you What do?	born you When were?
QUESTIONS: UNSCRAMBLE	**QUESTIONS: UNSCRAMBLE**
What time do you open?	*When* were you born?
close time you What do?	are you How?
QUESTIONS: UNSCRAMBLE	**QUESTIONS: UNSCRAMBLE**
What time do you close?	*How* are you?

Word Scramble: Common Questions GAME CARDS #2

you Where do work?

QUESTIONS: UNSCRAMBLE

Where do you work?

---

was vacation How your?

QUESTIONS: UNSCRAMBLE

How was your vacation?

---

like Do job your you?

QUESTIONS: UNSCRAMBLE

Do you like your job?

---

size your is What shoe?

QUESTIONS: UNSCRAMBLE

What is your shoe size?

---

are What hobbies your?

QUESTIONS: UNSCRAMBLE

What are your hobbies?

---

is family your How?

QUESTIONS: UNSCRAMBLE

How is your family?

---

to like you Do cook?

QUESTIONS: UNSCRAMBLE

Do you like to cook?

---

to like they Do read?

QUESTIONS: UNSCRAMBLE

Do they like to read?

---

have you pets Do any?

QUESTIONS: UNSCRAMBLE

Do you have any pets?

---

you a Are student?

QUESTIONS: UNSCRAMBLE

Are you a student?

---

are tall you How?

QUESTIONS: UNSCRAMBLE

How tall are you?

---

is How weather the?

QUESTIONS: UNSCRAMBLE

How is the weather?

Word Scramble: Common Questions GAME CARDS #3

is Where station the? **QUESTIONS: UNSCRAMBLE** *Where* is the station?	name your is first What? **QUESTIONS: UNSCRAMBLE** *What* is your first name?
very this Is food spicy? **QUESTIONS: UNSCRAMBLE** *Is* this food very spicy?	name last your is What? **QUESTIONS: UNSCRAMBLE** *What* is your last name?
feel Do sick you? **QUESTIONS: UNSCRAMBLE** *Do* you feel sick?	address is What your? **QUESTIONS: UNSCRAMBLE** *What* is your address?
the Do know you answer? **QUESTIONS: UNSCRAMBLE** *Do* you know the answer?	need I ticket Do a? **QUESTIONS: UNSCRAMBLE** *Do* I need a ticket?
you old are How? **QUESTIONS: UNSCRAMBLE** *How* old are you?	have you Do kids any? **QUESTIONS: UNSCRAMBLE** *Do* you have any kids?
is How the much bill? **QUESTIONS: UNSCRAMBLE** *How* much is the bill?	you a have reservation Do? **QUESTIONS: UNSCRAMBLE** *Do* you have a reservation?

Word Scramble: Common Questions **GAME CARDS #4**

at Who door the is?	food is favorite What your?
QUESTIONS: UNSCRAMBLE	**QUESTIONS: UNSCRAMBLE**
Who is at the door?	***What*** is your favorite food?
your is passport Where?	will When snow it?
QUESTIONS: UNSCRAMBLE	**QUESTIONS: UNSCRAMBLE**
Where is your passport?	***When*** will it snow?
appointment an have you Do?	do How work you late?
QUESTIONS: UNSCRAMBLE	**QUESTIONS: UNSCRAMBLE**
Do you have an appointment?	***How*** late do you work?
is appointment When your?	working you today Are?
QUESTIONS: UNSCRAMBLE	**QUESTIONS: UNSCRAMBLE**
When is your appointment?	***Are*** you working today?
have you a headache Do?	live Do here they?
QUESTIONS: UNSCRAMBLE	**QUESTIONS: UNSCRAMBLE**
Do you have a headache?	***Do*** they live here?
start When class does?	lunch What is time?
QUESTIONS: UNSCRAMBLE	**QUESTIONS: UNSCRAMBLE**
When does class start?	***What*** time is lunch?

Word Scramble: Common Questions GAME CARDS #5

hard Do work they? **QUESTIONS: UNSCRAMBLE** *Do* they work hard?	a you ride need Do? **QUESTIONS: UNSCRAMBLE** *Do* you need a ride?
like Would you tea some? **QUESTIONS: UNSCRAMBLE** *Would* you like some tea?	call Can you I cab a? **QUESTIONS: UNSCRAMBLE** *Can* I call you a cab?
you bread buy Did any? **QUESTIONS: UNSCRAMBLE** *Did* you buy any bread?	the you party go Did to? **QUESTIONS: UNSCRAMBLE** *Did* you go to the party?
milk they some get Did? **QUESTIONS: UNSCRAMBLE** *Did* they get some milk?	enjoying he Is himself? **QUESTIONS: UNSCRAMBLE** *Is* he enjoying himself?
a Are doctor you? **QUESTIONS: UNSCRAMBLE** *Are* you a doctor?	the she Does party like? **QUESTIONS: UNSCRAMBLE** *Does* she like the party?
flight your is When? **QUESTIONS: UNSCRAMBLE** *When* is your flight?	have you a Do car? **QUESTIONS: UNSCRAMBLE** *Do* you have a car?

Word Scramble: Common Questions **GAME CARDS #6**

help Can you I?	the How movie was?
QUESTIONS: UNSCRAMBLE	**QUESTIONS: UNSCRAMBLE**
Can I help you?	***How*** was the movie?
I on this try Can?	book How your is?
QUESTIONS: UNSCRAMBLE	**QUESTIONS: UNSCRAMBLE**
Can I try this on?	***How*** is your book?
it is much How?	you would What like?
QUESTIONS: UNSCRAMBLE	**QUESTIONS: UNSCRAMBLE**
How much is it?	***What*** would you like?
be will paying you How?	did you do What?
QUESTIONS: UNSCRAMBLE	**QUESTIONS: UNSCRAMBLE**
How will you be paying?	***What*** did you do?
check I Can by pay?	window the May open I?
QUESTIONS: UNSCRAMBLE	**QUESTIONS: UNSCRAMBLE**
Can I pay by check?	***May*** I open the window?
mind smoke Do if I you?	is What like London?
QUESTIONS: UNSCRAMBLE	**QUESTIONS: UNSCRAMBLE**
Do you mind if I smoke?	***What*** is London like?

Word Scramble: Common Questions GAME CARDS #7

like you pizza Do?	she does Where work?
QUESTIONS: UNSCRAMBLE	**QUESTIONS: UNSCRAMBLE**
Do you like pizza?	***Where*** does she work?
swim he Can?	you tall How are?
QUESTIONS: UNSCRAMBLE	**QUESTIONS: UNSCRAMBLE**
Can he swim?	***How*** tall are you?
people they nice Are?	this much How is?
QUESTIONS: UNSCRAMBLE	**QUESTIONS: UNSCRAMBLE**
Are they nice people?	***How*** much is this?
work Do to drive they?	you married Are?
QUESTIONS: UNSCRAMBLE	**QUESTIONS: UNSCRAMBLE**
Do they drive to work?	***Are*** you married?
friendly your Is dog?	old are How kids your?
QUESTIONS: UNSCRAMBLE	**QUESTIONS: UNSCRAMBLE**
Is your dog friendly?	***How*** old are your kids?
keys are my Where?	do you What do?
QUESTIONS: UNSCRAMBLE	**QUESTIONS: UNSCRAMBLE**
Where are my keys?	***What*** do you do?

Word Scramble: Common Questions GAME CARDS #8

the is When meeting?	**When** is the meeting?
we Are yet there?	**Are** we there yet?
will arrive When bus the?	**When** will the bus arrive?
have May check I the?	**May** I have the check?
the is Where bathroom?	**Where** is the bathroom?
our Is ready room?	**Is** our room ready?
date What today's is?	**What** is today's date?
rent is much the How?	**How** much is the rent?
you How do much weigh?	**How** much do you weigh?
the are What amenities?	**What** are the amenities?
are late you Why?	**Why** are you late?
do you do How?	**How** do you do?

Word Scramble: Common Questions **GAME CARDS #9**

it dinner Is for time?	the Which store is way?
QUESTIONS: UNSCRAMBLE	**QUESTIONS: UNSCRAMBLE**
Is it time for dinner?	*Which* way is the store?
for dinner What's?	live you Where do?
QUESTIONS: UNSCRAMBLE	**QUESTIONS: UNSCRAMBLE**
What's for dinner?	*Where* do you live?
phone the on Who's?	your job What's?
QUESTIONS: UNSCRAMBLE	**QUESTIONS: UNSCRAMBLE**
Who's on the phone?	*What's* your job?
done your Is homework?	you Where go did?
QUESTIONS: UNSCRAMBLE	**QUESTIONS: UNSCRAMBLE**
Is your homework done?	*Where* did you go?
favorite What's your song?	play you tennis Can?
QUESTIONS: UNSCRAMBLE	**QUESTIONS: UNSCRAMBLE**
What's your favorite song?	*Can* you play tennis?
library is Where the?	you golf play Can?
QUESTIONS: UNSCRAMBLE	**QUESTIONS: UNSCRAMBLE**
Where is the library?	*Can* you play golf?

Some, A, An **GAME CARDS #1**

There has been ___ progress on the testing. **some** a an	I need to put ___ gas in the car. **some** a an	There's ___ grain of sand in my eye. some **a** an
I need ___ butter to bake this pie. **some** a an	I have ___ gallon of gas left in the tank. some **a** an	I got ___ tea at the store. **some** a an
This recipe calls for ___ stick of butter. some **a** an	We've had ___ beautiful weather lately. **some** a an	I'd like ___ cup of tea. some **a** an
Solar panels provide ___ of our electricity. **some** a an	We had ___ snow last weekend. **some** a an	I had ___ good luck finding a new job. **some** a an
I found ___ old lamp in the attic. some a **an**	I got ___ sand in the car. **some** a an	I have ___ knowledge of opera. **some** a an

Verbs: Definition

PRE-INTERMEDIATE

LESSON PREPARATION:

Photocopy and cut out the GAME CARDS.

Divide the class into 2 teams or divide the class into groups of about 4 students and have each student play for themself.

BEGIN:

Stack the GAME CARDS, face down, on the table.

Student A takes the top card and reads the top sentence and the 3 choices to Student B. Student B must choose the correct answer that completes the sentence to earn the card and thus the point.

If Student B chooses the wrong answer, the card is put off to the side and no point is earned.

Student B then chooses a new card and reads to Student C, and so on until there are no more GAME CARDS left.

The student or team that earns the most GAME CARDS at the end of the game wins.

OBJECTIVE:

To expand the vocabulary for commonly used verbs.

If you are teaching a new class, this lesson is a good way to assess the vocabulary level of your students.

PRIVATE LESSONS:

These GAME CARDS can also be used as flash cards for an enjoyable and effective way to review grammar with your one-to-one students.

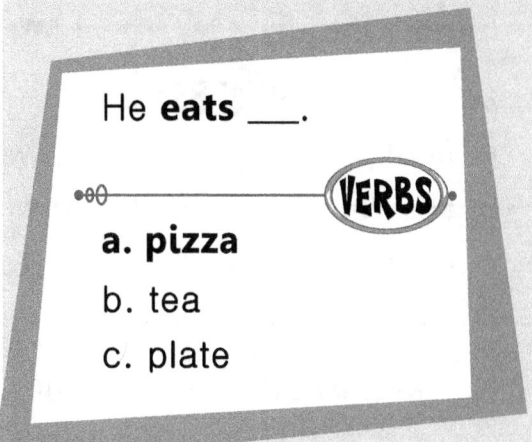

Verbs: Definitions **Game Cards #1**

He **eats** ___.

a. pizza
b. tea
c. plate

We **buy** ___.

a. money
b. food
c. vacations

My dog **digs** ___.

a. gardens
b. bones
c. holes

They **ride** the ___.

a. train
b. taxi
c. car

They **steal** ___.

a. robbers
b. money
c. jewelry store

I **do** my ___.

a. classroom
b. computer
c. homework

Class **begins** at ___.

a. the morning
b. room 101
c. 1:00 pm

We **fly** on a ___.

a. plane
b. train
c. bus

I'll **dive** into the ___.

a. swimsuit
b. pool
c. gymnasium

I **know** the ___.

a. floor
b. answer
c. eggs

I **sweep** the ___.

a. walls
b. windows
c. floors

She **draws** ___.

a. pictures
b. paintings
c. pencils

He **catches** the ___.

a. ball
b. bat
c. team

They will **build** a ___.

a. cake
b. house
c. book

I **dream** when I ___.

a. swim
b. eat
c. sleep

Verbs: Definitions **Game Cards #2**

She **fell** from ___.

VERBS

a. a tree
b. a river
c. the floor

___ can **fly**.

VERBS

a. Fish
b. Birds
c. Dogs

I will **go** to the ___.

VERBS

a. radio
b. television
c. movies

We **feed** the ___.

VERBS

a. dogs
b. food
c. bowl

Don't **forget** your ___.

VERBS

a. feet
b. keys
c. nose

I'll **grind** some ___.

VERBS

a. tea
b. tobacco
c. coffee beans

I **feel** ___.

VERBS

a. a cold
b. sick
c. headache

The pond **freezes** in ___.

VERBS

a. Spring
b. Autumn
c. Winter

He **grows** ___.

VERBS

a. roses
b. fish
c. children

The cat **fights** with the ___.

VERBS

a. food
b. milk
c. dog

I have to **get** a ___.

VERBS

a. job
b. money
c. bank

My picture **hangs** on the ___.

VERBS

a. floor
b. wall
c. ceiling

I can never **find** my ___.

VERBS

a. keys
b. hair
c. house

I like to **get** ___ on my birthday.

VERBS

a. work
b. classes
c. presents

I **have** a ___.

VERBS

a. flu
b. cold
c. dizzy

Verbs: Definitions **Game Cards #3**

Hide the ___.
a. goldfish
b. sweaters
c. money

Do you **know** the ___?
a. talk
b. answer
c. response

You should always **tell** the ___.
a. truth
b. answer
c. parents

He **hit** the ___.
a. ball
b. bat
c. stadium

It's nice to **lay** on the ___.
a. floor
b. beach
c. street

Don't **gamble** away our ___.
a. kids
b. chairs
c. money

Hold my ___.
a. nose
b. hand
c. toes

He will **lead** the ___ to victory.
a. team
b. game
c. championship

I'm going to **make** ___.
a. pans
b. plates
c. dinner

I think I **hurt** my ___.
a. hair
b. shirt
c. back

Don't **leave** the ___ open.
a. light
b. door
c. phone

Wring out that ___.
a. rag
b. soap
c. brush

Can you **keep** ___?
a. a secret
b. an answer
c. a problem

Could you **lend** me some ___?
a. gum
b. money
c. tea

I'm going to **meet** ___ tonight.
a. the radio
b. my goldfish
c. some friends

Verbs: Definitions **Game Cards #4**

Can you **prove** he's ___? *VERBS*
a. laughing
b. at lunch
c. the murderer

The sun **rises** ___. *VERBS*
a. in the east
b. under water
c. at the airport

I'll **mail** a ___ for her birthday. *VERBS*
a. ham
b. card
c. horse

Put on your ___. *VERBS*
a. jacket
b. zipper
c. hair

I think he'll **run** for ___. *VERBS*
a. preacher
b. president
c. the post office

I'm **sewing** a ___ for Halloween. *VERBS*
a. candy
b. pumpkin
c. costume

Sally **quit** ___ for her health. *VERBS*
a. eating
b. smoking
c. sleeping

He can **say** the ___. *VERBS*
a. alphabet
b. English
c. question

Americans often **shake** ___. *VERBS*
a. legs
b. feet
c. hands

I **read** the ___ on Sundays. *VERBS*
a. menu
b. dictionary
c. newspaper

Did you **see** the ___? *VERBS*
a. cold
b. sunrise
c. morning

The farmer **shears** the ___. *VERBS*
a. sheep
b. geese
c. cows

I **ride** a ___ at the farm. *VERBS*
a. fish
b. bird
c. horse

The kids **play** ___ and seek. *VERBS*
a. find
b. hide
c. search

Don't **shine** that light in ___. *VERBS*
a. my eyes
b. the kitchen
c. the evening

Verbs: Definitions Game Cards #5

She **showed** us the ___. a. air b. ground **c. sights**	He is **sleeping** in the ___. a. sink **b. tent** c. freezer	I was **stung** by a ___. **a. bee** b. mouse c. butterfly
My ___ **shrunk** in the dryer. **a. sweater** b. sneakers c. sheets	She can **speak** ___. a. China **b. French** c. Greece	**Take** out the ___. It stinks. a. car b. dinner **c. garbage**
Please **shut** the ___. **a. door** b. floor c. lights	He **speeds** on the ___. a. corner **b. freeway** c. driveway	The ducks **swim** in the ___. a. tree b. yard **c. pond**
We **sing** in the ___. **a. choir** b. office c. hospital	Don't **spend** too much ___. a. shopping **b. money** c. shoes	I **take** ___ every week. a. piano keys b. piano schools **c. piano lessons**
My ___ is going to **sink**. a. kite **b. boat** c. surfboard	The ballet dancers **spin** ___. a. in b. down **c. around**	She **teaches** ___. **a. math** b. recess c. the school

Verbs: Definitions Game Cards #6

We **tell** ___ at night.
a. time
b. the truth
c. ghost stories

Don't **wake** ___.
a. the alarm
b. Grandpa
c. the couch

I need to **wind** this old ___.
a. clock
b. oven
c. lamp

I hope I **win** the ___.
a. luck
b. lottery
c. casino

I'm **wearing** my new ___.
a. car
b. bike
c. shoes

I must **withdraw** some ___.
a. money
b. checks
c. credit cards

We want to **throw** a ___ tonight.
a. party
b. championship
c. game

She's **weaving** a ___.
a. pot
b. basket
c. glass

She **wrote** a ___.
a. pen
b. pencil
c. paper

I **understand** what you're ___.
a. speaking
b. saying
c. talking

I'm **marrying** my ___.
a. fiancé
b. dog
c. wedding

Don't **withhold** ___ at the trial.
a. guilt
b. innocent
c. evidence

Police officers **uphold** the ___.
a. law
b. rules
c. directions

I **weep** during ___.
a. comedies
b. sad movies
c. documentaries

The knight wanted to **slay** the ___.
a. forest
b. wizard
c. dragon

Verbs: Definitions Game Cards #7

She **drives** a ___.
a. car
b. bike
c. skateboard

I can't **hear** the ___.
a. table
b. radio
c. lamp

We're **selling** ___ for charity.
a. oil
b. water
c. cookies

He **cut** ___.
a. the cake
b. some soup
c. a glass of milk

Grandma likes to **knit** ___.
a. shoes
b. glasses
c. scarves

The police officer **shot** the ___.
a. jail
b. criminal
c. evidence

She **drinks** ___.
a. toast
b. spaghetti
c. orange juice

I **let** them have the ___.
a. car
b. highway
c. traffic light

She **sits** in her ___.
a. sink
b. chair
c. desk

My foot doesn't **fit** this ___.
a. hat
b. shoe
c. glove

I will **pay** the ___.
a. rent
b. check
c. payment

Please **stand** in a ___.
a. line
b. box
c. triangle

Please **give** me your ___.
a. housework
b. headache
c. homework

Ring the ___ and I'll let you in.
a. gate
b. phone
c. doorbell

I **tore** my ___.
a. watch
b. shirt
c. glasses

Idioms of Comparison

197

INTERMEDIATE

LESSON PREPARATION:

Photocopy and cut out the GAME CARDS.

Divide the class into 2 teams or divide the class into groups of about 4 students and have each student play for themself.

An IDIOMS LIST is provided (328).

BEGIN:

Stack the GAME CARDS, face down, on the table.

Student A chooses a card and reads the incomplete idiom to Student B. Student B must correctly choose the word or phrase that completes the idiom to earn the card and thus the point. *A brief definition of the idiom is included to help students make an informed choice.*

If Student B chooses incorrectly, the card is put off to the side and no point is earned.

Student B then chooses a new card and reads to Student C, and so on until there are no more GAME CARDS left.

The student or team that earns the most GAME CARDS at the end of the game wins.

OBJECTIVE:

To gain cultural insight through the understanding of idioms. Upon completion of this lesson, students should:

1. Be more familiar with using common Idioms.

2. Expand their vocabulary.

PRIVATE LESSONS:

These GAME CARDS can also be used as flash cards for an enjoyable and effective way to review idioms with your one-to-one students.

As **clean** as a ___.

a. whistle
b. shirt
c. window

Very clean

Idioms of Comparison **GAME CARDS #1**

As **clean** as a ___.

a. whistle
b. shirt
c. window

Very clean

As **white** as a ___.

a. snowflake
b. sheet
c. wall

Very pale (i.e. from sickness or fright)

As **wise** as an ___.

a. octopus
b. elephant
c. owl

Very wise

As **strong** as a ___.

a. horse
b. camel
c. gorilla

Very strong

As **easy** as ___.

a. kindergarten
b. ABC
c. walking

Very easy

As **good** as ___.

a. diamonds
b. pearls
c. gold

Very well-behaved (as in children)

As **pale** as a ___.

a. ghost
b. swan
c. cloud

Very pale (i.e. from sickness or fright)

As **easy** as ___.

a. cookies
b. cake
c. pie

Very easy

As **flat** as a ___.

a. crepe
b. pancake
c. piece of toast

Very flat

As **fresh** as a ___.

a. daisy
b. rose
c. tulip

Alert and energetic

As **dry** as ___.

a. dust
b. cotton
c. a bone

Very dry

As **tough** as ___.

a. trees
b. nails
c. steel

Strong willed

Idioms of Comparison **GAME CARDS #2**

As **free** as a ___.

a. dog
b. bird
c. butterfly

To have no obligations

As **busy** as a ___.

a. bee
b. bear
c. bird

Very busy, having a lot to do

As **cold** as ___.

a. Alaska
b. snow
c. ice

Cold weather or personality

As **red** as a ___.

a. lobster
b. fire truck
c. strawberry

Very sunburned

As **dead** as a ___.

a. rock
b. grave
c. doornail

Completely dead, no signs of life

As **drunk** as a ___.

a. monk
b. skunk
c. punk

Very drunk

As **sharp** as a ___.

a. spike
b. sword
c. razor

Smart, quick-witted

As **pretty** as a ___.

a. jewel
b. picture
c. flower

Very pretty

As **regular** as ___.

a. clockwork
b. the sun
c. the stars

A consistent schedule

As **clear** as a ___.

a. window
b. stream
c. bell

Easily understood

As **poor** as a ___.

a. barn owl
b. tree frog
c. church mouse

Having little or no money

As **sly / cunning** as a ___.

a. fox
b. wolf
c. coyote

Very clever

Idioms of Comparison GAME CARDS #3

As **hot** as ___.

a. a fire
b. a stove
c. an oven

Hot weather or temperature

As **quiet** as a ___.

a. snake
b. mouse
c. fish

To move very quietly

Like **taking** candy from a ___.

a. baby
b. blind man
c. candy shop

Very easy to do

As **proud** as a ___.

a. parent
b. preacher
c. peacock

Very proud

Like a **moth** to a ___.

a. flame
b. fire
c. lamp

To be attracted to something

As **different** as ___.

a. up and down
b. night and day
c. black and white

Completely different

As **sharp** as a ___.

a. knife
b. tack
c. pin

Very smart, clever

As **slow** as ___.

a. honey
b. ketchup
c. molasses

To move very slowly

As **gentle** as a ___.

a. lamb
b. rabbit
c. kitten

Very gentle

As **fit** as a ___.

a. fiddle
b. flute
c. French horn

In perfect health or physical condition

As **sick** as a ___.

a. cat
b. dog
c. bird

Very sick

As **pleased** as ___.

a. pork chops
b. peaches
c. punch

Very pleased or happy

Idioms of Comparison GAME CARDS #4

As thick as ___.

a. thieves
b. trees
c. fog

A close friendship, closely allied

To sleep like a ___.

a. bear
b. rock
c. tree

To sleep very well, soundly, or deeply

To go as the ___.

a. cheetah runs
b. eel swims
c. crow flies

The most direct route from A to B

As light as a ___.

a. snowflake
b. balloon
c. feather

Very lightweight or airy

To smoke like a ___.

a. chimney
b. pipe
c. factory

To smoke too many cigarettes or cigars

To fit like a ___.

a. sock
b. glove
c. hat

To be a perfect fit

To spread like ___.

a. wildfire
b. a cold
c. weeds

To spread quickly (e.g. like gossip)

To sell like ___.

a. French toast
b. hotcakes
c. donuts

To sell a lot and quickly

Like herding ___.

a. puppies
b. frogs
c. cats

Difficulty organizing people

It's like comparing apples and ___.

a. oranges
b. bananas
c. pears

Two items that can't be compared

Like a bull in a ___.

a. library
b. museum
c. china shop

A loud, clumsy or awkward person

To be out like a ___.

a. lamp
b. flame
c. light

To quickly fall into a deep sleep

Idioms of Comparison **GAME CARDS #5**

To **sing** like a ___.	Like **peas** in a ___.	Like there's no ___.
a. violin b. fairy **c. bird** *To sing beautifully, to divulge secrets*	a. stew **b. pod** c. soup *To look very similar or exactly alike*	**a. tomorrow** b. today c. yesterday *To do something energetically*
To **shake** like a ___.	Like **water** off a ___.	To **look** like something the ___.
a. blade of grass b. flower **c. leaf** *To tremble from cold or fear*	**a. duck's back** b. dolphin's nose c. whale's tail *Not bothered by criticism*	a. dog chewed up **b. cat dragged in** c. cow slept on *Look very disheveled*
To **sleep** like a ___.	Like putting **lipstick** on ___.	To **stand out** like a ___ **thumb**.
a. stick **b. log** c. leave *To sleep very well, soundly, or deeply*	a. an alligator b. a monkey **c. a pig** *Trying to disguise the real situation*	**a. sore** b. green c. fat *To be different from one's surroundings*
To **look / feel** like a ___.	Like the **cat** that **swallowed** the ___.	To **look** like **death** ___.
a. million bucks b. bag of gold coins c. diamond ring *To look / feel great*	a. swallow **b. canary** c. pigeon *To look mischievous*	a. over easy b. on toast **c. warmed over** *To look extremely sick*

Idioms of Comparison **GAME CARDS #6**

To **play** (someone) like a ___.
a. ukulele
b. mandolin
c. fiddle

To manipulate someone

Raining ___.
a. cats and dogs
b. coffee and tea
c. rocks and stones

To rain heavily

To **eat** like a ___.
a. bear
b. pig
c. dog

No table manners or to eat a lot

Like a **thief** in ___.
a. the alley
b. jail
c. the night

To come swiftly and stealthily

To **sing** like a ___.
a. parrot
b. canary
c. pigeon

To inform the police about a crime

To **sweat** like a ___.
a. pig
b. horse
c. dog

To sweat a lot

To be **off** like a ___.
a. shot
b. sprinter
c. race horse

To leave very quickly or urgently

To **drink** like ___.
a. a camel
b. a fish
c. an elephant

To have too many alcoholic drinks

To **work** like a ___.
a. camel
b. horse
c. dog

To work very hard

To **hit** (me) like a ___.
a. bag of rocks
b. sack of stones
c. ton of bricks

To be very surprised or shocked

To **eat** like a ___.
a. bird
b. mouse
c. squirrel

To eat very little

As **safe** as ___. (Brit)
a. parks
b. houses
c. school buses

Very safe or secure

Idioms of Comparison GAME CARDS #7

As **blind** as a ___. **a. bat** b. snail c. mole *To have very weak vision*	To **sleep** like a ___. a. sloth b. cat **c. baby** *To sleep very well, soundly, or deeply*	As **thick** as ___. a. gravy **b. pea soup** c. clam chowder *Foggy weather that's hard to see through*
As **stubborn** as a ___. a. horse b. donkey **c. mule** *Very stubborn*	Like a **fish** out of ___. a. the sea **b. water** c. the pot *To feel out of place or awkward*	As **old** as the ___. **a. hills** b. moon c. forests *Very old*
As **cool** as a ___. **a. cucumber** b. carrot c. cabbage *Calm under pressure*	To **know** something like the ___. a. tip of one's nose **b. back of one's hand** c. top of one's head *Very familiar with*	As **dull** as ___. a. old sponges b. soap **c. dishwater** *A very boring person or experience*
To **eat** like a ___. a. bear b. whale **c. horse** *To eat a lot*	To **fight** like cats and ___. **a. dogs** b. mice c. birds *To fight a lot*	As **mad** as a ___. (Brit) a. batter **b. hatter** c. nutter *Very crazy, insane person*

Business Idioms

LESSON PREPARATION:

Photocopy and cut out the GAME CARDS.

Divide the class into 2 teams or divide the class into groups of about 4 students and have each student play for themself.

An IDIOMS LIST is provided (329).

BEGIN:

Stack the GAME CARDS, face down, on the table.

Student A chooses a card and reads the top sentence and the 3 possible definitions to Student B. Student B must choose the correct definition to earn the card and thus the point.

If Student B chooses the incorrect definition, the card is put off to the side and no point is earned.

Student B then chooses a new card and reads to Student C, and so on until there are no more GAME CARDS left.

The student or team that earns the most GAME CARDS at the end of the game wins.

ADVANCED

OBJECTIVE:

To gain cultural insight through the understanding of idioms. Upon completion of this lesson, students should:

1. Be more familiar with using business idioms.

2. Expand their vocabulary.

PRIVATE LESSONS:

These GAME CARDS can also be used as flash cards for an enjoyable and effective way to review idioms with your one-to-one students.

---

*Our company is **in the black**.*

a. profitable
b. unprofitable
c. going bankrupt

Business Idioms GAME CARDS #1

Our company is **in the black**.

a. profitable
b. unprofitable
c. going bankrupt

They keep **jacking up** the prices.

a. changing
b. raising
c. making mistakes

He **passes the buck** when there's work to do.

a. spends money
b. works very hard
c. shifts responsibility

Our company is **in the red**.

a. profitable
b. unprofitable
c. in the lead

They really **mean business**.

a. are serious
b. think about money
c. make big deals

He always **pulls his own weight**.

a. does his share of work
b. is very confident
c. avoids decisions

I would like to get this **in black and white**.

a. via e-mail
b. in a memo
c. in writing

My stocks **took a nosedive**.

a. lost value quickly
b. gained value
c. fluctuated in value

Red tape delayed her visa.

a. employee vacations
b. late payments
c. excessive bureaucracy

Business Idioms GAME CARDS #2

I was just given my **walking papers**.

a. notice of dismissal
b. formal transfer
c. a promotion

Our new co-worker is an **eager beaver**.

a. pushy salesperson
b. hard worker
c. clever negotiator

We **lost our shirts** in the merger.

a. lost most of the staff
b. closed a department
c. lost all of the money

My boss is always **talking shop**.

a. talking about work
b. office gossiping
c. talking about money

The layoffs will cut some **dead wood**.

a. unproductive staff
b. part-time staff
c. middle managers

We **made a bundle** last quarter.

a. made a lot of money
b. made a big mistake
c. had financial losses

Our new database isn't **passing muster**.

a. intuitive
b. successful
c. acceptable

I only invest in **blue chip companies**.

a. environmental
b. high technology
c. stable & profitable

I **made a killing** in the stock market.

a. went bankrupt
b. lost a lot of money
c. made a lot of money

Business Idioms GAME CARDS #3

I would like to give **my two cents**.

a. formal resignation
b. brief opinion
c. financial donation

Tell me about the meeting **in a nutshell**.

a. in detail
b. in private
c. in a few words

She's a **desk jockey**.

a. an office worker
b. a secretary
c. a radio personality

I **don't have a clue**.

a. have no idea
b. have no opinion
c. have no interest

It's time for some **belt-tightening**.

a. saving money
b. streamlining production
c. selling off stock

Our firm must **downsize**.

a. reduce its work force
b. save money
c. rent a small office

This decision is a **no-brainer**.

a. risky
b. stupid
c. obvious

The new soda flavor turned into a real **cash cow**.

a. huge investment
b. waste of money
c. money maker

Let's **get our ducks in a row**.

a. recruit more staff
b. improve security
c. get organized

Business Idioms **GAME CARDS #4**

I need some **face time** *with our clients.*  **a. to meet in person** b. a teleconference c. a video conference	*It's time to* **pull the plug** *on this product.*  a. to get results **b. to terminate** c. to advertise	*We can't* **bankroll** *more advertising.*  a. launch b. develop **c. pay for**
Our boss ended up being the **fall guy**.  **a. the scapegoat** b. the guinea pig c. the workhorse	*I'd like to get the most* **bang for my buck**.  **a. return on investment** b. high interest rates c. low price	*Last year was a* **banner year** *for our firm.*  **a. an outstanding year** b. a bad year c. the worst year
Fire away.  a. start firing people b. start brainstorming **c. speak when ready**	**Bait and switch** *is illegal.*  a. tax evasion b. sell stolen goods **c. falsely advertise sale items**	*I'd quit if it weren't for the* **golden handcuffs**.  a. medical insurance b. office friendships **c. financial incentives**

Business Idioms GAME CARDS #5

Our market research raised several **red flags**.

a. positive feedback
b. warning signs
c. new product ideas

We have a deadline but is there any **wiggle room**?

a. immediate solutions
b. possible short-cuts
c. flexibility

We've put a lot of **sweat equity** into our house.

a. a heating system
b. hard, unpaid labor
c. skilled labor costs

We got our new project **rubber stamped**.

a. funded
b. approved
c. started

I'm unhappy with my **take-home pay**.

a. money after bills
b. pay after deductions
c. commission or tips

Let's **put feelers out** to see if they'll make a deal.

a. arrange a meeting
b. discretely find out
c. negotiate a price

Don't **make waves** if you want a promotion.

a. be lazy
b. go to meetings
c. cause trouble

We had a **three martini lunch**.

a. weekend brunch
b. lunch and golf
c. leisurely business lunch

Let's try to **think outside of the box**.

a. look into outsourcing
b. hire freelancers
c. be innovative

Business Idioms **GAME CARDS #6**

Let's get down to **brass tacks**.

a. essential business
b. sales strategies
c. reducing costs

Don't get **hot under the collar**.

a. stressed
b. angry
c. nervous

She just hired a new **flunky**.

a. a college drop out
b. a college graduate
c. low-level employee

Our sales team is **batting a thousand**.

a. below quota
b. 100% success rate
c. getting new clients

We just need to get through **hump day**.

a. Monday
b. Wednesday
c. Friday

There is no **free lunch** at this firm.

a. long lunch hours
b. something for nothing
c. an expense account

We hired a new **bean counter**.

a. middle manager
b. stockbroker
c. accountant

What's our new **game plan**?

a. quota
b. deadline
c. strategy

That issue is on the **back burner** for now.

a. instant high priority
b. ignored, dismissed
c. temporary lower priority

Business Idioms **GAME CARDS #7**

This info came straight **from the horse's mouth**.

a. **the highest authority**
b. office gossip
c. certified mail

Please explain your plan **from soup to nuts**.

a. briefly
b. in great detail
c. **from beginning to end**

Their accountant is **cooking the books**.

a. **falsifying accounts**
b. making calculation errors
c. embezzling

I'll have a **golden parachute** if I'm laid off.

a. extended healthcare
b. **generous compensation**
c. job counseling

Our talks resulted in a **zero-sum game**.

a. one party gains all
b. one party loses all
c. **gains equal losses**

My department is run by **empty suits**.

a. **incompetent managers**
b. lazy managers
c. overseas managers

We want someone who can **hit the ground running**.

a. increase sales
b. **do the job now**
c. motivate their staff

We need to **talk turkey** at this meeting.

a. talk seriously
b. negotiate
c. brainstorm

We can barely **keep our head above water**.

a. **survive financially**
b. compete financially
c. pay our employees

Business Idioms **GAME CARDS #8**

She **wears many hats** at the company.

a. has several duties
b. is a freelancer
c. is very fashionable

So, what's **the bottom line**?

a. the main idea
b. the level of sales
c. annual expenses

They **bounce checks** all over town.

a. find good discounts
b. write bad checks
c. shop at boutiques

I try to **keep my nose to the grindstone**.

a. concentrate on work
b. learn new job skills
c. listen to my boss

The **hard sell** isn't always effective.

a. to sell aggressively
b. online marketing
c. telemarketing

Our company is having a **budget crunch**.

a. financial strategy
b. financial difficulty
c. financial surplus

We bought the building for **chicken feed**.

a. very little money
b. a lot of money
c. a reasonable price

He **cuts corners** when he's close to a deadline.

a. compromises quality
b. works efficiently
c. works over-time

The new toys **sold like hotcakes**.

a. were marked up
b. were on sale
c. sold out quickly

Business Idioms **GAME CARDS #9**

It was a **win-win situation**.

a. only one side won
b. all sides won
c. all sides compromised

Our boss has given **lip service** regarding bonuses.

a. promises
b. talk but no action
c. serious discussion

We need to find some **common ground**.

a. cheap real estate
b. mutual interest
c. affordable labor

We **threw cold water** on that proposal.

a. encouraged
b. dismissed
c. paid close attention

Those cell phones are **a dime a dozen**.

a. 10 cents for 12 units
b. common & cheap
c. of bad quality

I'm **climbing the corporate ladder**.

a. buying stocks
b. getting promoted quickly
c. cross-training

Find a solution or **heads will roll**.

Someone:
a. will be confused
b. will be punished
c. will have fear

Our firm **broke even** last year.

a. went into debt
b. income equaled expenses
c. earned profits

I found a solution in **the eleventh hour**.

a. ahead of schedule
b. at the last moment
c. after the deadline

Business Idioms GAME CARDS #10

Most job applications end up in **the circular file**.

a. before a committee
b. in the garbage can
c. in an intranet database

These are **Mickey Mouse** issues.

a. family-oriented
b. unimportant
c. amusing

Handle our customers with **kid gloves**.

a. tact & gentleness
b. flattery & compliments
c. a sense of humor

Can you give me a **ballpark figure**?

a. quarterly sales
b. an estimate
c. annual revenue

This is a **turnkey** business.

a. security company
b. ready to use now
c. high-tech operation

I heard they **got the axe**.

a. got fired
b. got demoted
c. got transferred

The $5,000 sign-on bonus was **gravy**.

a. earned
b. an unexpected benefit
c. invested

There is no **magic bullet** to solve our problem.

a. injection of money
b. perfect solution
c. brainstorming session

Our popularity grew by **word of mouth**.

a. radio commercials
b. casual conversations
c. telemarketing

Some, A, An **GAME CARDS #2**

Would you like to listen to ___ music? **some** a an	I bought ___ bananas at the store. **some** a an	Do you have ___ deck of cards? some **a** an
I'm listening to ___ song by the Beatles. some **a** an	I need ___ egg for this recipe. some a **an**	There are ___ children in the yard. **some** a an
Would you like to see ___ movie tonight? some **a** an	I need ___ eggs for this recipe. **some** a an	There's ___ kid in the pool. some **a** an
I'm making ___ sandwiches for lunch. **some** a an	I need ___ dozen eggs from the market. some **a** an	I have ___ ideas about our next vacation. **some** a an
I bought ___ bunch of grapes at the store. some **a** an	I'd like ___ ice cube for my tea. some a **an**	I have ___ idea for the New Year's Eve party. some a **an**

Body Idioms

LESSON PREPARATION:

Photocopy and cut out the GAME CARDS.

Divide the class into 2 teams or divide the class into groups of about 4 students and have each student play for themself.

An IDIOMS LIST is provided (330).

BEGIN:

Stack the GAME CARDS, face down, on the table.

Student A chooses a card and reads the incomplete idiom and the 3 choices to Student B. Student B must choose the correct word or phrase that completes the idiom to earn the card and thus the point. *A brief definition of the idiom is included to help students make an informed choice.*

If Student B completes the idiom incorrectly, the card is put off to the side and no point is earned.

Student B then chooses a new card and reads to Student C, and so on until there are no more GAME CARDS left.

The student or team that earns the most GAME CARDS at the end of the game wins.

ADVANCED

OBJECTIVE:

To gain cultural insight through the understanding of idioms. Upon completion of this lesson, students should:

1. Be more familiar with using body idioms.

2. Expand their vocabulary.

PRIVATE LESSONS:

These GAME CARDS can also be used as flash cards for an enjoyable and effective way to review idioms with your one-to-one students.

Our new office has more ___ **room**.

a. neck
b. elbow
c. arm

Space to move around

Body Idioms **GAME CARDS #1**

Our new office has more ___ **room**.

a. neck
b. elbow
c. arm

Space to move around

I'd **give my right ___** for a promotion.

a. eye
b. arm
c. foot

Do almost anything for something you want

My ___ **is to the wall**. Either I borrow more money or I lose my business.

a. face
b. back
c. heel

Run out of options

It took a lot of ___ **grease** to get the rust off of this car.

a. elbow
b. arm
c. back

Hard physical labor – especially to clean or polish

My new car **cost ___** but it was worth it.

a. an arm and a leg
b. a hand and a foot
c. a nose and an eye

Was very expensive

I was **stabbed in the ___** when my best friend stole my sweetheart.

a. back
b. heart
c. chest

Deceived by a trusted person

I'll keep him **at ___ length** until I know him better.

a. elbow's
b. leg's
c. arm's

Not allow someone to become too friendly or close

No matter where you go, you can't escape **the long ___ of the law**.

a. leg
b. hand
c. arm

The extent of legal authority or policing

"Can I get a tattoo, Mom?" "**Over my ___ body!**"

a. cold
b. buried
c. dead

Absolutely not. (A strong refusal)

Body Idioms GAME CARDS #2

I got **the cold** ___ after I rejected their proposal.

a. eye
b. shoulder
c. back

To ignore or behave coolly towards someone

I won't plan my trip. I'll just **play it by** ___.

a. hand
b. nose
c. ear

Improvise, act without preparation

She tried to **put her best** ___ **forward** at the job interview.

a. foot
b. face
c. nose

Make a good impression

I **rubbed** ___ with the top executives at the company BBQ.

a. shoulders
b. arms
c. wrists

Met or talked to famous or important people

I don't trust him. He is **two-**___.

a. faced
b. headed
c. mouthed

Deceitful, insincere, hypocritical

Our teacher **keeps us on our** ___ with frequent pop quizzes.

a. toes
b. ears
c. thumbs

Alert, ready to act

His success was the result of ___.

a. tears, sweat & blood
b. sweat, blood & tears
c. blood, sweat & tears

Hard work & sacrifice

When he burped during his speech, I couldn't **keep a straight** ___.

a. mouth
b. lip
c. face

Try to look serious and not laugh

We **dug in our** ___ and refused to work overtime.

a. feet
b. toes
c. heels

Strongly resisted

Body Idioms GAME CARDS #3

She **shot herself in the** ___ when she lied on her job application.

a. knee
b. foot
c. leg

She worked against her own interests

After work, I like to **put my** ___ **up** and watch TV.

a. head
b. knees
c. feet

Sit down and relax

She has her father **wrapped around her** ___.

a. thumb
b. wrist
c. finger

Easily manipulated

I could be a big star if I could just **get my** ___ **in the door**.

a. foot
b. hand
c. nose

A small start that could lead to future success

I had to **think on my** ___ during the oral quiz.

a. feet
b. toes
c. heels

Improvise, act without preparation

The only way I could afford that jacket is with a ___ **discount**.

a. 5 finger
b. 10 finger
c. 2 hand

Stealing

I **put my** ___ **in my mouth** when I called that lady 'Sir'.

a. thumb
b. hand
c. foot

Say something that offends or embarrasses

We **voted with our** ___ when the owner raised the rent.

a. legs
b. heels
c. feet

Showed lack of support by leaving or not buying

My job interview went well, so I'm **keeping my** ___ **crossed**.

a. eyes
b. knees
c. fingers

Hoping for luck or success

Body Idioms GAME CARDS #4

We've been **working our ___ to the bone** all week.

a. hands
b. fingers
c. elbows

Working very hard

Since I lost my job, I've been **living from hand to ___**.

a. stomach
b. mouth
c. chest

Only enough money for the essentials

Without funding, this program will be **on its last ___**.

a. legs
b. feet
c. heels

Nearly dead or over

If we **grease some ___** me might get the house built faster.

a. palms
b. hands
c. fingers

Bribe

Idle ___ are the devil's workshop.

a. hands
b. fingers
c. arms

Inactivity can lead to bad behavior

He **puts his money where his ___ is** regarding education.

a. mouth
b. heart
c. hand

Back up words with action or money

Vigilantes try to **take the law into their own ___**.

a. heads
b. arms
c. hands

To administer justice as one likes without regard for legality

---

Without proof, you **don't have a ___ to stand on**.

a. foot
b. toe
c. leg

No support for one's claims or assertions

These monthly reports are a **pain in the ___**.

a. foot
b. back
c. neck

Very annoying or irritating

Body Idioms **GAME CARDS #5**

I've tried to eat better but I have a **sweet ___**.

a. tongue
b. tooth
c. stomach

A fondness for sweets

Every time we go out I end up ___ **the bill**.

a. toeing
b. footing
c. legging

Paying the bill

His daughter is the **apple of his ___**.

a. heart
b. eye
c. hand

A cherished person

She's always dropping things. She's a **butter ___**.

a. fingers
b. thumbs
c. hands

Clumsy, often dropping things

I never stay in one place for long. I have **itchy ___**.

a. feet
b. toes
c. legs

Unable to settle down in one place

I was so mad, I was yelling **at the top of my ___**.

a. lungs
b. throat
c. heart

Yelling as loudly as possible

She's got her dad **under her ___**.

a. big toe
b. foot
c. thumb

Under someone's complete control

He has learned his speech **by ___**.

a. head
b. brain
c. heart

Memorize something completely

The company lost lots of money and **went ___ up**.

a. chest
b. chin
c. belly

Bankrupt

Body Idioms GAME CARDS #6

I was a **bundle of** ___ before my speech. a. muscles **b. nerves** c. bones *Very anxious or nervous*	Our new manager seems to be **dead from the ___ up**. a. nose **b. neck** c. mouth *Stupid*	My co-worker's constant complaining is starting to **get under my ___**. a. hair **b. skin** c. nerves *Become bothersome or irritating*
He's **carrying the weight of the world on his ___**. **a. shoulders** b. back c. head *Dealing with major problems or stress*	I can't talk now; I **have a frog in my ___**. **a. throat** b. neck c. chest *Difficulty or discomfort when speaking*	That documentary **grabbed us by the ___**. **a. throat** b. neck c. ears *Commanded complete attention*
We were **chilled to the ___** after coming in from the rain. a. heart b. joints **c. bone** *Felt very cold*	The movie was so sad that I got a **lump in my ___**. a. heart b. chest **c. throat** *Felt as if I would cry cry*	They really **hate his ___**. a. face b. nerves **c. guts** *Extreme hatred of another person*

Body Idioms **GAME CARDS #7**

Our soccer team is **___ and shoulders above the rest**.

a. neck
b. head
c. hips

To be better or superior

It's been hard **keeping ___ together** after the layoffs.

a. heart & mind
b. body & soul
c. hand & mouth

To barely survive financially

I **split my ___** when I heard the joke.

a. chest
b. sides
c. belly

Laughed very hard

Discussing his ex-wife **hit a raw ___**.

a. nerve
b. heart
c. lip

Mentioned a sensitive issue or subject

I finally got a **pat on the ___** for my hard work.

a. back
b. head
c. shoulder

Acknowledgment or praise of one's efforts

His plants look great. He must have a **green ___**.

a. thumb
b. hand
c. finger

Skilled with plants or gardening

He has acting **in his ___**.

a. heart
b. guts
c. blood

An inherited talent or characteristic

I needed a **___ to cry on** when my car was stolen.

a. arm
b. chest
c. shoulder

Someone who listens to problems and sympathizes

Lawyers are usually very **thick-___**.

a. hearted
b. headed
c. skinned

A person whose feelings are not easily hurt

Body Idioms GAME CARDS #8

A lot of people were **up in** ___ over the tax increase.

a. legs
b. arms
c. mouths

Outraged, indignant

He got **cold** ___ on his wedding day.

a. hands
b. ears
c. feet

Hesitant or unsure about continuing

She dances like she **has** ___.

a. 3 long legs
b. 20 big toes
c. 2 left feet

To be a bad dancer

I wish my boss would **get off my** ___ and let me work.

a. neck
b. back
c. chest

Stop nagging

The last chapter of the murder mystery **sent shivers down my** ___.

a. back
b. spine
c. neck

To be frightened

We **got off on the wrong** ___ at first, but we're friends now.

a. hand
b. foot
c. knee

Started a relationship badly

Our new boss seems to have **a chip on his** ___.

a. tooth
b. shoulder
c. head

Overly defensive

I've been **cooling my** ___ in the doctor's office for hours.

a. toes
b. ankles
c. heels

Be kept waiting for longer than expected

Even after retirement he still keeps a ___ **in every pie.**

a. thumb
b. hand
c. finger

Involved in several activities

Body Idioms **GAME CARDS #9**

He is from a family of **blue** ___.

a. noses
b. bloods
c. hairs

From an aristocratic family

We're practically **joined at the** ___.

a. ankles
b. hip
c. elbows

Spending all or most of the time together

To save this company, everyone must be willing to **get their ___ dirty**.

a. face
b. hands
c. feet

Do hard, unpleasant work

Keep your ___ **up**; things aren't so bad.

a. eyes
b. chin
c. nose

Stay optimistic

I was **soaked to the ___** after walking in the rain.

a. bones
b. skin
c. scalp

In clothing that is completely drenched

I can't tell if he's serious or **pulling my** ___.

a. arm
b. leg
c. nose

Teasing me or telling me falsehoods

I didn't want to go camping but they **twisted my** ___.

a. leg
b. arm
c. neck

Persuaded someone

This customer always complains. He's a real **thorn in my ___**.

a. eye
b. side
c. toe

A constant annoyance

They don't get along. They are always **at each other's** ___.

a. necks
b. throats
c. eyes

Always fighting or arguing

Adjectives of Nationality

LESSON PREPARATION:

Photocopy and cut out the GAME CARDS.

Divide the class into 2 teams or divide the class into groups of about 4 students and have each student play for themselves.

BEGIN:

Stack the GAME CARDS, face down, on the table.

Student A chooses a card and reads the top sentence to Student B. Student B must say the correct nationality to earn the card and thus the point.

If Student B says the wrong nationality, the card is put off to the side and no point is earned.

Student B then chooses a new card and reads to Student C, and so on until there are no more GAME CARDS left.

The student or team that earns the most GAME CARDS at the end of the game wins.

BEGINNER

OBJECTIVE:

To be more accurate when stating the nationality for most countries.

PRECURSOR TO:

Countries, Nationalities & Languages (7)

PRIVATE LESSONS:

These GAME CARDS can also be used as flash cards for an enjoyable and effective way to review grammar with your one-to-one students.

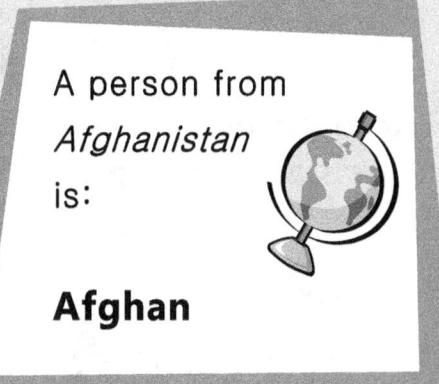

Adjectives of Nationality **GAME CARDS #1**

A person from *Afghanistan* is: **Afghan**	A person from *Australia* is: **Australian**	A person from *Belgium* is: **Belgian** 
A person from *Albania* is: **Albanian**	A person from *Austria* is: **Austrian** 	A person from *Bolivia* is: **Bolivian**
A person from *Algeria* is: **Algerian**	A person from *The Bahamas* is: **Bahamian** 	A person from *Botswana* is: **Batswana (pl.) Motswana (sing.)**
A person from *Argentina* is: **Argentine (or Argentinian)**	A person from *Bangladesh* is: **Bangladeshi** 	A person from *Brazil* is: **Brazilian** 
A person from *Armenia* is: **Armenian**	A person from *Barbados* is: **Barbadian** 	A person from *Bulgaria* is: **Bulgarian** 

Adjectives of Nationality **GAME CARDS #2** 229

A person from *Cambodia* is:

Cambodian

A person from *Colombia* is:

Colombian

A person from *Ecuador* is:

Ecuadorian

A person from *Romania* is:

Romanian

A person from *Costa Rica* is:

Costa Rican

A person from *Egypt* is:

Egyptian

A person from *Canada* is:

Canadian

A person from *Croatia* is:

Croatian

A person from *England* is:

English

A person from *Chile* is:

Chilean

A person from *Cuba* is:

Cuban

A person from *Ethiopia* is:

Ethiopian

A person from *China* is:

Chinese

A person from *Denmark* is:

Danish

A person from *Finland* is:

Finnish

Adjectives of Nationality **GAME CARDS #3**

A person from *France* is: **French**	A person from *Haiti* is: **Haitian**	A person from *India* is: **Indian**
A person from *Germany* is: **German**	A person from the *Netherlands / Holland* is: **Dutch**	A person from *Indonesia* is: **Indonesian**
A person from *Ghana* is: **Ghanaian**	A person from *Honduras* is: **Honduran**	A person from *Iran* is: **Iranian**
A person from *Greece* is: **Greek**	A person from *Hungary* is: **Hungarian**	A person from *Iraq* is: **Iraqi**
A person from *Guatemala* is: **Guatemalan**	A person from *Iceland* is: **Icelandic**	A person from *Ireland* is: **Irish**

Adjectives of Nationality GAME CARDS #4

A person from *Israel* is: **Israeli**	A person from *Kuwait* is: **Kuwaiti**	A person from *Malaysia* is: **Malaysian**
A person from *Italy* is: **Italian**	A person from *Korea* is: **Korean**	A person from *Mexico* is: **Mexican**
A person from *Jamaica* is: **Jamaican**	A person from *Lebanon* is: **Lebanese**	A person from *Morocco* is: **Moroccan**
A person from *Japan* is: **Japanese**	A person from *Libya* is: **Libyan**	A person from *Nepal* is: **Nepalese**
A person from *Kenya* is: **Kenyan**	A person from *Lithuania* is: **Lithuanian**	A person from *Nicaragua* is: **Nicaraguan**

Adjectives of Nationality GAME CARDS #5

A person from *Nigeria* is: **Nigerian**	A person from *Poland* is: **Polish**	A person from *Scotland* is: **Scottish**
A person from *Norway* is: **Norwegian**	A person from *Portugal* is: **Portuguese**	A person from *Senegal* is: **Senegalese**
A person from *Pakistan* is: **Pakistani**	A person from *Russia* is: **Russian**	A person from *Singapore* is: **Singaporean**
A person from *Panama* is: **Panamanian**	A person from *Rwanda* is: **Rwandan**	A person from *Slovenia* is: **Slovenian**
A person from *Peru* is: **Peruvian**	A person from *Saudi Arabia* is: **Saudi or Saudi Arabian**	A person from *Somalia* is: **Somali**

Adjectives of Nationality **GAME CARDS #6** 233

A person from *Ukraine* is:  **Ukrainian**	A person from *Syria* is:  **Syrian**	A person from *Uganda* is:  **Ugandan**
A person from *Spain* is:  **Spanish**	A person from *Taiwan* is: 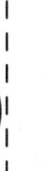 **Taiwanese**	A person from *Uruguay* is: **Uruguayan**
A person from *Sri Lanka* is:  **Sri Lankan**	A person from *Thailand* is: **Thai**	A person from *Bermuda* is: **Bermudian**
A person from *Sweden* is:  **Swedish**	A person from *Tunisia* is: **Tunisian**	A person from the *Sudan* is: **Sudanese**
A person from *Switzerland* is:  **Swiss**	A person from *Turkey* is:  **Turkish**	A person from *Wales* is: **Welsh**

Adjectives of Nationality GAME CARDS #7

A person from *Zambia* is: **Zambian**	A person from the *United Kingdom* is: **British**	A person from *Cameroon* is: **Cameroonian**
A person from the *United States* is: **American**	A person from *Burma / Myanmar* is: **Burmese**	A person from *Zimbabwe* is: **Zimbabwean**
A person from the *Philippines* is: **Philippine**	A person from *Cyprus* is: **Cypriot**	A person from *Venezuela* is: **Venezuelan**
A person from *Belize* is: **Belizean**	A person from the *Czech Republic* is: **Czech**	A person from *Vietnam* is: **Vietnamese**
A person from *Serbia* is: **Serb / Serbian**	A person from *Slovakia* is: **Slovak**	A person from *South Africa* is: **South African**

World Capitals

LEVEL: ALL

OBJECTIVE:

Word Capitals can be a light lesson or a component to a board game.

Upon completion of this lesson, students should be more familiar with the names and pronunciation of nations' capitals.

LESSON PREPARATION:

Photocopy and cut out the GAME CARDS.

Divide the class into 2 teams or divide the class into groups of about 4 students and have each student play for themself.

BEGIN:

Stack the GAME CARDS, face down, on the table.

Student A takes the top card and reads the top sentence to Student B. Student B must name the correct nation's capital to earn the card and thus the point.

If Student B gives the wrong answer, the card is put off to the side and no point is earned.

Student B then chooses a new card and reads to Student C, and so on until there are no more GAME CARDS left.

The student or team that earns the most GAME CARDS at the end of the game wins.

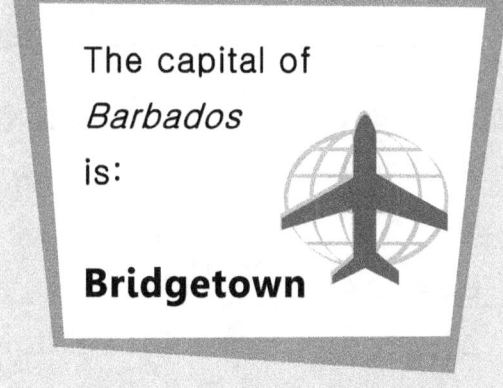

The capital of *Barbados* is:

Bridgetown

World Capitals GAME CARDS #1

The capital of *Afghanistan* is: **Kabul**	The capital of *Australia* is: **Canberra**	The capital of *Belgium* is: **Brussels**
The capital of *Albania* is: **Tirana**	The capital of *Austria* is: **Vienna**	The capital of *Bolivia* is: **La Paz (Sucre)**
The capital of *Algeria* is: **Algiers**	The capital of *The Bahamas* is: **Nassau**	The capital of *Botswana* is: **Gaborone**
The capital of *Argentina* is: **Buenos Aires**	The capital of *Bangladesh* is: **Dhaka**	The capital of *Brazil* is: **Brasilia**
The capital of *Armenia* is: **Yerevan**	The capital of *Barbados* is: **Bridgetown**	The capital of *Bulgaria* is: **Sofia**

World Capitals **GAME CARDS #2**

The capital of *Cambodia* is: **Phnom Penh**	The capital of *Colombia* is: **Bogotá**	The capital of *Ecuador* is: **Quito**
The capital of *Cameroon* is: **Yaoundé**	The capital of *Costa Rica* is: **San José**	The capital of *Egypt* is: **Cairo**
The capital of *Canada* is: **Ottawa**	The capital of *Croatia* is: **Zagreb**	The capital of *England* is: **London**
The capital of *Chile* is: **Santiago**	The capital of *Cuba* is: **Havana**	The capital of *Ethiopia* is: **Addis Ababa**
The capital of *China* is: **Beijing**	The capital of *Denmark* is: **Copenhagen**	The capital of *Finland* is: **Helsinki**

World Capitals GAME CARDS #3

The capital of *France* is: **Paris**	The capital of the *Netherlands / Holland* is: **Amsterdam (The Hague)**	The capital of *India* is: **New Delhi**
The capital of *Germany* is: **Berlin**	The capital of *Honduras* is: **Tegucigalpa**	The capital of *Indonesia* is: **Jakarta**
The capital of *Ghana* is: **Accra**	The capital of *Hungary* is: **Budapest**	The capital of *Iran* is: **Tehran**
The capital of *Greece* is: **Athens**	The capital of *Samoa* is: **Apia**	The capital of *Iraq* is: **Baghdad**
The capital of *Iceland* is: **Reykjavik**	The capital of *Sudan* is: **Khartoum**	The capital of *Ireland* is: **Dublin**

World Capitals GAME CARDS #4

The capital of *Israel* is: **Jerusalem**	The capital of *Kuwait* is: **Kuwait City**	The capital of *Mexico* is: **Mexico City**
The capital of *Italy* is: **Rome**	The capital of *North Korea* is: **Pyongyang**	The capital of *Morocco* is: **Rabat**
The capital of *Jamaica* is: **Kingston**	The capital of *Lebanon* is: **Beirut**	The capital of *Nepal* is: **Kathmandu**
The capital of *Japan* is: **Tokyo**	The capital of *Libya* is: **Tripoli**	The capital of *Nicaragua* is: **Managua**
The capital of *Kenya* is: **Nairobi**	The capital of *Lithuania* is: **Vilnius**	The capital of *Nigeria* is: **Abuja**

World Capitals GAME CARDS #5

The capital of *Norway* is: **Oslo**	The capital of *Poland* is: **Warsaw**	The capital of *Scotland* is: **Edinburgh**
The capital of *Pakistan* is: **Islamabad**	The capital of *Portugal* is: **Lisbon**	The capital of *Senegal* is: **Dakar**
The capital of *Panama* is: **Panama City**	The capital of *Russia* is: **Moscow**	The capital of *Singapore* is: **Singapore**
The capital of *Peru* is: **Lima**	The capital of *Rwanda* is: **Kigali**	The capital of *Slovenia* is: **Ljubljana**
The capital of *Switzerland* is: **Bern**	The capital of *Saudi Arabia* is: **Riyadh**	The capital of *Somalia* is: **Mogadishu**

World Capitals GAME CARDS #6

The capital of *South Africa* is: **Pretoria (Cape Town)**	The capital of *Syria* is: **Damascus**	The capital of *Uganda* is: **Kampala**
The capital of *Spain* is: **Madrid**	The capital of *Taiwan* is: **Taipei**	The capital of *Uruguay* is: **Montevideo**
The capital of *Sri Lanka* is: **Colombo**	The capital of *Thailand* is: **Bangkok**	The capital of *Venezuela* is: **Caracas**
The capital of *Sweden* is: **Stockholm**	The capital of *Tunisia* is: **Tunis**	The capital of *Vietnam* is: **Hanoi**
The capital of *Belize* is: **Belmopan**	The capital of *Turkey* is: **Ankara**	The capital of *Wales* is: **Cardiff**

World Capitals GAME CARDS #7

The capital of *Zambia* is: **Lusaka**

The capital of *South Korea* is: **Seoul**

The capital of the *Philippines* is: **Manila**

The capital of *Zimbabwe* is: **Harare**

The capital of *Myanmar (Burma)* is: **Rangoon**

The capital of *Haiti* is: **Port-au-Prince**

The capital of *Ukraine* is: **Kyiv (Kiev)**

The capital of *Cyprus* is: **Nicosia**

The capital of *Guatemala* is: **Guatemala City**

The capital of *Serbia* is: **Belgrade**

The capital of the *Czech Republic* is: **Prague**

The capital of *Malaysia* is: **Kuala Lumpur**

The capital of *Romania* is: **Bucharest**

The capital of *Slovakia* is: **Bratislava**

The capital of the *United States* is: **Washington D.C.**

The U.S. & Capitals

LESSON PREPARATION:

Photocopy and cut out the GAME CARDS.

Divide the class into 2 teams or divide the class into groups of about 4 students and have each student play for themself.

BEGIN:

Stack the GAME CARDS, face down, on the table.

Student A takes the top card and reads the top sentence to Student B. Depending on the card, Student B must either:

1. Correctly spell the state or
2. Give the correct state capital

to earn the card and thus the point.

If Student B is incorrect, the card is put off to the side and no point is earned.

Student B then chooses a new card and reads to Student C, and so on until there are no more GAME CARDS left.

The student or team that earns the most GAME CARDS at the end of the game wins.

LEVEL: ALL

OBJECTIVE:

Upon completion of this lesson, students should:

1. Be well acquainted with the letters of the alphabet.

2. Be more familiar with the names, pronunciation, and spelling of U.S. states.

3. Be more familiar with the names and pronunciation of U.S. state capitals.

PRIVATE LESSONS:

These GAME CARDS can also be used as flash cards for an enjoyable and effective way to review spelling with your one-to-one students.

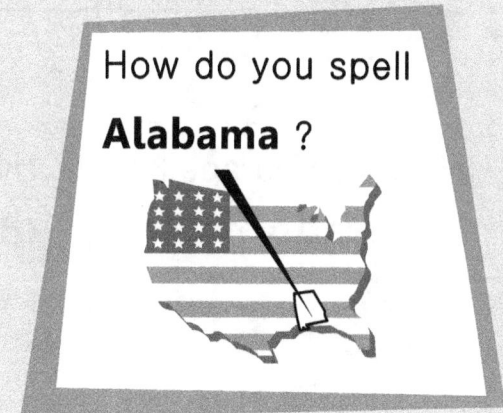

The U.S. & Capitals **GAME CARDS #1**

How do you spell **Alabama**?

How do you spell **Delaware**?

How do you spell **Indiana**?

How do you spell **Alaska**?

How do you spell **Florida**?

How do you spell **Iowa**?
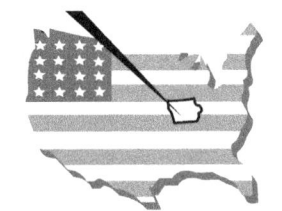

How do you spell **Arizona**?

How do you spell **Georgia**?

How do you spell **Kansas**?

How do you spell **California**?

How do you spell **Hawaii**?

How do you spell **Kentucky**?

How do you spell **Colorado**?
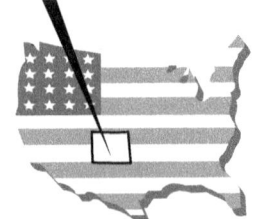

How do you spell **Idaho**?

How do you spell **Louisiana**?

The U.S. & Capitals **GAME CARDS #2**

How do you spell **Maine**? 	How do you spell **Michigan**? 	How do you spell **Nebraska**? 
How do you spell **Illinois**? 	How do you spell **Minnesota**? 	How do you spell **Nevada**? 
How do you spell **Connecticut**? 	How do you spell **Mississippi**? 	How do you spell **New Hampshire**? 
How do you spell **Maryland**? 	How do you spell **Missouri**? 	How do you spell **New Jersey**? 
How do you spell **Massachusetts**? 	How do you spell **Montana**? 	How do you spell **New Mexico**? 

The U.S. & Capitals **GAME CARDS #3**

How do you spell **New York**?

How do you spell **Oregon**?

How do you spell **Tennessee**?

How do you spell **North Carolina**?

How do you spell **Pennsylvania**?

How do you spell **Texas**?

How do you spell **North Dakota**?

How do you spell **Rhode Island**?

How do you spell **Utah**?
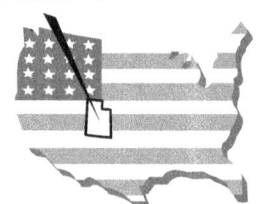

How do you spell **Ohio**?

How do you spell **South Carolina**?

How do you spell **Vermont**?

How do you spell **Oklahoma**?

How do you spell **South Dakota**?

How do you spell **Virginia**?

The U.S. & Capitals **GAME CARDS #4**   247

How do you spell **Washington** ? 	The capital of *Alabama* is:  a. Mobile b. Birmingham **c. Montgomery**	The capital of *Delaware* is:  **a. Dover** b. Seaford c. Middleton
How do you spell **West Virginia** ? 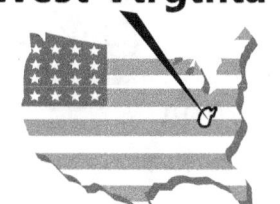	The capital of *Alaska* is:  **a. Juneau** b. Fairbanks c. Anchorage	The capital of *Florida* is:  a. Miami b. Orlando **c. Tallahassee**
How do you spell **Wisconsin** ? 	The capital of *Arizona* is:  a. Yuma **b. Phoenix** c. Flagstaff	The capital of *Georgia* is:  a. Macon **b. Atlanta** c. Savannah
How do you spell **Wyoming** ? 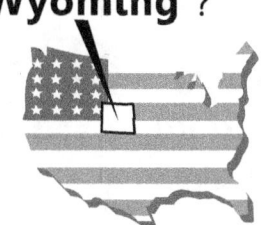	The capital of *Arkansas* is:  a. Omaha b. Nashville **c. Little Rock**	The capital of *Connecticut* is: a. Bristol **b. Hartford** c. New Haven
How do you spell **Arkansas** ? 	The capital of *Colorado* is:  **a. Denver** b. Aspen c. Boulder	The capital of *California* is: a. Burbank **b. Sacramento** c. Los Angeles

The U.S. & Capitals GAME CARDS #6

The capital of *Montana* is:
a. Helena
b. Billings
c. Missoula

The capital of *New Mexico* is:
a. Gallup
b. Santa Fe
c. Albuquerque

The capital of *Oklahoma* is:
a. Lawton
b. Tulsa
c. Oklahoma City

The capital of *Nebraska* is:
a. Omaha
b. Bellevue
c. Lincoln

The capital of *New York* is:
a. Albany
b. Long Island
c. New York City

The capital of *Oregon* is:
a. Salem
b. Portland
c. Eugene

The capital of *Nevada* is:
a. Reno
b. Carson City
c. Las Vegas

The capital of *North Carolina* is:
a. Raleigh
b. Charlotte
c. Fayetteville

The capital of *Pennsylvania* is:
a. Pittsburg
b. Harrisburg
c. Philadelphia

The capital of *New Hampshire* is:
a. Berlin
b. Concord
c. Manchester

The capital of *North Dakota* is:
a. Fargo
b. Bismarck
c. Jamestown

The capital of *Rhode Island* is:
a. Warwick
b. Cranston
c. Providence

The capital of *New Jersey* is:
a. Trenton
b. Newark
c. Sussex

The capital of *Ohio* is:
a. Columbus
b. Cleveland
c. Cincinnati

The capital of *South Carolina* is:
a. Columbia
b. Greenville
c. Charleston

The U.S. & Capitals **GAME CARDS #7**

The capital of *South Dakota* is:

a. Pierre
b. Sioux Falls
c. Aberdeen

The capital of *Virginia* is:

a. Richmond
b. Virginia Beach
c. Williamsburg

The capital of *Tennessee* is:

a. Nashville
b. Memphis
c. Chattanooga

The capital of *Washington* is:

a. Seattle
b. Olympia
c. Spokane

The capital of *Texas* is:

a. Austin
b. Houston
c. Dallas

The capital of *West Virginia* is:

a. Beckley
b. Charleston
c. Huntington

The capital of *Utah* is:

a. Provo
b. Sandy
c. Salt Lake City

The capital of *Wisconsin* is:

a. Madison
b. Sandy
c. Milwaukee

The capital of *Vermont* is:

a. Montpelier
b. Burlington
c. Newport

The capital of *Wyoming* is:

a. Cheyenne
b. Casper
c. Laramie

Mystery Cards

LESSON PREPARATION:

Photocopy and cut out the GAME CARDS.

BEGIN:

Stack the GAME CARDS, face down, on the Mystery Card box on the gameboard.

The Active Player can read these cards themself or another student can read these cards to the Active Player.

If the Mystery Card is a positive "thumbs up" card then the Active Player must:

1. In the case of the game Around the World: advance 2 spaces.

2. In the case of the game Shop Owner: collect some amount of money.

If the Mystery Card is a negative "thumbs down" card then the Active Player must:

1. In the case of the game Around the World: go back 2 spaces.

2. In the case of the game Shop Owner: lose some amount of money.

LEVEL: ALL

OBJECTIVE:

The Mystery Cards *is not a standalone lesson.*

This unit is for adding random luck to the BOARD GAMES that include a Mystery Card option:

1. AROUND THE WORLD (261)

2. SHOP OWNER (275)

Mystery Cards **GAME CARDS #1**

Someone brought donuts to work.	Your boss will be out of the office for the rest of the week.	You won the lottery.
The weather is sunny and warm today.	You just got a promotion.	Today is your birthday.
You were able to find a seat on the train.	You just got a raise.	Your in-laws are finally leaving.
You got 8 hours of sleep last night.	Your vacation starts tomorrow.	You're eating more fresh fruits and vegetables.
The baby sleeps through the night now.	It's lunch time!	You've joined a gym.

Mystery Cards GAME CARDS #2

You can retire soon. 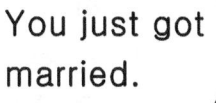	You lost 10 pounds. 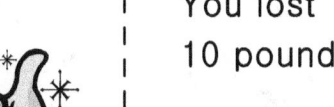	You inherited a lot of money. 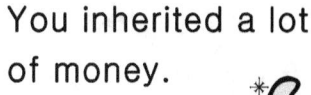
You just got married.	Your kids got straight A's on their report cards. 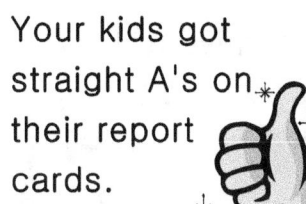	Your child is graduating from college.
You're going to the movies with your sweetheart. 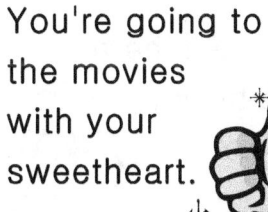	You passed your English test. 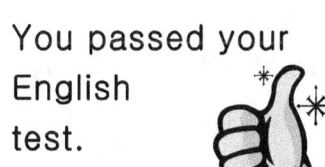	You've lowered your cholesterol.
You've paid off your credit card debt.	You're meeting an old friend for lunch. 	This weekend is a 3-day weekend.
You won a new speedboat on a game show. 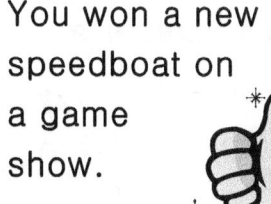	You are taking an art class.	You've made the final payment on your house. 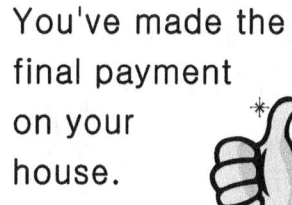

Mystery Cards **GAME CARDS #3**

You completed the Boston Marathon.	Your doctor has given you a clean bill of health.	Your children have promised not to put you in a nursing home.
You floss your teeth every day.	You have a good credit history.	Your sweetheart made you a nice dinner.
Someone just made a fresh pot of coffee.	You've just finished mowing the lawn.	You became a member of Mensa.
TGIF! (Thank God it's Friday!)	The ice cream truck is coming.	Your'e a Little League Baseball coach.
You heard your favorite song on the radio.	You've been invited to a 4th of July BBQ.	You volunteer at a local soup kitchen.

Mystery Cards **GAME CARDS #4** 255

You're taking an afternoon nap.	You got bumped from economy to first class.	Your favorite TV show is on tonight.
You installed solar panels on your roof.	It's time for Happy Hour.	You're reading more books and watching less TV.
You reduce, reuse, and recycle.	Someone gave you flowers.	All of your children have moved out of the house.
Tonight is Family Game Night.	Your team won the championship.	You're going for a hike today.
You got a huge income tax refund.	You're learning how to dance.	You adopted a puppy.

Mystery Cards GAME CARDS #5

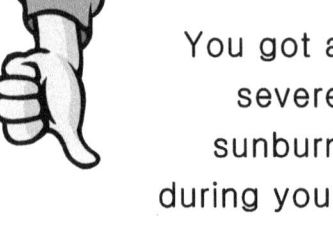 You got a severe sunburn during your vacation.

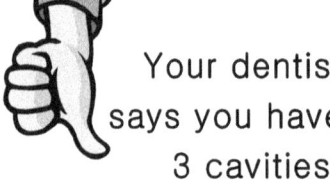 Your dentist says you have 3 cavities.

 Your computer crashed.

 The airline lost your luggage.

 The neighbor's dog keeps digging up your flowers.

 You lost a button on your jacket.

 You got a ticket for not wearing your seat belt.

 Your hotel room has a view of the parking lot.

 Your basement is flooded.

 Your child has chickenpox.

 The baby's diaper needs changing.

 Your library books are overdue.

 Your waiter brought you the wrong food.

 There's a fly in your soup.

 You spilled hot coffee on your lap.

Mystery Cards GAME CARDS #6

You forgot your wedding anniversary.	Your company is downsizing.	You can't find a matching pair of socks.
You've found your first gray hair.	Your child dropped out of college and joined the circus.	You got stuck in rush hour traffic.
The copy machine is on the fritz.	There is a very long line at the bank.	There are no free seats on the bus.
It's April 10th and you haven't filed your taxes.	Your co-workers are out sick, so you have to do their work.	Someone is talking too loudly on their cell phone.
Your sister, brother-in-law, and their 5 kids need a place to stay.	A telemarketer called you during dinner.	You caught your co-worker's cold.

Mystery Cards **GAME CARDS #7**

 The dog ate your homework.

 The heel of your shoe broke off.

 The water main was turned off during your shower.

 You took the wrong bus to class.

 The toaster burned your toast.

 A barking dog kept you up all night.

 Your alarm clock didn't go off this morning.

 It's raining and you forgot your umbrella.

 You were pulled over for speeding.

 You missed your train to work.

 All your pens dried out and stopped working.

 The back tire of your bicycle is flat.

 You've got a stain on your shirt.

 The battery in your cell phone went dead.

 Your child spilled grape juice on your new suit.

Mystery Cards **GAME CARDS #8**

 Your shoelace broke.

 You forgot to brush your teeth.

 Someone's car alarm is keeping you awake.

 You have a 10-hour layover in Detroit.

 One of your checks bounced.

 There's a garbage strike.

 Your new shoes really hurt your feet.

 You burned a hole in your jacket when you ironed it.

 Your dog had an accident on the carpet.

 Your car broke down on the freeway.

 Your team lost the championship.

 You have bad credit.

 A passing car splashed mud on you.

 Your neighbor is leaf blowing early Sunday morning.

 You failed your English test.

 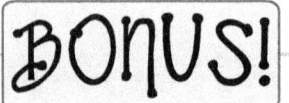

Some, A, An **GAME CARDS #3**

Do you have ___ address to send this letter to?
some a **an**

Please get ___ potatoes for dinner.
some a an

I have ___ homework to do tonight.
some a an

I need ___ jam for my toast.
some a an

I need ___ pound of potatoes for dinner.
some **a** an

I had ___ ear of corn for dinner.
some a **an**

There's ___ jar of jam on the table.
some **a** an

He collected ___ data about our competition.
some a an

I brought ___ chewing gum for the flight.
some a an

There's ___ ice in the freezer.
some a an

There was ___ garbage in the street.
some a an

Would you like ___ stick of chewing gum?
some **a** an

She has ___ job at a computer company.
some **a** an

We got ___ new office equipment.
some a an

I'm making ___ omlette for lunch.
some a **an**

AROUND THE WORLD

2-6 PLAYERS (ALL LEVELS)

LESSON PREPARATION:

Choose 3 sets of GAME CARDS from the previous chapters and 1 set of Mystery Cards (251) for the Mystery box on the GAMEBOARD. Stack each set of GAME CARDS, face down, on the card boxes on the GAMEBOARD.

A die (327) and place markers (282 or 304) are also needed.

BEGIN:

Each player places their marker on START and rolls the die to see who goes first. The player who rolls the highest number rolls again and moves their marker that number of spaces on the GAMEBOARD.

If the Active Player lands on one of the following spaces:

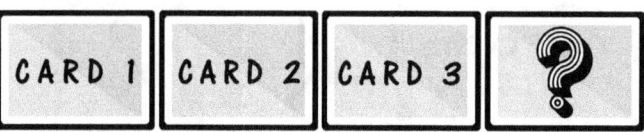

another player picks the top card from the corresponding box on the GAMEBOARD and reads it to the Active Player.

If the Active Player answers the question correctly, they **advance 2 spaces** and their turn is over, regardless of where they land.

OBJECTIVE:

The first player to reach FINISH wins.

PLACE MARKERS:

Place markers are available on pages 282 or 304. Coins, buttons, etc. can also be used as place markers.

GAMEBOARD LAYOUT:

Photocopy the 4 GAMEBOARD sheets, trim away the edges along the dotted lines, and tape together with clear tape.

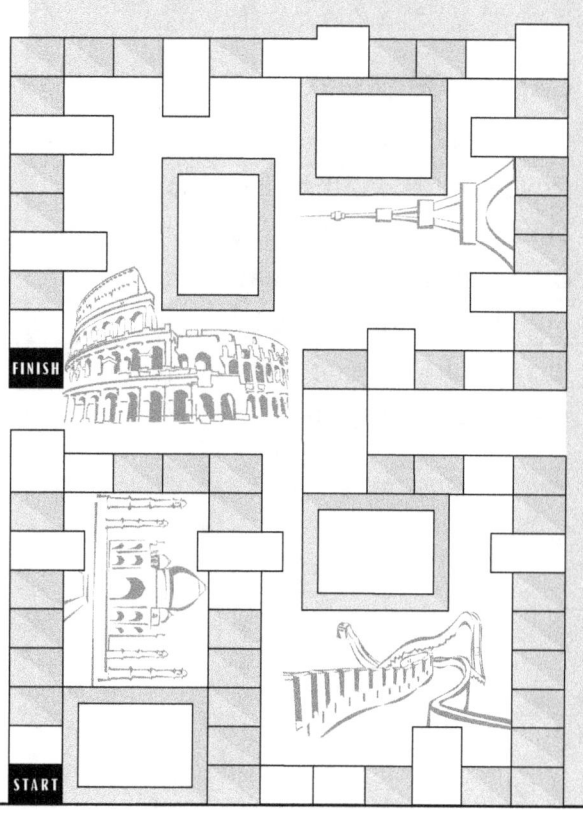

AROUND THE WORLD

A CLASS OF 2 STUDENTS:

The teacher joins the game. Both students play for themselves and alternate between themselves to answer the teacher's questions. If answered correctly, the teacher **advances 2 spaces**. If answered incorrectly, the student **moves back 2 spaces**.

MYSTERY CARDS:

Possible substitutions for the MYSTERY CARDS are: WORLD CAPITALS (235), ADJECTIVES OF NATIONALITY (227), or THE U.S. & CAPITALS (243).

GAME CARD COVERS:

If you're using thin photocopy paper, you can place a Game Card Cover (274) on each stack of GAME CARDS to prevent the answers from being read through the paper of the top card.

If the question is answered incorrectly, the Active Player **moves back 2 spaces** and their turn is over, regardless of where they land.

TRADE PLACES: The Active Player must choose another player to swap markers with, even if the Active Player is in the lead.

GO TO: If the Active Player lands on one of these spaces, they must go where directed, even if it means moving backwards.

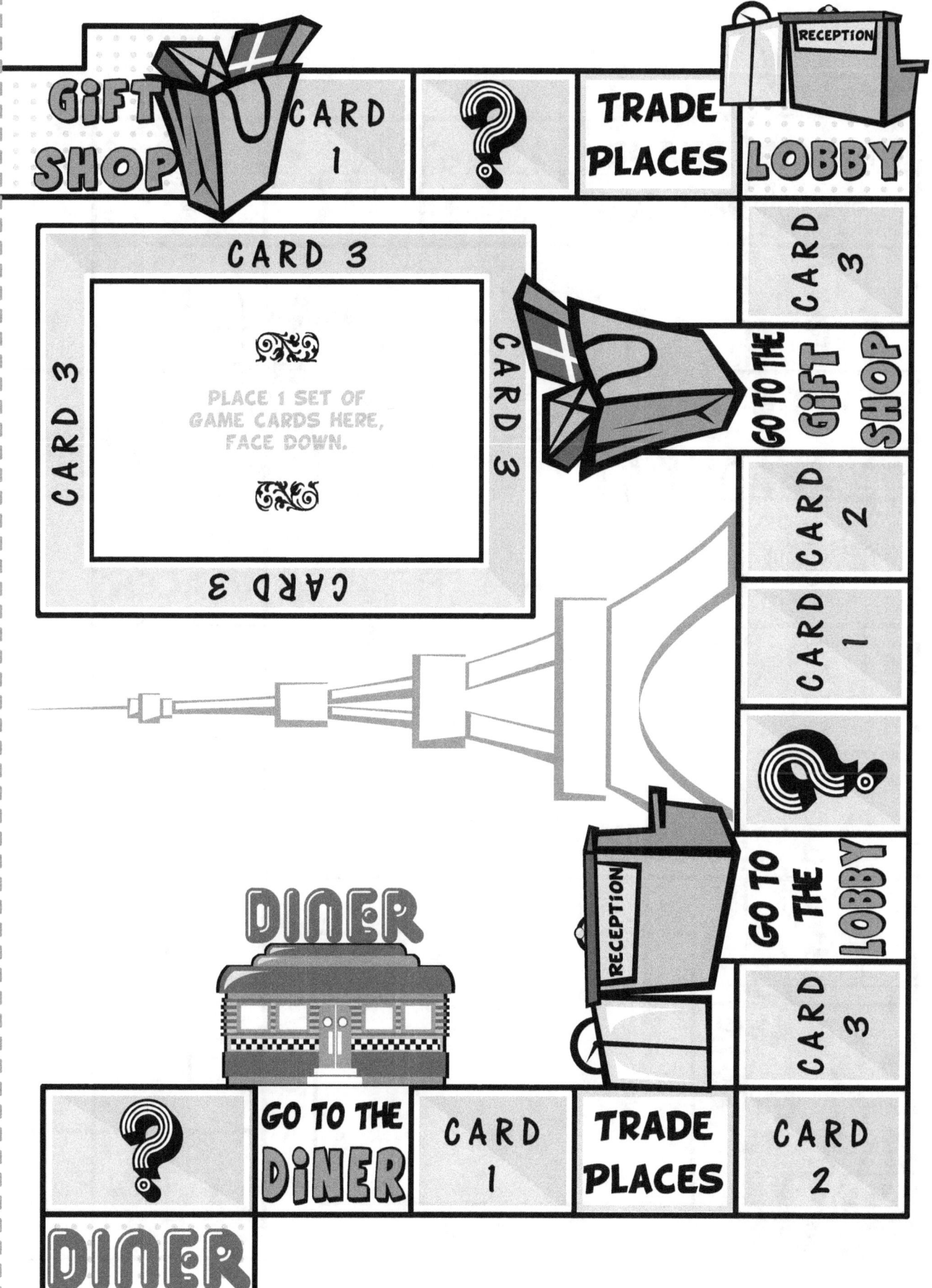
(Upper Right Corner)

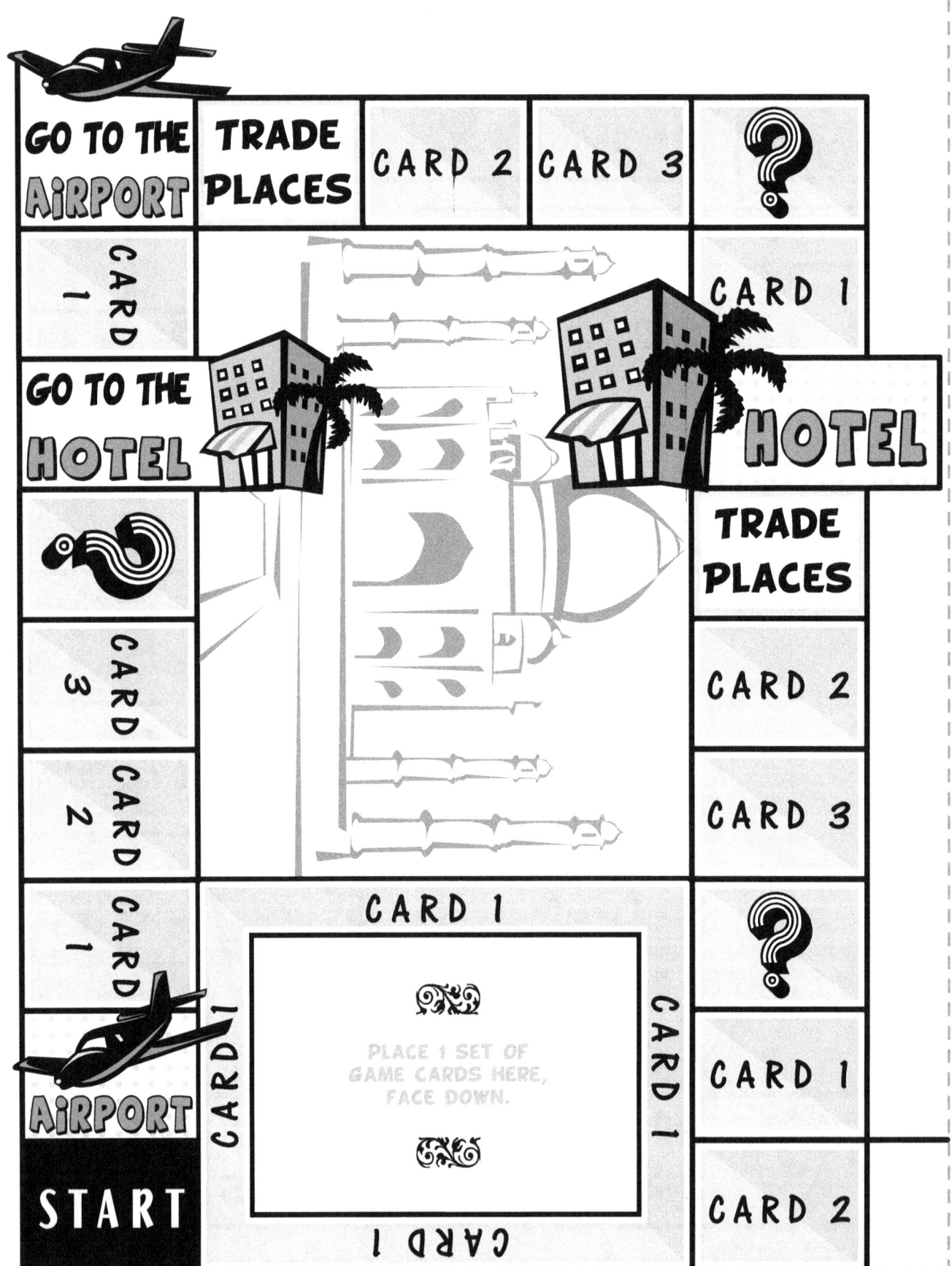

(Lower Left Corner)

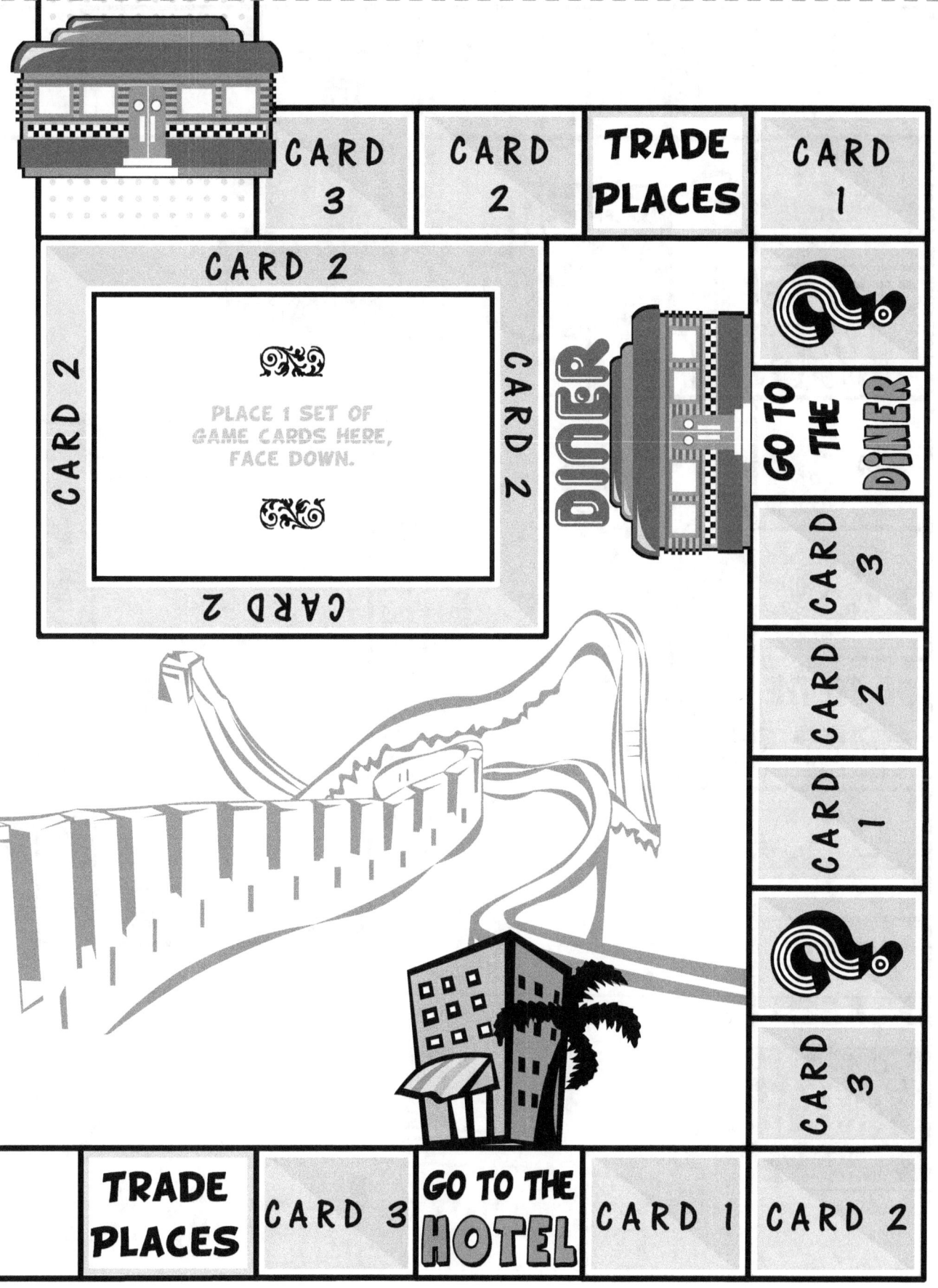

(Lower Right Corner)

(Upper Left Corner)

FRUIT SMASH

2-6 PLAYERS (ALL LEVELS)

LESSON PREPARATION:

Photocopy and cut out 6 copies of the FRUIT CARDS sheet (273) and place them, face up, on the FRUIT BIN box on the GAMEBOARD.

Choose 6 sets of GAME CARDS from the previous chapters and place them, face down, on the various fruit boxes.

A die (327) and place markers (282 or 304) are also needed.

BEGIN:

Each player places their marker on START and rolls the die to see who goes first. The first player rolls again and moves their marker that number of spaces on the GAMEBOARD.

If the player lands on a fruit space:

another player picks a card from the corresponding fruit box and reads it to the Active Player.

If the Active Player answers the question correctly, they earn that piece of fruit from the FRUIT BIN and their turn is over. Earned FRUIT CARDS must be placed face up for everyone to see.

OBJECTIVE:

To be the first player to collect at least 1 each of the 6 pieces of fruit.

PLACE MARKERS:

Coins, buttons, etc. can also be used as place markers.

GAMEBOARD LAYOUT:

Photocopy the 4 GAMEBOARD sheets, trim away the edges along the dotted lines, and tape together with clear tape.

FRUIT SMASH

268

A CLASS OF 2 STUDENTS:

The teacher joins the game. Each student plays for themself and alternates with the other student to answer the teacher's questions.

If the student answers correctly, the teacher collects the fruit. If the student answers incorrectly, the teacher returns any one of the student's pieces of fruit to the FRUIT BIN.

GAME CARD COVERS:

If you're using thin photocopy paper, you can place a Game Card Cover (274) on each stack of GAME CARDS to prevent the answers from being read through the paper of the top card.

If the question is answered incorrectly, the Active Player earns nothing and their turn is over.

FRUIT SMASH: The Active Player takes 1 FRUIT CARD of their choice from another player of their choice and returns it to the FRUIT BIN.

GIVE A FRUIT: The Active Player must choose 1 FRUIT CARD of their own to give to another player of their choice.

FRUIT SWAP: The Active Player chooses 1 FRUIT CARD of their own to swap for 1 FRUIT CARD from another player of their choice. The Active Player decides which FRUIT CARDS will be swapped.

TAKE A FRUIT: The Active Player takes 1 FRUIT CARD of their choice from another player of their choice.

(Lower Left Corner)

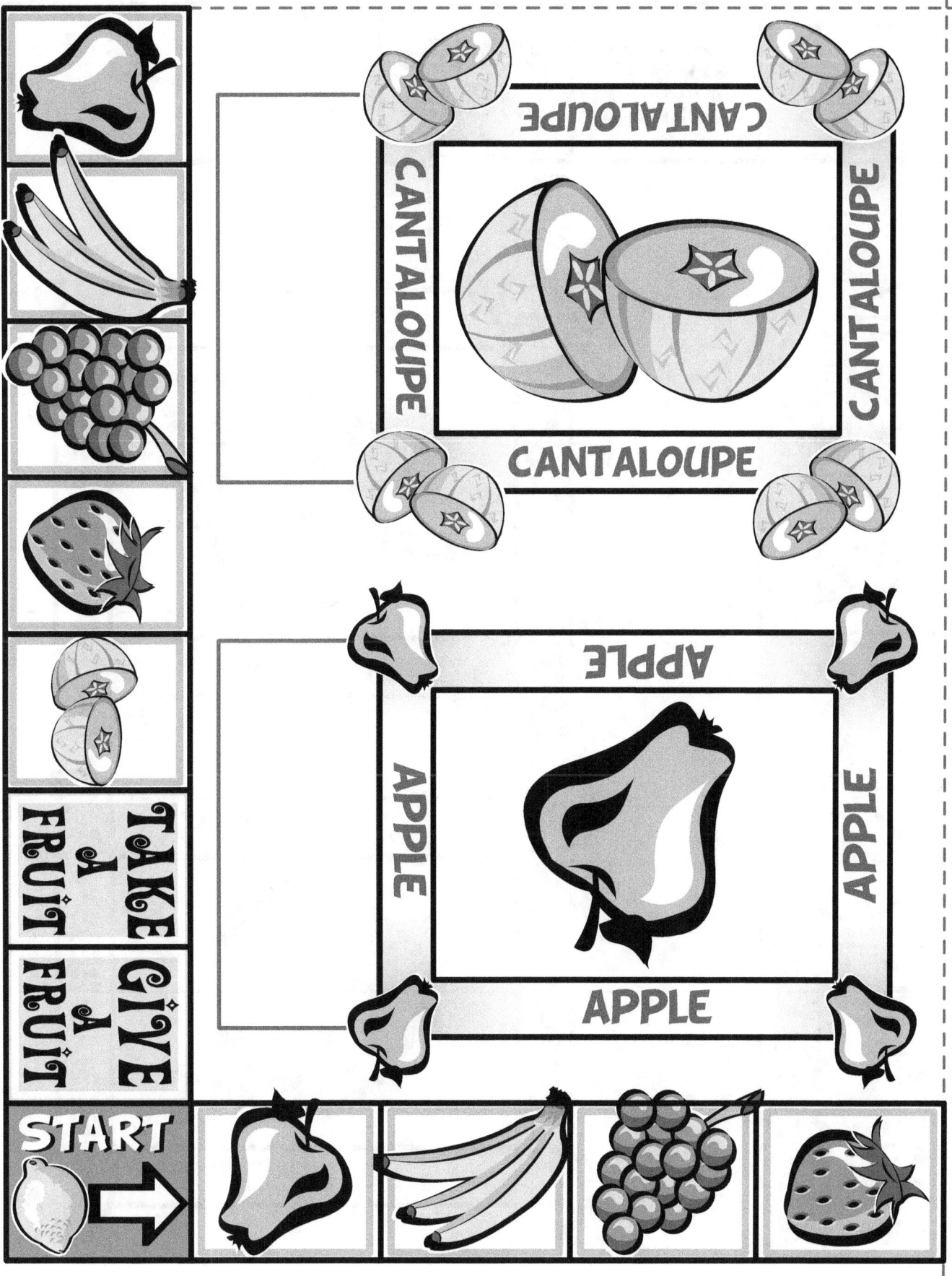

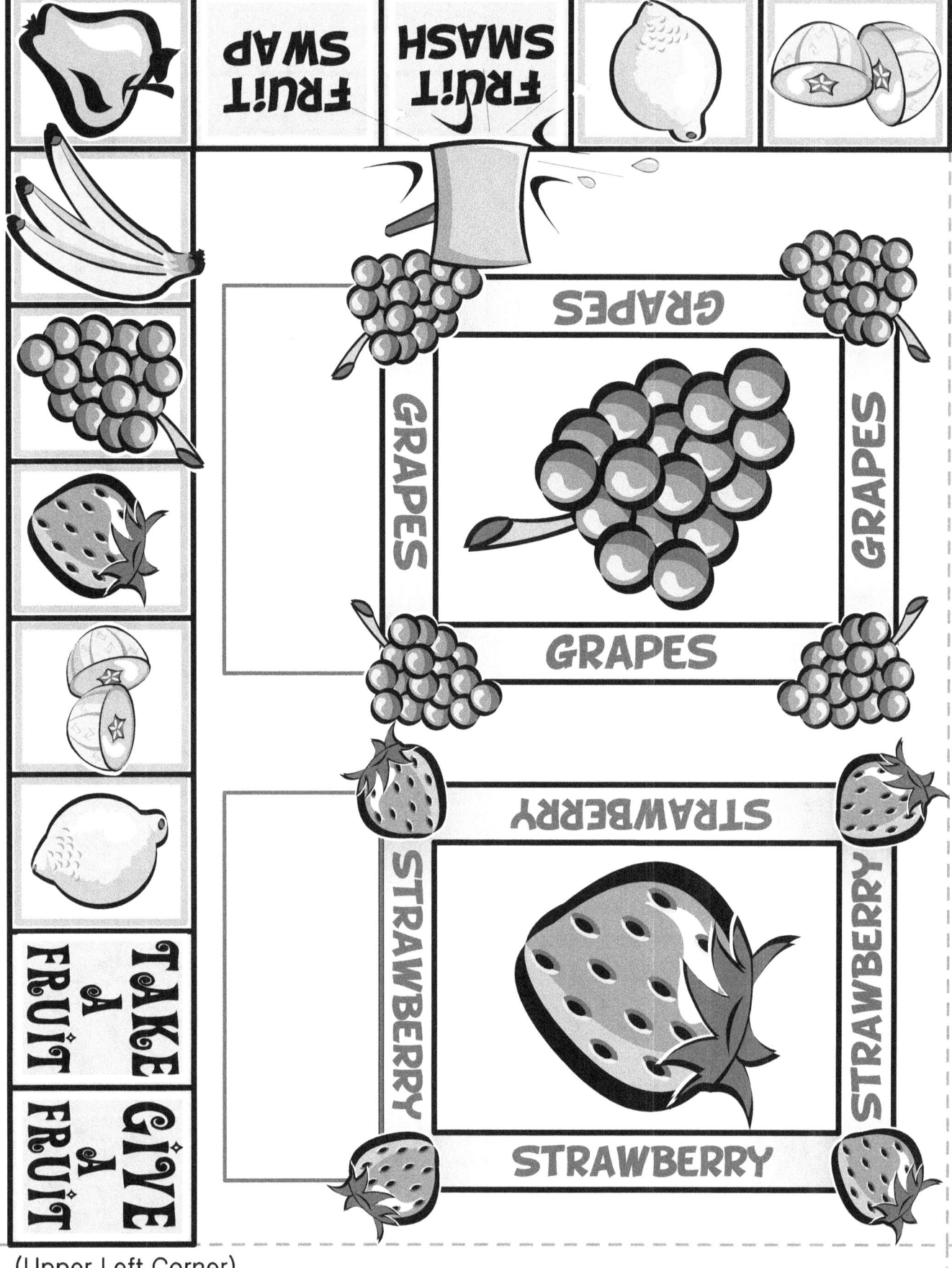

(Upper Left Corner)

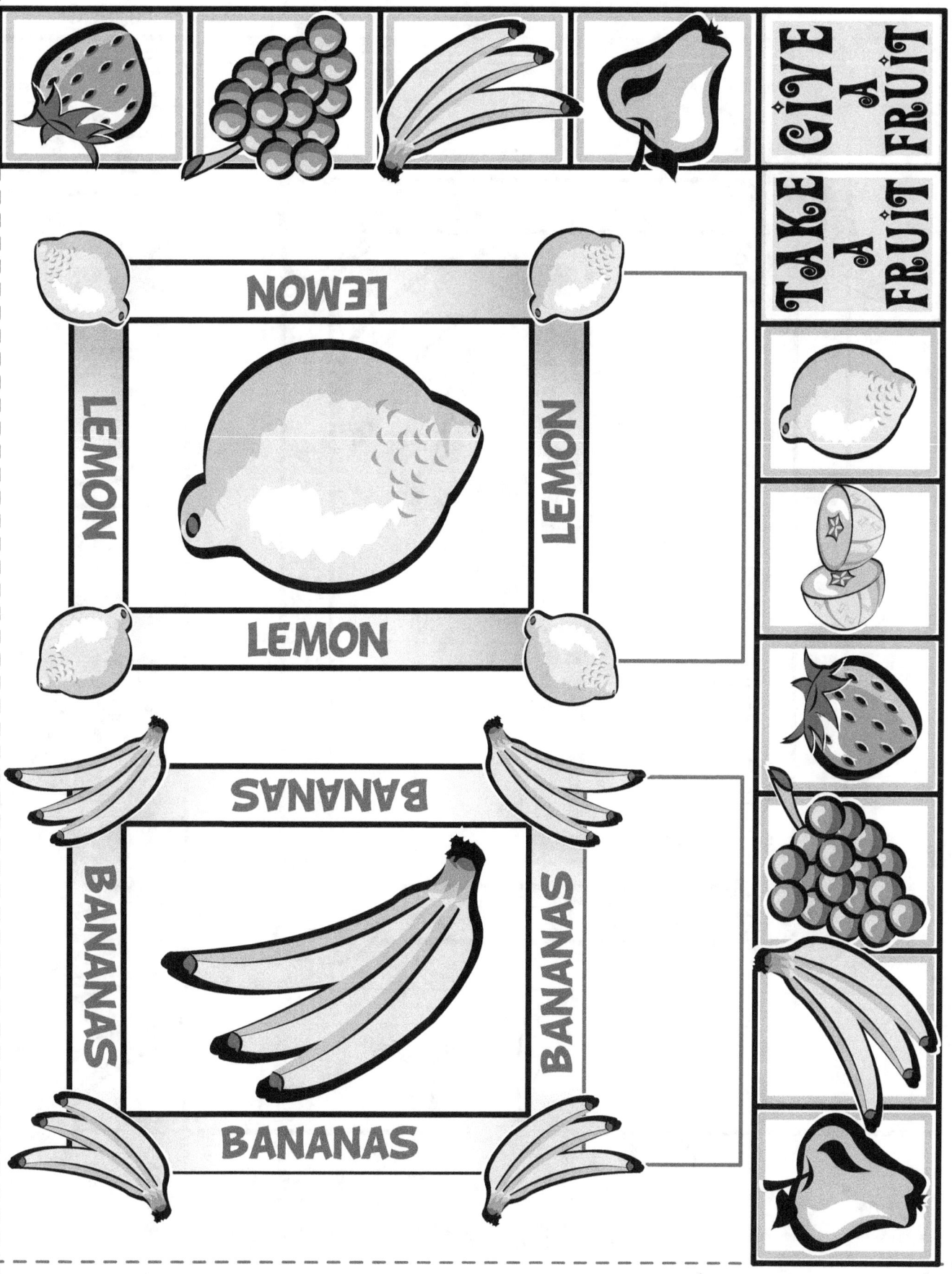

(Upper Right Corner)

(Lower Right Corner)

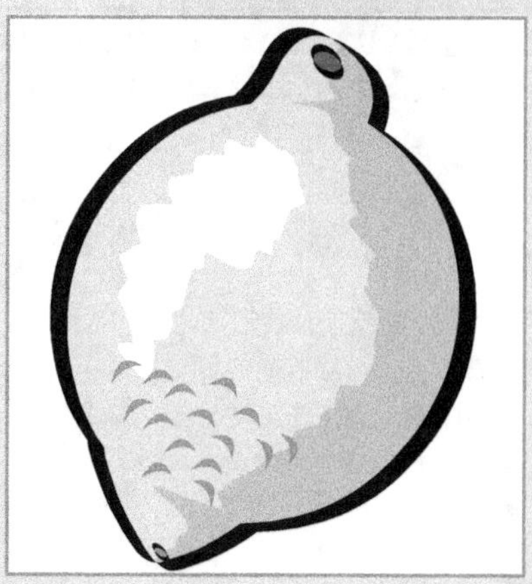

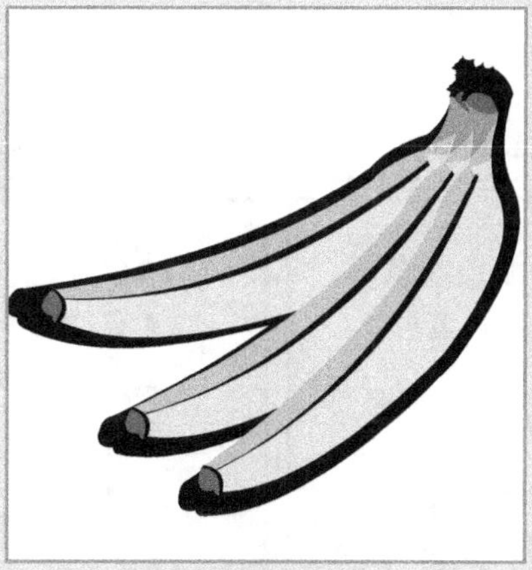

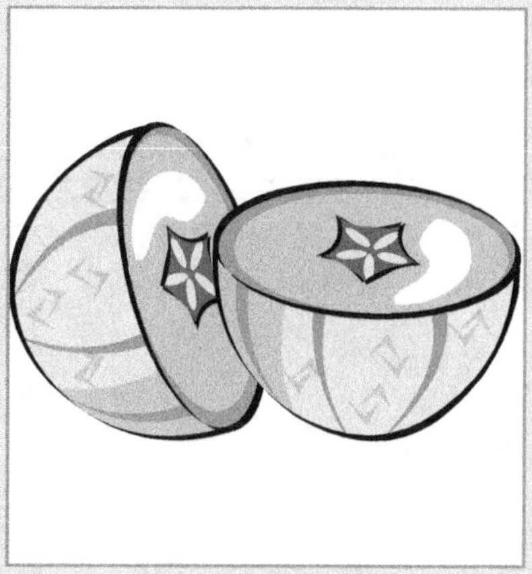

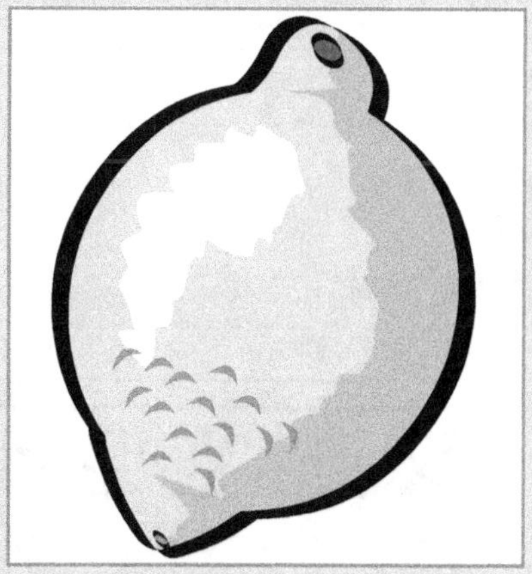

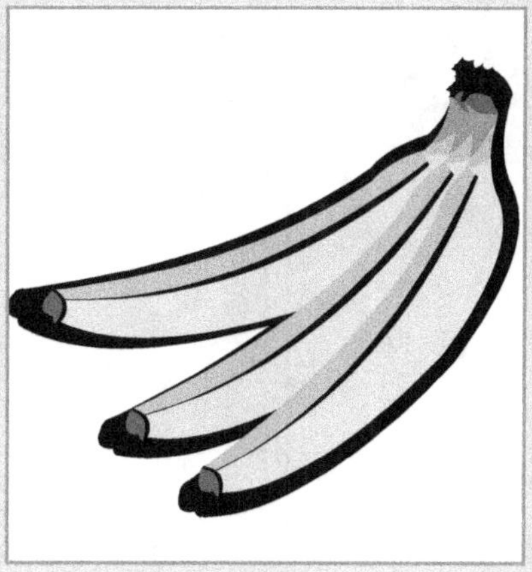

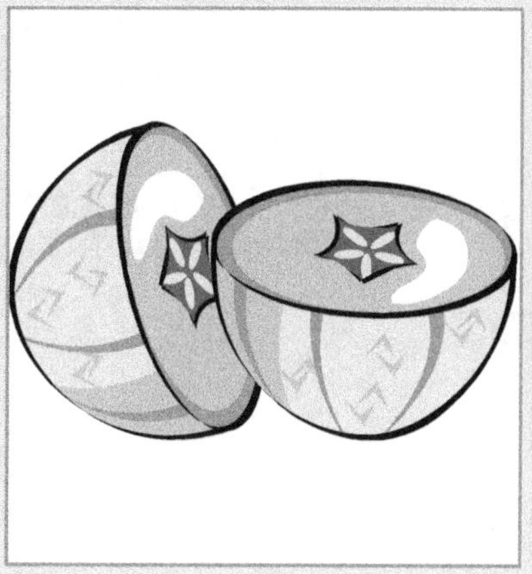

FRUIT SMASH: **FRUIT CARDS** 273

GAME CARD COVERS

GRAMMAR GAMES
FOR TEACHERS OF ADULT ESL
Game Card Cover & Label

GRAMMAR GAMES
FOR TEACHERS OF ADULT ESL
Game Card Cover & Label

GRAMMAR GAMES
FOR TEACHERS OF ADULT ESL
Game Card Cover & Label

GRAMMAR GAMES
FOR TEACHERS OF ADULT ESL
Game Card Cover & Label

GRAMMAR GAMES
FOR TEACHERS OF ADULT ESL
Game Card Cover & Label

GRAMMAR GAMES
FOR TEACHERS OF ADULT ESL
Game Card Cover & Label

SHOP OWNER

LESSON PREPARATION:

Photocopy and cut out 1 copy of the PLACE MARKERS & SHOP CARDS sheet (282). If you don't already have play money, photocopy and cut out 15-25 copies of the U.S. CURRENCY sheet (326). A die (327) is also needed.

Choose 3 sets of GAME CARDS from the previous chapters and 1 set of Mystery Cards (251) for the Mystery box on the GAMEBOARD.

Stack each set of GAME CARDS, face down, on the card boxes on the GAMEBOARD.

Assign 1 student to be The Banker.

BEGIN:

Each player places their marker on **START** and rolls the die to see who goes first. The player who rolled the highest number rolls again and moves their marker that number of spaces on the GAMEBOARD.

If the Active Player lands on any of the following spaces:

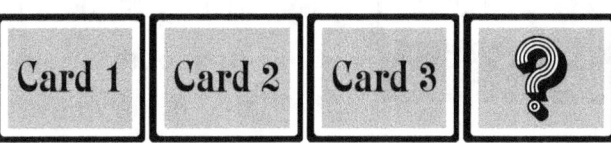

another player reads the top card from the corresponding stack.

2-6 PLAYERS (ALL LEVELS)

OBJECTIVE:

The player with the most cash at the end of the game wins.

THE BANKER:

The Banker distributes Shop Cards (282) and **pays money** to players when they:

1. Answer Game Cards correctly
2. Sell property
3. Win at the Stock Market

The Banker **collects money** from players when they:

1. Answer Game Cards incorrectly
2. Buy property
3. Lose at the Stock Market

The Banker gives $40 to each player to start the game. *The Banker must be careful not to confuse their own personal money with The Bank's money.*

SHOP OWNER

A CLASS OF 2 STUDENTS:

The teacher joins the game. Each student plays for themselves and alternates with the other student to answer the teacher's questions.

If the student answers correctly, the **teacher collects** the money from The Bank. If the student answers incorrectly, that **student pays** the money to The Bank.

MYSTERY CARDS:

Possible substitutions for the MYSTERY CARDS are: WORLD CAPITALS (235), ADJECTIVES OF NATIONALITY (227), or THE U.S. & CAPITALS (243).

GAME CARD COVERS:

If you're using thin photocopy paper, you can place a Game Card Cover (274) on each stack of GAME CARDS to prevent the answers from being read through the paper of the top card.

The Active Player must give the correct answer to **earn** the money written on that space; otherwise, they must **pay** that amount of money to The Bank.

GIFT BOX: The Active Player pays the dollar amount written on that space to the player directly to their right – not to The Bank.

LOTTERY TICKET: The Active Player puts $1.00 on the JACKPOT box on the GAMEBOARD.

JACKPOT: The Active Player collects all the money that is on the JACKPOT box.

STOCK MARKET: The Active Player must roll the die again.

If the Active Player rolls 1, 3 or 5, they **pay** $1.00, $3.00 or $5.00 respectively to The Bank. If the Active Player rolls 2, 4, or 6, The Bank **pays** them $2.00, $4.00 or $6.00 respectively.

SHOP OWNER

If the Active Player lands on a business:

1. If no one already owns the business, the Active Player can buy the business for the amount listed below; in the case of the **HOT DOG STAND**, $5.00. The Active Player then receives a Shop Card from The Bank as proof of ownership.

The Active Player is not obligated to buy the business.

2. If the Active Player owns the business but wishes to sell it, The Bank will pay 50% of the original price; in the case of the **HOT DOG STAND**, $2.50. The Active Player may sell their business during any of their turns, whether or not they land on the actual property space.

3. If the business has already been purchased, the Active Player pays the owner of that business (not The Bank) the amount listed at the top; in the case of the **HOT DOG STAND**, $1.00.

At the end of the game, each student counts their cash (not including business values). The student with the most cash at the end of the game wins.

SHOP CARDS:

When a player buys a business, The Bank gives them a SHOP CARD as proof of ownership.

GAMEBOARD LAYOUT:

Photocopy the 4 GAMEBOARD sheets, trim away the edges along the dotted lines, and tape together with clear tape.

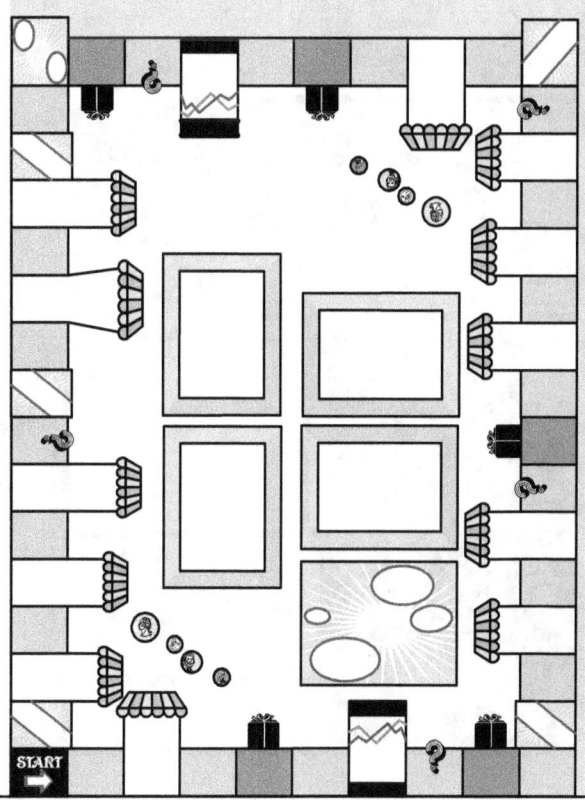

(Lower Left Corner)

Board spaces (starting from lower left corner, going up, then right along top edge implied)

- $0.81
- ICE CREAM PARLOR — $2.00 — $10.00 ($5.00)
- Card 1 — $1.68
- CANDY STORE — $1.60 — $8.00 ($4.00)
- Card 2 — $0.92
- FLOWER SHOP — $2.80 — $14.00 ($7.00)
- Buy A LOTTERY TICKET $1
- START →
- Card 1 — $2.01
- HOT DOG STAND — $1.00 — $5.00 ($2.50)
- Card 2 — $1.76
- BIRTHDAY GIFT — $2.02

Card 1 placement area

Card 1

PLACE 1 SET OF GAME CARDS HERE, FACE DOWN.

Coin values

- Quarter = .25
- Dime = .10
- Nickel = .05
- Penny = .01

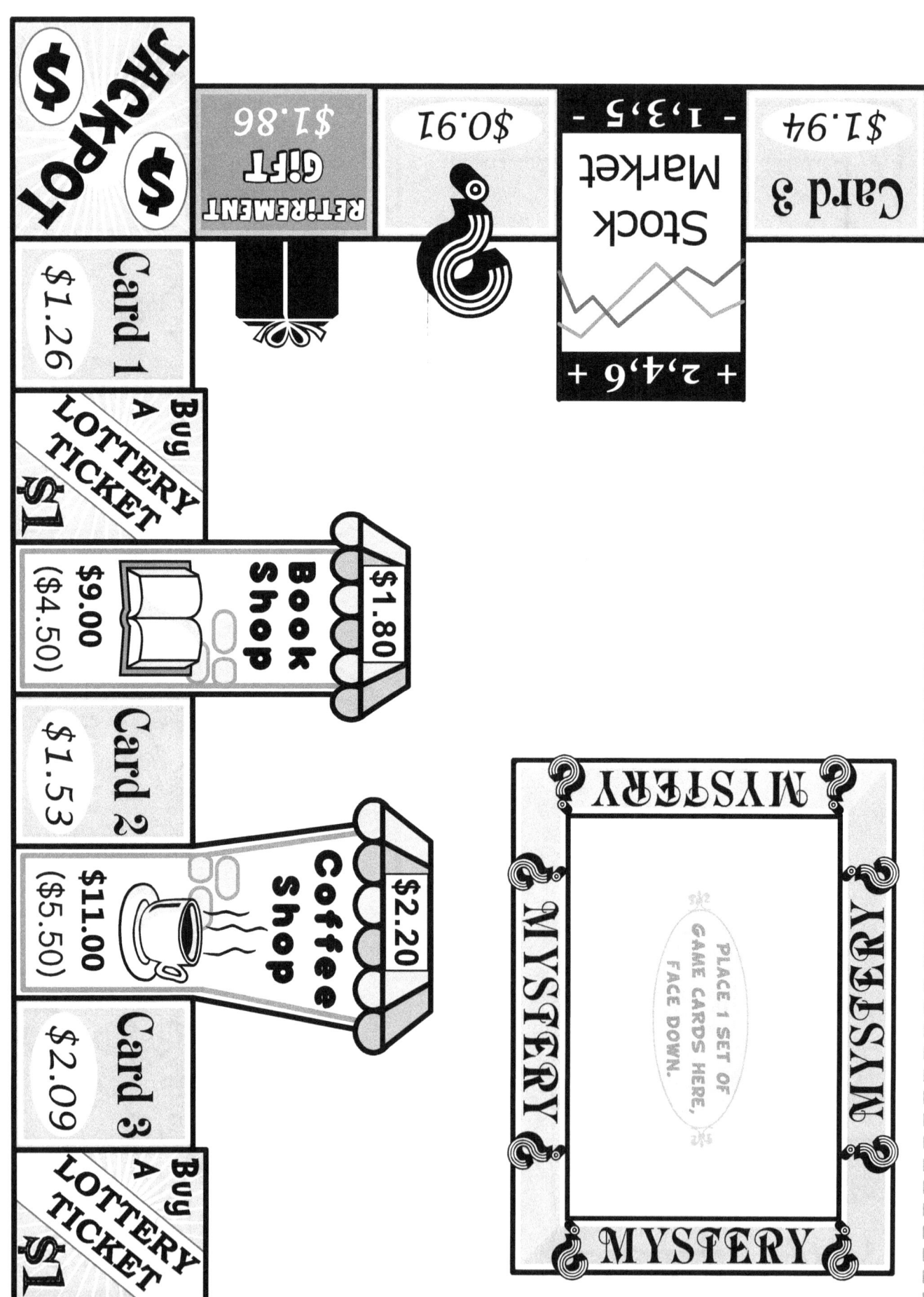

(Upper Left Corner)

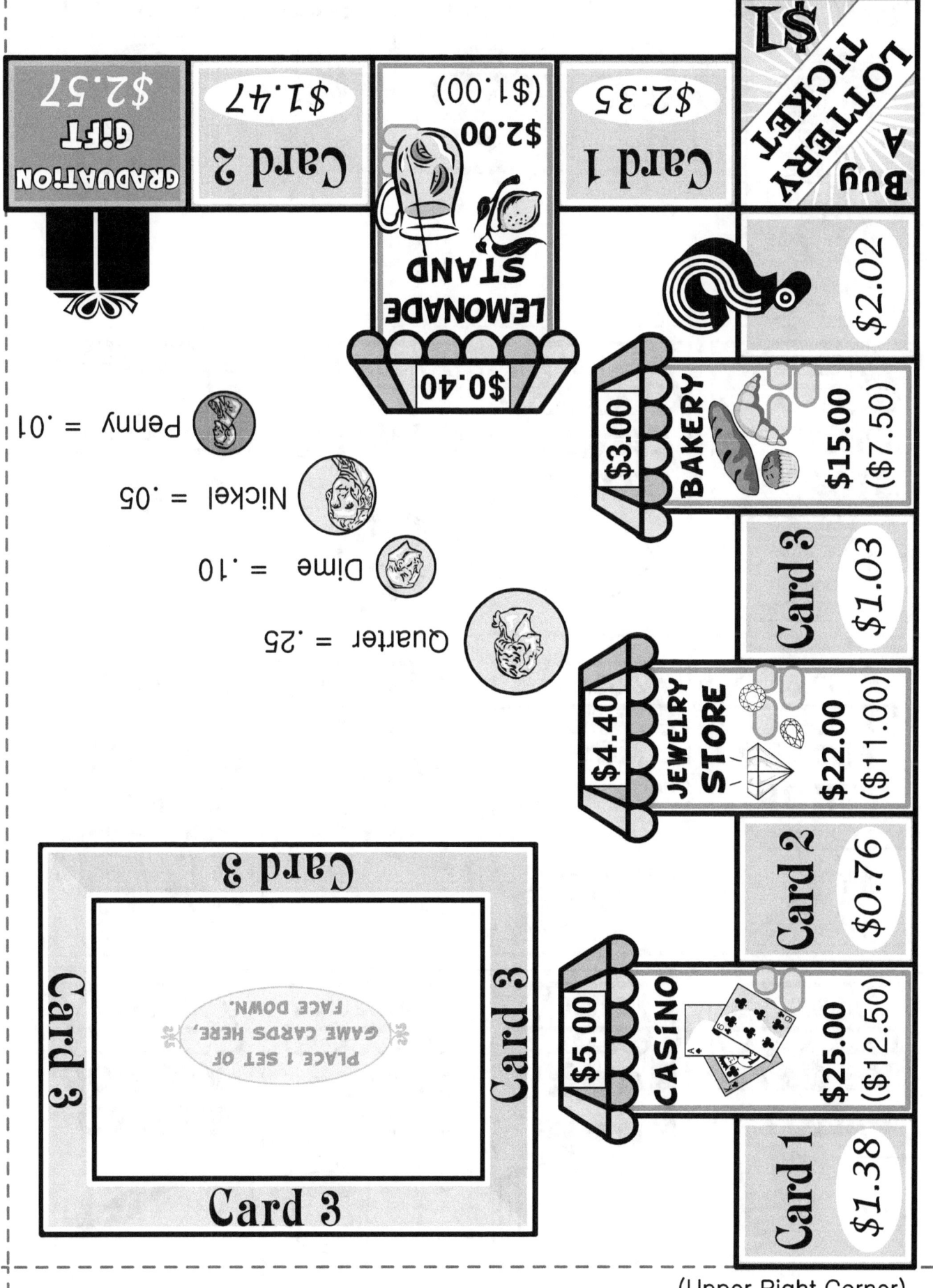

282 — SHOP OWNER: **PLACE MARKERS & SHOP CARDS**

$2.40 — DRUG STORE

$1.60 — CANDY STORE

$5.00 — CASINO

$4.40 — JEWELRY STORE

$2.80 — FLOWER SHOP

$3.00 — MOVIE THEATER

$3.00 — BAKERY

$0.40 — LEMONADE STAND

$2.00 — ICE CREAM PARLOR

$1.80 — Book Shop

$2.20 — Coffee Shop

$1.00 — HOT DOG STAND

CONNECT FIVE

283

2-4 PLAYERS (ALL LEVELS)

LESSON PREPARATION:

Photocopy and cut out 3 copies of the GAME PIECES (290) and 4 copies of the NUMBER CARDS (289). Choose 6 sets of GAME CARDS from the previous chapters.

BEGIN:

Divide the class into 2 teams of 2 players. Each player sits opposite their teammate.

Each team chooses their GAME PIECES. Coins, buttons, etc. can be used in place of the GAME PIECES. For example, Team A can be pennies and Team B can be nickels.

Stack the NUMBER CARDS, face down, on the table. Each Player takes 3 NUMBER CARDS without showing them to anyone. Player 1 from Team A lays down one of their NUMBER CARDS, face up.

Another player reads the corresponding GAME CARD. If Player 1 answers the question correctly, they can put one of their GAME PIECES over that number anywhere on the gameboard. The NUMBER CARD is then put off to the side and Player 1's turn is over.

OBJECTIVE:

The first player or team to arrange 5 of their GAME PIECES in a row (horizontally, vertically or diagonally) wins.

(RIGHT)

(WRONG)

CONNECT FIVE

ENVELOPE:

If you're using thin photocopy paper or if you have the windows open, try using a manila envelope to keep the NUMBER CARDS from blowing away or being read through the paper. The players simply reach their hand in the envelope to get their cards.

FOR 2 OR 3 PLAYERS:

The same rules apply but each player plays for themself rather than with a partner.

SWAP & WILD CARDS:

Swap & Wild cards are free turns that don't require answering any GAME CARD questions.

GAMEBOARD LAYOUT:

Photocopy the 4 GAMEBOARD sheets, trim away the edges along the dotted lines, and tape together with clear tape.

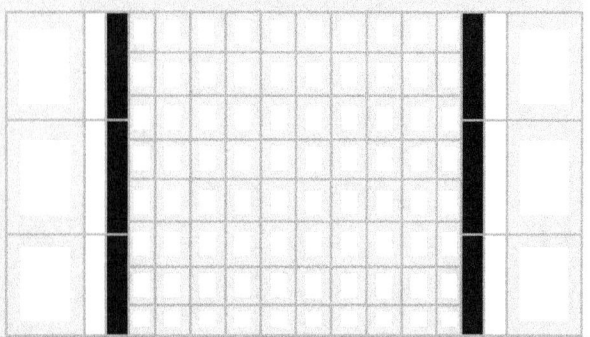

If Player 1 answers the question incorrectly, the NUMBER CARD is put off to the side and Player 1's turn is over.

Player 1 takes another NUMBER CARD from the stack to replace the NUMBER CARD they have just played.

Player 1 from Team B goes next followed by Player 2 from Team A and finally Player 2 from Team B. The turns should alternate between the 2 teams.

SWAP: The Active Player swaps any one of their GAME PIECES already on the GAMEBOARD with any one of their opponent's GAME PIECES already on the GAMEBOARD.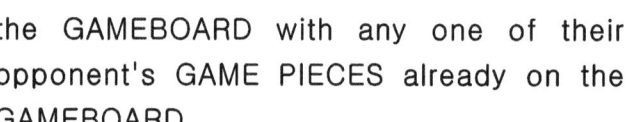

WILD: The Active Player places 1 new GAME PIECE on any free space on the GAMEBOARD.

The first team to create a row of 5 GAME PIECES wins. The GAMEBOARD is then cleared and the NUMBER CARDS are collected for the next round.

If the GAMEBOARD is covered but neither team has created a row of 5 GAME PIECES, it's a draw and neither team wins. The GAMEBOARD is cleared for the next round.

(Lower Right Corner)

1	2	3	4	5	6
6	5	4	3	2	1
1	2	3	4	5	6
6	5	4	3	2	1
1	2	3	4	5	6
6	5	4	3	2	1

CARD 2   CARD 3   CARD 3

ARDS here.
l above.

Place GAME CARDS here.
Write label above.

(Upper Right Corner)

1	2	3	4	5	6
6	5	4	3	2	1
1	2	3	4	5	6
6	5	4	3	2	1
1	2	3	4	5	6
6	5	4	3	2	1

CARD 4

Place GAME CARDS here.
Write label above.

CARD 5

Place GAME C
Write labe

(Upper Left Corner)

1	2	3	4	5	6
6	5	4	3	2	1
1	2	3	4	5	6
6	5	4	3	2	1
1	2	3	4	5	6
6	5	4	3	2	1

CARD 5

CARD 6

ARDS here.
l above.

Place GAME CARDS here.
Write label above.

(Lower Left Corner)

1	2	3	4	5	6
6	5	4	3	2	1
1	2	3	4	5	6
6	5	4	3	2	1
1	2	3	4	5	6
6	5	4	3	2	1

CARD 1

Place GAME CARDS here.
Write label above.

CARD 2

Place GAME C
Write labe

CONNECT FIVE: **NUMBER CARDS** 289

1	2	3	4	5
6	1	2	3	4
5	6	1	2	3
4	5	6	1	2
3	4	5	6	1
2	3	4	5	6
1	2	3	4	5
6	S	W	S	W

CONNECT FIVE: **GAME PIECES**

WHODUNIT?

2-4 PLAYERS (ALL LEVELS)

LESSON PREPARATION:

Photocopy and cut out 1 copy of the SUSPECT, WEAPON and CRIME SCENE cards (294-297).

Photocopy enough STUDY SHEETS (293) and GAME SHEETS #1 and #2 (298, 299) for each player.

A die (327) and place markers (304) are also needed.

BEGIN:

Choose 1 card at random from each of the 3 categories - SUSPECT, WEAPON and CRIME SCENE. Set them off to the side, face down. These are the 3 cards that the players must try to guess.

| SUSPECT | WEAPON | CRIME SCENE |

Deal the rest of the cards (including the Murder Victim card) out to each player. Each player checks off their GAME CARDS on their GAME SHEETS, without showing either their cards or sheets to anyone.

Each player places their marker on **START** and rolls the die to see who goes first. The player who rolls the highest number rolls again and moves their marker that number of spaces on the GAMEBOARD.

START ? →

OBJECTIVE:

To be the first player to solve a mystery by determining the:

1. SUSPECT
2. WEAPON
3. CRIME SCENE

GAME SHEETS

GAME SHEETS are used to keep track of clues and cards.

They can also be folded in half to help hide each player's GAME CARDS from view of the other players.

A CLASS OF 2 STUDENTS:

The Teacher can join the game if there are only 2 players.

USE DISCRETION:

Although it's handled playfully, the subject matter of this game may be disturbing for some people.

WHODUNIT?

GAMEBOARD LAYOUT:

Photocopy the 4 GAMEBOARD sheets, trim away the edges along the dotted lines, and tape together with clear tape.

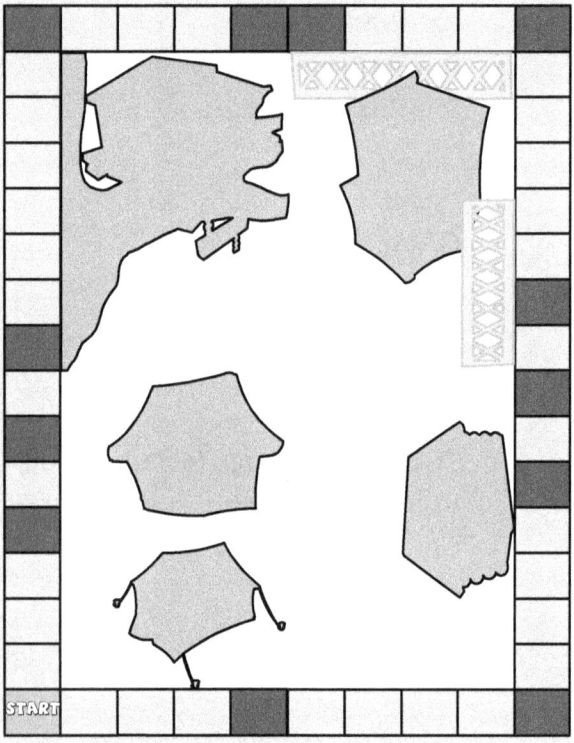

MURDER VICTIM CARD:

A player cannot attempt to solve the mystery while they possess the Murder Victim card. At the end of the game, each player reveals their cards to see who had the Murder Victim card.

TAKE 1 CARD: The Active Player receives 1 card from the player of their choice. The chosen player decides which card to give.

GIVE 1 CARD: The Active Player gives 1 card of their choice to another player of their choice.

SWAP 1 CARD: The Active Player swaps 1 card of their choice with another player of their choice. The chosen player decides which of their own cards to swap.

❓: The Active Player asks one YES/NO question to another player of their choice. Ideally, the question should be asked in such a way that benefits the Active Player but no one else. Players must answer the questions honestly but aren't required to say more than 'yes' or 'no'.

If the Active Player is ready to solve the mystery, the Teacher compares the three cards set off to the side with the player's answer. If the player is incorrect, the game continues without the Teacher saying which cards were incorrect.

If the Active Player guesses correctly, the game is over.

WHODUNIT? STUDY SHEET

BY THE END OF THIS GAME, THERE WILL BE A MURDER... BUT WHO? MAYBE HIM... MAYBE HER... MAYBE ME... MAYBE... YOU!

THERE IS A MURDERER ON THE SLEEPY SUBURBAN STREET OF PINE CONE ROAD. IT'S UP TO YOU TO ASK QUESTIONS AND GATHER CLUES TO FIND OUT:

1. Who the murderer is
2. What weapon they're using and
3. The scene of the crime.

ONLY ASK QUESTIONS THAT CAN BE ANSWERED WITH A "YES" OR "NO". HERE ARE SOME EXAMPLES:

A question can be direct:

"Do you have the Tent card?"
"Do you have the Murder Victim card?"
"Do you have the Colonel Portly card?"

Or less direct:

"Do you have 2 RUSTIC crime scenes?"
"Did you have a DURABLE weapon?"
"Do you have an HONEST, female suspect?"
"Did you just give a SHARP weapon to John?"
"Do you have a suspect with a moustache?"
"Have you got a weapon that is also food?"
"Did you receive a weapon that keeps food cold?"
"Do you have a female suspect with light hair?"
"Do you have a suspect with the last name of 'Butterfingers'?"

GRAMMAR GAMES FOR TEACHERS OF ADULT ESL

WHODUNIT? **SUSPECT CARDS #1**

THE WIDOW MRS. PRUDENCE TRUSTWORTHY

1. Thrifty
2. Honest
3. Forgetful

SUSPECT

COLONEL PORTLY

1. Stingy
2. Witty
3. Quiet

SUSPECT

MR. JOLLY BUTTERFINGERS

1. Intelligent
2. Clumsy
3. Friendly

SUSPECT

MRS. FAITH BUTTERFINGERS

1. Optimistic
2. Clumsy
3. Honest

SUSPECT

SNOWBALL THE CAT

1. Demanding
2. Playful
3. Quiet

SUSPECT

SLOBBERS THE DOG

1. Forgetful
2. Friendly
3. Playful

SUSPECT

WHODUNIT? SUSPECT CARDS #2

MR. SLIM LANKY

1. Optimistic
2. Witty
3. Greedy

SUSPECT

MS. SUNNY SMART

1. Intelligent
2. Snoopy
3. Witty

SUSPECT

BABY SMART

1. Demanding
2. Friendly
3. Snoopy

SUSPECT

BABY BUTTERFINGERS

1. Greedy
2. Clumsy
3. Playful

SUSPECT

GOLDIE THE GOLDFISH

1. Forgetful
2. Playful
3. Quiet

SUSPECT

MR. PIOUS McTIGHTWAD

1. Honest
2. Thrifty
3. Stingy

SUSPECT

 296   WHODUNIT? **WEAPON CARDS**

BUTCHER KNIFE

1. Durable
2. Metallic
3. Sharp

WEAPON

POISONED CAKE

1. Chocolate
2. Delicious
3. Sweet

WEAPON

SAUSAGE LINKS

1. Spicy
2. Greasy
3. Delicious

WEAPON

REFRIGERATOR

1. Heavy
2. Electric
3. Metallic

WEAPON

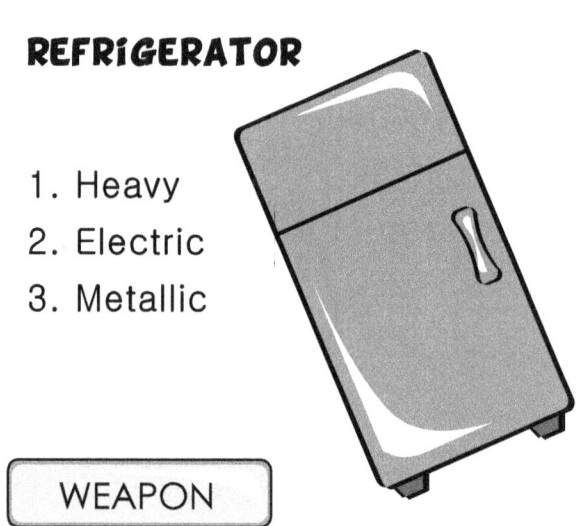

SEWING SHEARS

1. Sharp
2. Shiny
3. Durable

WEAPON

POTTED PLANT

1. Heavy
2. Sharp
3. Pointy

WEAPON

WHODUNIT? **CRIME SCENE CARDS** 297

TREE HOUSE — CRIME SCENE
1. Cramped 2. Rustic 3. Bright

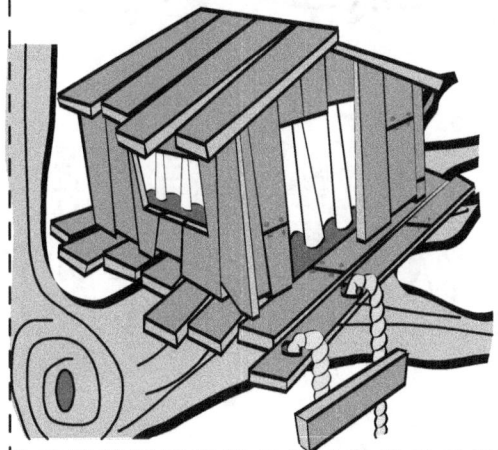

TENT — CRIME SCENE
1. Cramped 2. Colorful 3. Damp

DUPLEX — CRIME SCENE
1. Colorful 2. Bright 3. Cozy

COTTAGE — CRIME SCENE
1. Charming 2. Bright 3. Cozy

LOG CABIN — CRIME SCENE
1. Charming 2. Rustic 3. Damp

MURDER

VICTIM

WHODUNIT? GAME SHEET #1   Suspects

BABY BUTTERFINGERS

1. Greedy
2. Clumsy
3. Playful
☐

SNOWBALL THE CAT
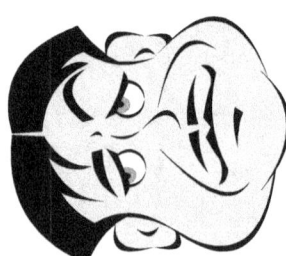
1. Demanding
2. Playful
3. Quiet
☐

COLONEL PORTLY

1. Stingy
2. Witty
3. Quiet
☐

MR. JOLLY BUTTERFINGERS

1. Intelligent
2. Clumsy
3. Friendly
☐

MS. SUNNY SMART

1. Intelligent
2. Snoopy
3. Witty
☐

THE WIDOW MRS. PRUDENCE TRUSTWORTHY

1. Thrifty
2. Honest
3. Forgetful
☐

SLOBBERS THE DOG

1. Forgetful
2. Friendly
3. Playful
☐

GOLDIE THE GOLDFISH

1. Forgetful
2. Playful
3. Quiet
☐

MR. SLIM LANKY

1. Optimistic
2. Witty
3. Greedy
☐

MRS. FAITH BUTTERFINGERS
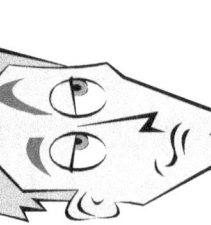
1. Optimistic
2. Clumsy
3. Honest
☐

BABY SMART

1. Demanding
2. Friendly
3. Snoopy
☐

MR. PIOUS McTIGHTWAD

1. Honest
2. Thrifty
3. Stingy
☐

WHODUNIT? GAME SHEET #2

Weapons & Crime Scenes

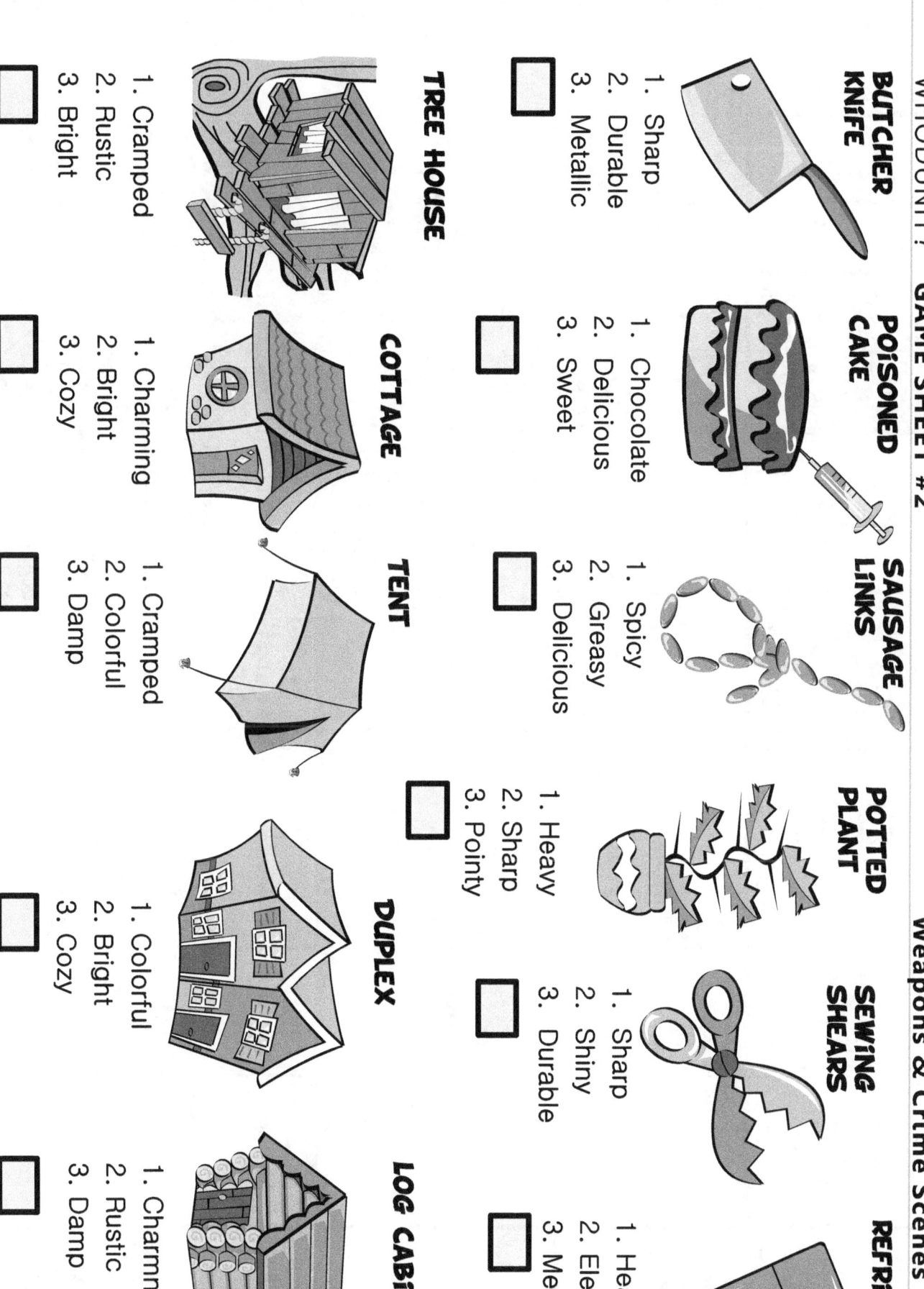

BUTCHER KNIFE
1. Sharp
2. Durable
3. Metallic
☐

POISONED CAKE
1. Chocolate
2. Delicious
3. Sweet
☐

SAUSAGE LINKS
1. Spicy
2. Greasy
3. Delicious
☐

POTTED PLANT
1. Heavy
2. Sharp
3. Pointy
☐

SEWING SHEARS
1. Sharp
2. Shiny
3. Durable
☐

REFRIGERATOR
1. Heavy
2. Electric
3. Metallic
☐

TREE HOUSE
1. Cramped
2. Rustic
3. Bright
☐

COTTAGE
1. Charming
2. Bright
3. Cozy
☐

TENT
1. Cramped
2. Colorful
3. Damp
☐

DUPLEX
1. Colorful
2. Bright
3. Cozy
☐

LOG CABIN
1. Charming
2. Rustic
3. Damp
☐

(Lower Left Corner)

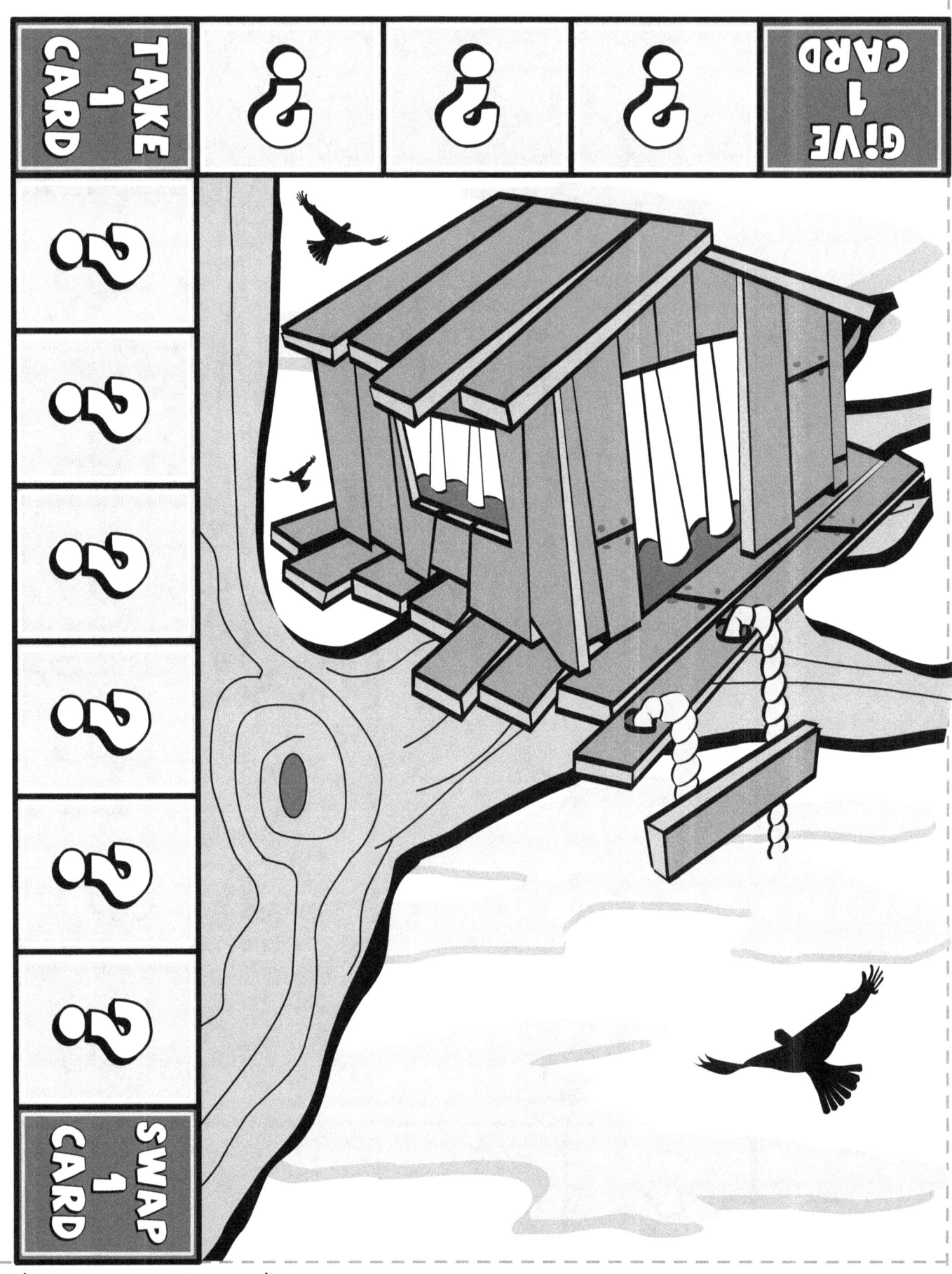

(Upper Right Corner)

WHODUNIT? **PLACE MARKERS**

PLAY BALL!

8-12 PLAYERS (ALL LEVELS)

LESSON PREPARATION:

Make 1 photocopy of the SCOREBOARD sheet (315) and enough VOCABULARY sheets (314) for each student and yourself.

Photocopy and cut out 1 copy of the PLAYER CARDS (311, 312) and WILD CARDS (313).

Choose 4 sets of GAME CARDS from the previous chapters. Mix 3 or 4 WILD CARDS in with each set of GAME CARDS.

BEGIN:

Stack the GAME CARDS face down on the Single, Double, Triple, and Home Run boxes on your GAMEBOARD.

Divide the class into 2 teams of 4-6 players. Have each student select a PLAYER CARD from their team; STiK-EE Candy Co. or GOO-EE Candy Co.

Decide which team goes up to bat first (e.g., coin toss). The first player from the first team up to bat decides what base they want. A member of the opposite team reads a GAME CARD from that base.

If the Batter answers incorrectly, their team receives 1 OUT and the Batter's turn is over. A new player from the same team goes up to bat.

OBJECTIVE:

The team that earns the most runs (points) wins.

The rules of baseball have been streamlined to accommodate educational goals and time constraints.

For example, in baseball each batter is allowed 3 strikes before they're out. However, for this game, each batter is only allowed 1 strike before they're out.

GAME CARD COVERS:

If you're using thin photocopy paper, you can place a Game Card Cover (274) on each stack of GAME CARDS to prevent the answers from being read through the paper of the top card.

INNINGS:

Each team bats until they have 3 outs. Then, it's the opposing team's turn to bat. When both teams have had one turn at bat, they have played one inning. A baseball game consists of 9 innings, thus giving each team 9 turns at bat.

PLAY BALL!

GAMEBOARD LAYOUT:

Photocopy the 4 GAMEBOARD sheets, trim away the edges along the dotted lines, and tape them together with clear tape.

WILD CARDS:

If the Batter gets a WILD CARD, they must do whatever is written on the card.

A WILD CARD is a free card that does not require answering any questions.

When a team gets 3 OUTS, their turn at bat is over and the opposing team goes to bat.

If the Batter answers correctly, they can move their PLAYER CARD to that base.

Base Runners go to the next base *only if it's required to free up a base for their teammate.*

For example, if the Batter correctly answers a question for a SINGLE and there is already a Base Runner on First Base, the Base Runner on First Base goes to Second Base to allow the Batter to go to First Base.

If the Batter hits a SINGLE with a Base Runner on Second, the Batter goes to First Base but the Base Runner stays on Second Base.

If the Batter hits a HOME RUN with a Base Runner on Second Base and another Base Runner on Third. The Base Runner on Third goes to Home Plate first, followed by the Base Runner on Second and finally the Batter; thus earning 3 RUNS (points) for their team.

The team that earns the most RUNS wins.

(Lower Right Corner)

FIRST BASE

FIRST BASE

FIRST BASE

FIRST BASE

FIRST BASE

Place EASY Game Cards here.

SINGLE = FIRST BASE

DOUBLE = SECOND BASE

THIRD BASE

TRIPLE   Place CHALLENGING Game Cards here.   **TRIPLE**

THIRD BASE

THIRD BASE

(Upper Left Corner)

TRIPLE = THIRD BASE

HOME RUN = HOME PLATE / 1 POINT

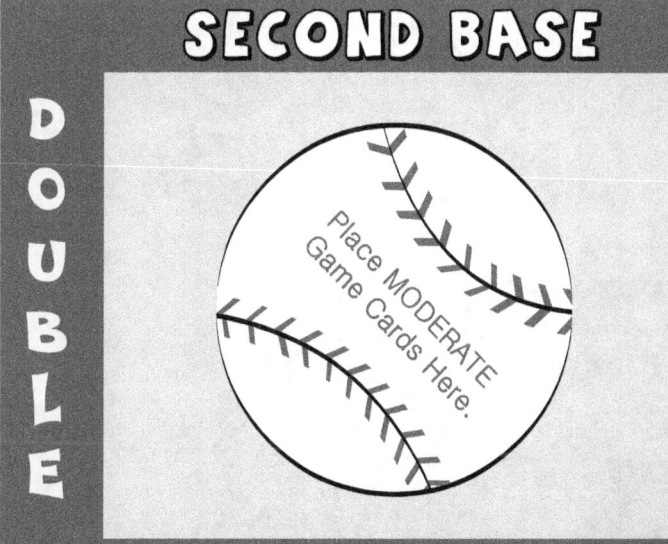

(Upper Right Corner)

HOME RUN

HOME PLATE

HOME PLATE

Place DIFFICULT Game Cards here.

HOME RUN

THE BATTER

THE PITCHER

HOME PLATE

(Lower Left Corner)

PLAY BALL! **PLAYER CARDS** GOO-EE CANDY CO. 311

FLOYD WEBBER : PRESIDENT & CEO

CARMEN GARCIA : HEAD OF SALES

MARIE LAROCHE : PUBLIC RELATIONS

SCOTT WILLIAMS : WEB DESIGNER

JASMIN SINGH : ADVERTISING

CARLO MARTINELLI : CANDY TASTER

✂ 312 PLAY BALL! **PLAYER CARDS** STiK-EE CANDY CO.

SACHIKO HARADA : PRESIDENT & CEO

iAN MCGILL : HEAD OF DISTRIBUTION

HAKIM NASSAR : HEAD OF MARKETING

ALINA BLAU : QUALITY CONTROL

JOYCE JONES : CUSTOMER SERVICE

CARL BURTON : ACCOUNTANT

PLAY BALL! **WILD CARDS** 313

YOU HIT A SINGLE  GO TO **FIRST BASE**.	**YOU HIT A SINGLE**  GO TO **FIRST BASE**.	**YOU HIT A SINGLE**  GO TO **FIRST BASE**.
YOU HIT A DOUBLE  GO TO **SECOND BASE**.	**YOU HIT A DOUBLE**  GO TO **SECOND BASE**.	**STRIKE! YOU'RE OUT!**  YOUR TURN IS **OVER**. YOUR TEAM HAS AN **OUT**.
YOU HIT A TRIPLE  GO TO **THIRD BASE**.	**YOU HIT A TRIPLE**  GO TO **THIRD BASE**.	**STRIKE! YOU'RE OUT!**  YOUR TURN IS **OVER**. YOUR TEAM HAS AN **OUT**.
YOU HIT A HOME RUN  ALL BASERUNNERS EARN A RUN.	**YOU HIT A HOME RUN**  ALL BASERUNNERS EARN A RUN.	**YOU HIT A HOME RUN**  ALL BASERUNNERS EARN A RUN.
STRIKE! YOU'RE OUT!  YOUR TURN IS **OVER**. YOUR TEAM HAS AN **OUT**.	**STRIKE! YOU'RE OUT!**  YOUR TURN IS **OVER**. YOUR TEAM HAS AN **OUT**.	**STRIKE! YOU'RE OUT!**  YOUR TURN IS **OVER**. YOUR TEAM HAS AN **OUT**.

PLAY BALL! VOCABULARY STUDY SHEET

PLAY BALL! To begin or continue playing a baseball game.

BATTER The player at HOME PLATE who is hitting (or BATTING) for their team.

UP TO BAT / AT BAT / BATTING The BATTER stands at HOME PLATE and attempts to hit a baseball with a long wooden club called a bat.

BASE RUNNER A player who's on a base or running to a base.

FIELDERS The players who are on the field while the opposing team is BATTING.

STRIKE! When the BATTER swings at the ball and misses.

HOME PLATE The corner of the baseball diamond where the BATTER stands and where a BASE RUNNER must successfully reach to earn a HOME RUN.

(HIT) A SINGLE A one-base hit. The BATTER successfully gets to First Base after hitting the ball.

(HIT) A DOUBLE A two-base hit. The BATTER successfully gets to Second Base after hitting the ball.

(HIT) A TRIPLE A three-base hit. The BATTER successfully gets to Third Base after hitting the ball.

(HIT) A HOME RUN A four-base hit. The batter successfully clears all the bases – First, Second, Third, & HOME PLATE, and earns 1 RUN (point) for their team.

A RUN When any BASE RUNNER successfully reaches HOME PLATE, thus earning 1 point for their team. This can be done when a BATTER HITS A HOME RUN or a BASE RUNNER runs to HOME PLATE from First, Second or Third Base after another BATTER successfully hits the ball.

OUT A BATTER is OUT when they are unsuccessful at getting a base hit or a HOME RUN. When the team AT BAT gets 3 OUTS they must go out on the field, while the opposing team is now UP TO BAT.

INNINGS The divisions of a baseball game where each team has a turn AT BAT and a turn in the field. Baseball has 9 INNINGS. The total number of RUNS for each team per INNING are listed on the SCOREBOARD.

SCOREBOARD Where the number of RUNS is listed for each INNING.

GRAMMAR GAMES FOR TEACHERS OF ADULT ESL

PEPPERMINT FIELD

TEAM	1	2	3	4	5	6	7	8	9	FINAL SCORE

INNINGS

PLAY BALL! **SCOREBOARD**

SOCCER TOURNAMENT

2-8 PLAYERS (ALL LEVELS)

LESSON PREPARATION:

Make 1 photocopy of the SCOREBOARD (323). Photocopy and cut out 1 copy of the BALL & STEAL CARDS (324).

Choose 3 sets of GAME CARDS from the previous chapters. Mix 3 or 4 STEAL CARDS in with each set of GAME CARDS.

Take 1 set of GAME CARDS and put half of them, face down, on one 20 YARD LINE box and the other half on the other 20 YARD LINE box. Take the other 2 sets of GAME CARDS and do the same with the 40 YARD LINE and the GOAL! boxes.

BEGIN:

Divide the class into 2 teams. Have each team come up with a team name and write their team name on either side of the GAMEBOARD and on the SCOREBOARD.

Place the SOCCER BALL on the (light gray) Center Circle. Decide which team will go first (e.g., coin toss).

A member from the opposing team reads a GAME CARD from the 20 YARD LINE box closest to their own GOAL.

If the Active Player answers correctly, they move the SOCCER BALL to the 20 YARD LINE (medium gray) Circle in the direction of the opposing team's GOAL.

OBJECTIVE:

The team that scores the most GOALS! wins.

GAMEBOARD LAYOUT:

Photocopy the 4 GAMEBOARD sheets, trim away the edges along the dotted lines, and tape together with clear tape.

SOCCER TOURNAMENT

GAME CARD COVERS:

If you're using thin photocopy paper, you can place a Game Card Cover (274) on each stack of GAME CARDS to prevent the answers from being read through the paper of the top card.

A CLASS OF 2 STUDENTS:

This game can be played with only 2 students (1 student on each team). However, the game is more enjoyable with 2 or more students per team.

STEAL:

If the Active Player draws the STEAL card, their turn is immediately over, the SOCCER BALL remains in it's current position, and the opposing team gets a chance to move the SOCCER BALL towards their opponent's GOAL.

A new member from the same team then answers a question from the 40 YARD LINE box in the direction of the opposing team's GOAL.

If this question is answered correctly, the SOCCER BALL is moved to the 40 YARD LINE (dark gray) Circle in the direction of the opposing team's GOAL. A new member from the same team then answers a question from the GOAL! box.

If this question is answered correctly, 1 goal (1 point) is earned and marked on the SCOREBOARD under that team's name.

All question boxes must be answered in order. For example, if the soccer ball is on the 20 YARD LINE circle, a 40 YARD LINE question can't be skipped in an attempt to answer a GOAL! question sooner.

After a goal is earned, the SOCCER BALL is returned to the Center Circle. The team that didn't score the last goal answers from the 20 YARD LINE question box in the direction of their opponent's GOAL.

If a question is answered incorrectly, the SOCCER BALL remains in its current position giving the opposing team a chance to move the ball in the opposite direction, towards their opponent's GOAL.

The team that earns the most goals wins.

(Upper Left Corner)

20 YARD LINE
20 YARD LINE
20 YARD LINE
20 YARD LINE

PLACE 1/2 OF ONE SET OF GAME CARDS HERE. PLACE THE OTHER 1/2 ON THE OTHER 20 YARD LINE BOX.

GOAL!

1/2 OF
GAME CARDS
THE OTHER
OPPONENT'S
BOX.

TEAM NAME

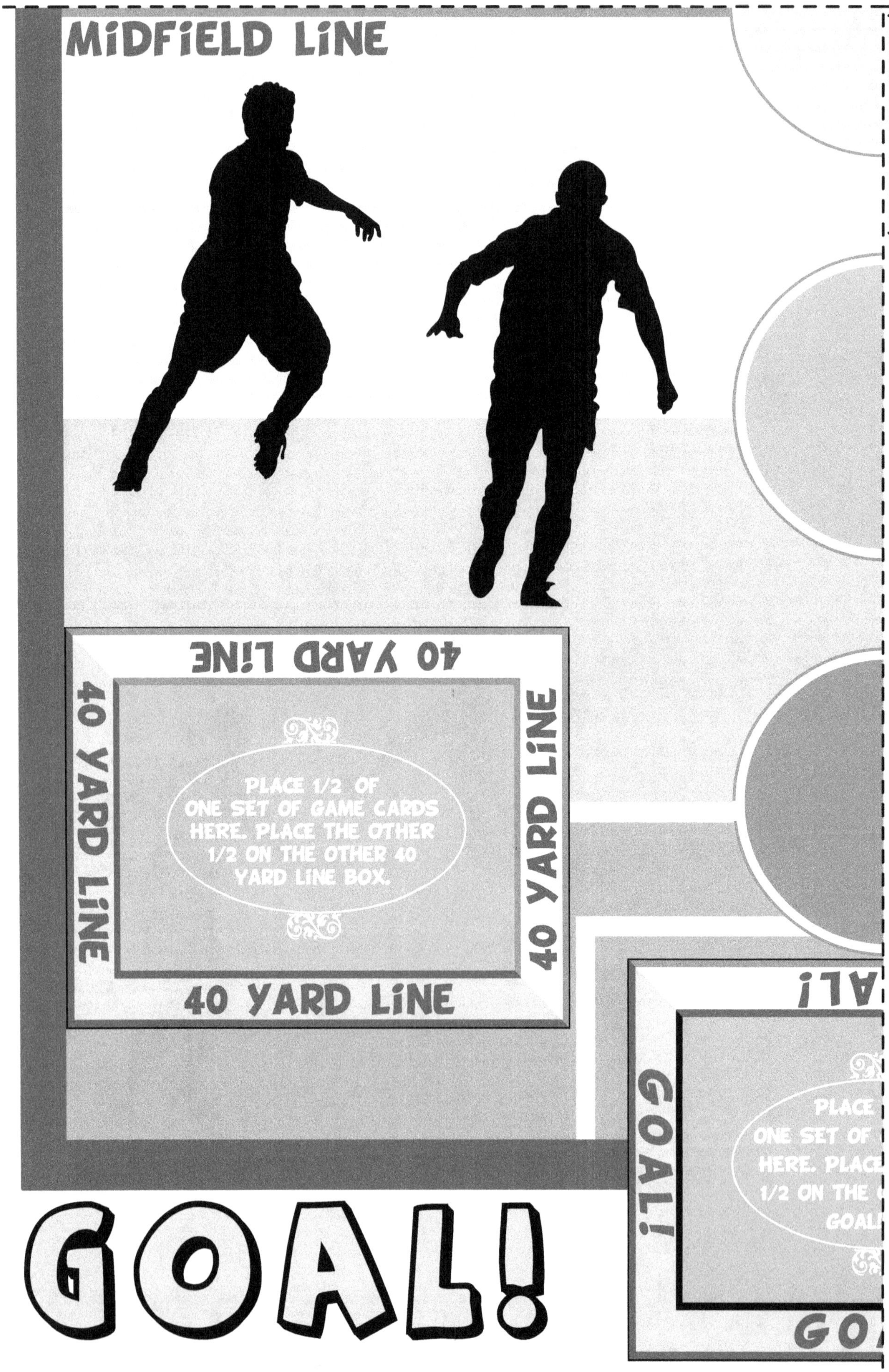

(Lower Left Corner)

MIDFIELD LINE

40 YARD LINE

40 YARD LINE

40 YARD LINE

40 YARD LINE

PLACE 1/2 OF ONE SET OF GAME CARDS HERE. PLACE THE OTHER 1/2 ON THE OTHER 40 YARD LINE BOX.

GOAL!

GOAL!

GOAL!

PLACE ONE SET OF HERE. PLAC 1/2 ON THE GOAL

(Lower Right Corner)

20 YARD LINE
20 YARD LINE
20 YARD LINE
20 YARD LINE

PLACE 1/2 OF ONE SET OF GAME CARDS HERE. PLACE THE OTHER 1/2 ON THE OTHER 20 YARD LINE BOX.

GOAL!
GOAL!
GOAL!

1/2 OF
GAME CARDS
THE OTHER
OPPONENT'S
BOX.

TEAM NAME

MIDFIELD LINE

40 YARD LINE

PLACE 1/2 OF ONE SET OF GAME CARDS HERE. PLACE THE OTHER 1/2 ON THE OTHER 40 YARD LINE BOX.

GOAL!

(Upper Right Corner)

SCOREBOARD

	TEAM NAME	TEAM NAME
GOAL 1	☐	☐
GOAL 2	☐	☐
GOAL 3	☐	☐
GOAL 4	☐	☐
GOAL 5	☐	☐
GOAL 6	☐	☐
GOAL 7	☐	☐
GOAL 8	☐	☐

 324

SOCCER TOURNAMENT: **BALL & STEAL CARDS**

APPENDIX

APPENDIX

U.S. Currency	326
Paper Die Pattern	327

IDIOMS LIST

Idioms of Comparison	328
Business Idioms	329
Body Idioms	330

326 U.S. CURRENCY

PAPER DIE PATTERN

1. Photocopy this page.
2. Cut along the solid, outside edge.
3. Fold along the dotted lines.
4. Use clear tape to tape together.

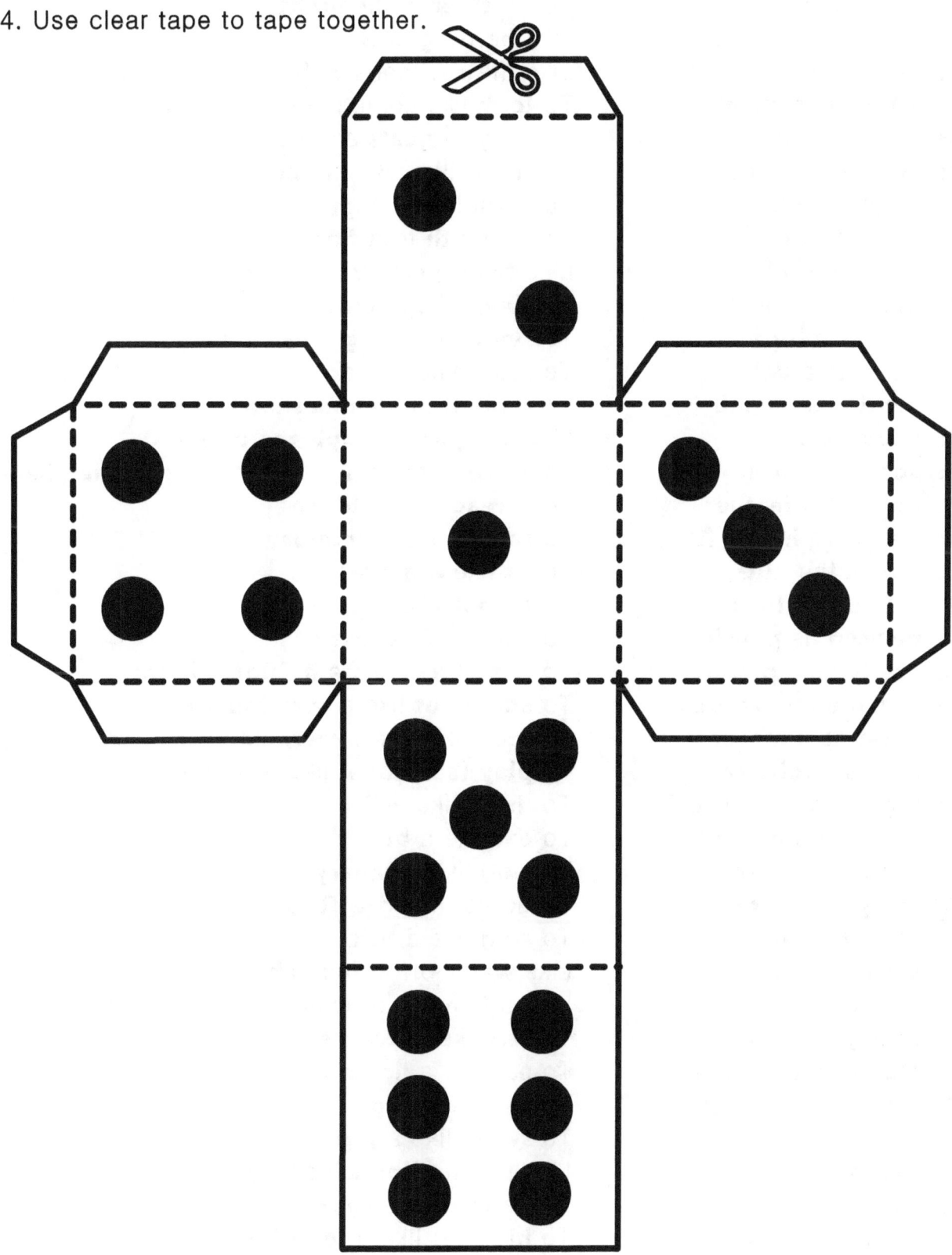

Idioms of Comparison

As **blind** as a **bat**	As **poor** as a **church mouse**
As **busy** as a **bee**	As **different** as **night** and **day**
As **clean** as a **whistle**	Like **peas** in a **pod**
As **clear** as a **bell**	Like there's **no tomorrow**
As **cold** as **ice**	Like a **thief** in the **night**
As **cool** as a **cucumber**	Like **herding cats**
As **dead** as a **doornail**	Like the **cat** that **swallowed** the **canary**
As **drunk** as a **skunk**	To **look** like something the **cat dragged in**
As **dry** as **a bone**	**Raining** like **cats** and **dogs**
As **dull** as **dishwater**	To **fight** like **cats** and **dogs**
As **easy** as **ABC**	To **work** like a **dog**
As **easy** as **pie**	Like a **moth** to a **flame**
As **fit** as a **fiddle**	Like **taking candy** from a **baby**
As **flat** as a **pancake**	To **sleep** like a **baby**
As **free** as a **bird**	To **sleep** like a **log**
As **fresh** as a **daisy**	To **sleep** like a **rock**
As **gentle** as a **lamb**	Like a **bull** in a **china shop**
As **good** as **gold**	Like **comparing apples** to **oranges**
As **hot** as an **oven**	To **know** something like the **back of one's hand**
As **light** as a **feather**	To **spread** like **wildfire**
As **mad** as a **hatter** (British)	To **smoke** like a **chimney**
As **old** as the **hills**	To **fit** like a **glove**
As **pale** as a **ghost**	To be **out** like a **light**
As **pleased** as **punch**	To **shake** like a **leaf**
As **pretty** as a **picture**	To **look / feel** like a **million dollars**
As **proud** as a **peacock**	To **stand out** like a **sore thumb**
As **quiet** as a **mouse**	To **look** like **death warmed over**
As **red** as a **lobster**	To **play** (someone) like a **fiddle**
As **regular** as **clockwork**	To **drink** like a **fish**
As **safe** as **houses** (British)	To **eat** like a **bird**
As **sharp** as a **razor**	To **sing** like a **canary**
As **sharp** as a **tack**	To **go** as the **crow flies**
As **sick** as a **dog**	To **sing** like a **bird**
As **slow** as **molasses**	Like **water** off a **duck's back**
As **sly / cunning** as a **fox**	Like a **fish** out of **water**
As **strong** as a **horse**	To **sell** like **hotcakes**
As **stubborn** as a **mule**	To **eat** like a **horse**
As **thick** as **pea soup**	To **eat** like a **pig**
As **thick** as **thieves**	To **sweat** like a **pig**
As **tough** as **nails**	Like putting **lipstick** on a **pig**
As **white** as a **sheet**	To be **off** like a **shot**
As **wise** as an **owl**	To **hit** (me) like a **ton of bricks**

IDIOMS LIST — Business Idioms

- **above board** honest
- **bean counter** an accountant
- **belt-tightening** saving money
- **bounce checks** write bad checks
- **brass tacks** essential business
- **cash cow** money maker
- **chicken feed** very little money
- **cut corners** compromise quality
- **dead wood** unproductive staff
- **desk jockey** an office worker
- **don't have a clue** have no idea
- **eager beaver** hard worker
- **fire away** speak when ready
- **flunky** low-level employee
- **game plan** strategy
- **got the axe** got fired
- **hard sell** to sell aggressively
- **heads will roll** someone will be punished
- **hot under the collar** angry
- **hump day** Wednesday
- **in a nutshell** in a few words
- **in the black** profitable
- **in the red** unprofitable
- **in black and white** in writing
- **jacking up** raising
- **kid gloves** tact & gentleness
- **lip service** talk but no action
- **make waves** cause trouble
- **magic bullet** perfect solution
- **mean business** are serious
- **Mickey Mouse** unimportant
- **my two cents** brief opinion
- **no-brainer** obvious
- **red flags** warning signs
- **red tape** excessive bureaucracy
- **rubber stamped** approved
- **talk turkey** talk seriously
- **talking shop** talking about work
- **took a nosedive** lost value quickly
- **three martini lunch** leisurely business lunch
- **bait and switch** falsely advertise sale items
- **bang for [my] buck** return on [my] investment
- **climbing the corporate ladder** getting promoted quickly
- **from the horse's mouth** from the highest authority
- **golden parachute** generous compensation
- **keep [our] head above water** survive financially
- **keep [your] nose to the grindstone** concentrate on work
- **pulls [his] own weight** does [his] share of work
- **a dime a dozen** common & cheap
- **back burner** temporary of lower priority
- **bankroll** pay for
- **banner year** an outstanding year
- **ballpark figure** an estimate
- **batting a thousand** 100% success rate
- **blue chip companies** stable & profitable
- **broke even** income equaled expenses
- **budget crunch** financial difficulty
- **common ground** mutual interest
- **cooking the books** falsifying accounts
- **downsize** reduce the work force
- **empty suits** incompetent managers
- **face time** meet in person
- **fall guy** the scapegoat
- **free lunch** something for nothing
- **from soup to nuts** from beginning to end
- **get [our] ducks in a row** get organized
- **golden handcuffs** financial incentives
- **gravy** an unexpected benefit
- **hit the ground running** do the job now
- **lost [our] shirts** lost all of [our] money
- **made a bundle** made a lot of money
- **made a killing** made a lot of money
- **passes the buck** shifts responsibility
- **passing muster** acceptable
- **put feelers out** discretely find out
- **sold like hotcakes** sold out quickly
- **sweat equity** hard, unpaid labor
- **take-home pay** pay after deductions
- **the bottom line** the main idea
- **the circular file** the garbage can
- **the eleventh hour** at the last moment
- **think outside of the box** be innovative
- **throw cold water** dismiss
- **turn-key** ready to use now
- **walking papers** notice of dismissal
- **wears many hats** has several duties
- **wiggle room** flexibility
- **win-win situation** all sides win
- **word of mouth** casual conversations
- **zero-sum game** gains equal losses

GRAMMAR GAMES FOR TEACHERS OF ADULT ESL

Body Idioms #1

a chip on [his] shoulder overly defensive
apple of [his] eye a cherished person
a shoulder to cry on someone who listens to problems and sympathizes
at arm's length not become too friendly or close
at each other's throats always fighting or arguing
at the top of [my] lungs yelling as loudly as possible
[my] back is to the wall run out of options
blood, sweat & tears requiring effort & sacrifice
blue bloods from an aristocratic family
bundle of nerves very anxious or nervous
butter fingers clumsy and often dropping things
by heart memorize something completely
carrying the weight of the world on [his] shoulders
  dealing with large problems or stress
chilled to the bone feel very cold
chin up stay optimistic
cold feet hesitant or unsure about continuing
cooling [my] heels kept waiting for longer than expected
cost an arm and a leg very expensive
dead from the neck up a stupid person
don't have a leg to stand on unable to prove a claim or an assertion
dug in [our] heels strongly resisted
elbow grease hard physical labor – especially to clean or polish
elbow room enough space to move around
finger in every pie involved in several activities
five finger discount stealing
footing the bill paying the bill
get [my] foot in the door a small start that could lead to future success
get [their] hands dirty do hard, unpleasant work
get off [my] back stop nagging
get under [my] skin become bothersome or irritating
give [my] right arm do almost anything for something you want
got off on the wrong foot started a relationship badly
grabbed [us] by the throat commanded complete attention
grease some palms using bribery to gain an unfair advantage
has two left feet a bad dancer, clumsy or awkward
hate [his] guts extreme hatred of another person
have a frog in [my] throat difficulty or discomfort when speaking
have a green thumb very good with plants
head & shoulders above the rest better or superior, the best
hit a raw nerve mentioned a sensitive issue or subject

Body Idioms #2

idle hands   inactivity can lead to bad behavior
in [his] blood   an inherited talent or characteristic
itchy feet   unable to settle down in one place
joined at the hip   spending all or most of the time together
keep a straight face   look serious while trying not to laugh
keeps [us] on our toes   alert, ready to act
keeping body & soul together   barely surviving financially
keeping [my] fingers crossed   hoping for luck or success
living from hand to mouth   only enough money for the essentials
lump in [my] throat   feel as if one is going to cry
on its last legs   nearly dead
over my dead body   absolutely not (a strong refusal)
pain in the neck   very annoying or irritating
pat on the back   praise or congratulations
play it by ear   improvise, act without preparation
pulling [my] leg   tease someone by telling them falsehoods
put [her] best foot forward   make a good impression
put [my] feet up   sit down and relax
put [my] foot in [my] mouth   say something that offends or embarrasses
puts [his] money where [his] mouth is   backs up words with action or money
rub shoulders   meet or talk to famous or important people
sent shivers down [my] spine   was frightened
shot [her]self in the foot   do something against one's own interests
soaked to the skin   in clothing that is completely drenched
[I] split [my] sides   laughed very hard
stabbed in the back   deceived by a trusted person
sweet tooth   a fondness for sweets
take the law into [their] own hands   to administer justice without regard for legality
the cold shoulder   ignore, behave coolly towards someone
the long arm of the law   the extent of legal authority or policing
thick-skinned   a person whose feelings are not easily hurt
think on [my] feet   improvise, act without preparation
thorn in [my] side   a constant annoyance
twisted [my] arm   persuaded or coerced by someone
two-faced   deceitful, insincere, hypocritical
under [her] thumb   under someone's complete control
up in arms   very angry and vocal about something
voted with [our] feet   showed one's opinion by leaving
went belly up   went bankrupt
working [our] fingers to the bone   working very hard
wrapped around [her] finger   easily manipulated

Also On Sale Now

Enjoy the convenient, low-cost, space-efficient alternative to buying multiple Bingo games. *Professor Melonhead's Bingo Book* contains 11 educational Bingo games covering the alphabet (upper & lower case), numbers (0-99 & 100-999), telling time (digital & analog clocks), 3-letter words, U.S. currency (including coin recognition), pictures of nouns, and the standard alphanumeric version. Each Bingo game contains 20 game sheets and accompanying game chips that can be easily photocopied for repeated use.

Retail Price $39.99   **Available at most online book retailers.**

Also On Sale Now

This book is a compilation of effective and engaging, pre-tested, game-based ESL activities for teachers of adult students. These activities are designed for active class participation in the form of group work, competing teams, or working with partners. Various grammar points, survival English, business English, and conversational English are covered as well as specific vocabulary building. Most activities include optional Study Sheets and/or Worksheets for the instructor's convenience.

Retail Price $39.99   Available at most online book retailers.

www.ingramcontent.com/pod-product-compliance
Lightning Source LLC
Chambersburg PA
CBHW082029300426
44117CB00015B/2416